# GOOD SPORTS: A LARGE PRINT ANTHOLOGY OF GREAT SPORTS WRITING

## Volume II: Tennis, Basketball, Golf, Horse Racing & The Olympics and Other Special Events

Other Anthologies published in Large Print from G.K. Hall:

# GOOD SPORTS: A LARGE PRINT ANTHOLOGY OF GREAT SPORTS WRITING

## Volume II: Tennis, Basketball, Golf, Horse Racing & The Olympics and Other Special Events

### Edited by
### RENEE SHUR AND JUDITH LEET

G.K.HALL &CO.

Boston, Massachusetts

1992

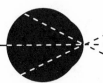

**This Large Print Book carries the
Seal of Approval of N.A.V.H.**

G.K. Hall Large Print Book Series.

Printed on acid free paper in the United States of America.

Set in 16 pt. Plantin.

**Library of Congress Cataloging-in-Publication Data**
(Revised for vol. 2)

Good sports : a large print anthology of great sports writing.

    (G.K. Hall Large print book series)
    Large print reprints of previously published articles
including fiction.
    Vol. 2 edited by Renee Shur and Judith Leet.
    Contents: Vol. 1. Baseball, boxing, fishing & football
—Tennis, basketball, golf, horse racing & the Olympics and
other special events.
    1. Sports.  2. Large type books.  I. Leet, Judith.
II. Shur, Renee.  III. Series.
GV707.L37  1990         796               90–40339
ISBN 0-8161-4735-3
ISBN 0-8161-5059-1 (v. 2)

# Acknowledgments

Randy Roberts and James Olson, "Sports and Self in Modern America," pp. 213-20 from *Winning Is the Only Thing: Sports in America since 1945.* Copyright © 1989 by The Johns Hopkins University Press, Baltimore/London. Reprinted by permission.

Michael Mewshaw, "Wimbledon." From *Short Circuit,* copyright © 1983. Reprinted by permission of the William Morris Agency, Inc., on behalf of the author and HarperCollins Publishers.

Larry Engelmann, "The Goddess." Excerpted from *The Goddess and the American Girl: The Story of Suzanne Lenglen and Helen Wills* by Larry Engelmann. Copyright © 1988 by Larry Engelmann. Reprinted by permission of Oxford University Press, Inc.

Frank Deford, "I'll Play My Own Sweet Game." From *Big Bill Tilden,* copyright © 1976 by Frank Deford. Reprinted by permission of Simon & Schuster, Inc.

Herbert Warren Wind, "About Chris Evert" orig-

# Contents

# THE OLYMPICS AND OTHER SPECIAL EVENTS

# EPILOGUE

# Editors' Note

Sports is an endlessly popular interest of Americans of every social strata. Americans watch the best athletes on television, participate in sports personally, talk about sports events at great length with friends and strangers, and follow their favorite teams in newsprint each day without fail.

This is the second of a two-volume anthology that assembles a collection of writing on sport by the finest writers, both those who specialize in sportswriting (Paul Gallico, Grantland Rice, Herbert Warren Wind, Red Smith) and those who only occasionally write on sports (John Updike, Donald Hall, John McPhee, Carol Flake, Michael Mewshaw). All these writers have in common a feeling for language as a means of recreating and interpreting a sports event in ways that many readers will find fresh and compelling.

In this second volume, we have concentrated on tennis, basketball, golf, horse racing, and the Olympics and other special events. Many selections concentrate on outstanding athletes at the top of their form; other pieces discuss the early development, struggles, and discipline of the young athlete; yet other selections describe the years following the great years—the inevitable decline in strength and reflexes, and new directions after the peak years.

Some pieces discuss the social climate (the role of sports in the United States today and the obstacles faced by young Jesse Owens, the strain of training and the personal toll on athletes (basketball player Connie Hawkins's difficult adjustment to the world of sports), the tournaments and other special events such as Wimbledon, the Olympics, the New York Marathon, and the Indianapolis 500, and the new visibility of women in sports. In these pieces, many facets of sports are analyzed and illuminated; both the newcomer to sports and the sports fan will gain a deeper understanding of the athlete's competitive world from the varied perspectives of these writers. We contrast ever-dependable good sportsmanship of a Chris Evert and a Bob Jones with those athletes like John McEnroe who are remembered for their temperamental disturbances on the court.

Sports represents excitement and entertainment, but more than that, it is the admiration the fan feels for those athletes who have developed skills and endurance, both physical and mental, that the rest of us collectively would like to have possessed. But since we are not blessed with these endowments, we do the next best thing and try to understand what is like to be a Bill Russell or a Jack Nicklaus.

# INTRODUCTION

# RANDY ROBERTS
# AND JAMES OLSON

# Sports and Self in Modern America

*In this introductory essay Randy Roberts and James Olson reflect on the role of sports in America today. Searching for the underlying reasons for the explosion in participation and spectatorship, they conclude that sports has come to define a new sense of community and personal identity in a mobile, suburban culture where traditional definitions no longer apply. From the fitness craze—epitomized by Jim Fixx, the guru of running—to Little Leagues and Little Dribblers to Monday night televised foolball, sports is a "common currency" that transcends social class, race, and ethnic background. For immigrants and minorities sports is an accessible entry into society at large. Similarly, sports is an arena in which women's struggle for equality and separate identity is being played out.*

It was a perfect July day in Vermont—clear and cool. Jim Fixx, on the eve of a long-awaited vacation, put on his running togs and headed down a rural road for his daily run, expecting to do the usual twelve to fifteen miles. At fifty-two years of age, Fixx was a millionaire, the best-selling author of *The Complete Book of Running,* and the reigning guru of the American exercise cult. In 1968 he had weighed 214 pounds, smoked two packs of cigarettes a day, and worried about his family health history. Fixx's father had died of a heart attack at the age of forty-three. So Fixx started running and stopped smoking. He lost 60 pounds and introduced America to the virtues of strenuous exercise: longevity, freedom from depression, energy, and the "runner's high." He regularly ran 80 miles a week. When he hit the road on July 21, 1984, Fixx weighed 154 pounds and seemed the perfect image of fitness. Twenty minutes into the run he had a massive heart attack and died on the side of the road. A motorcyclist found his body later that afternoon.

Fixx's death shocked middle- and upper-class America. Of all people, how could Jim Fixx have died of a heart attack? Millions of joggers, runners, swimmers, cyclists, tri-athletes, walkers, weight-lifters, and aerobic dancers had convinced themselves that exercise preserved youth and postponed death. It was the yuppie panacea; "working out" made them immune to the ravages of time.

The autopsy on Fixx was even more disturbing. In spite of all the running, his circulatory system was in a shambles. Fixx's cholesteral levels had been dangerously high. One coronary artery was 98 percent blocked, a second one 85 percent blocked, and a third one 50 percent blocked. In the previous two to eight weeks, the wall of his left ventricle had badly deteriorated.

On that clear Vermont day, Jim Fixx shouldn't have been running; he should have been undergoing triple-bypass surgery.

Even more puzzling, Fixx had been complaining for months of chest pains while running—clear signs of a deadly angina, the heart muscle protesting lack of oxygen. Friends had expressed concern and urged him to get a check-up. He resisted, attempting to will good health. In January 1984 he had agreed to a treadmill test, but he skipped the appointment that afternoon, running 16 miles instead. Why had someone so committed to health ignored such obvious warnings? How had sports, exercise, and fitness become such obsessions in the United States?

Modern society was the culprit. In an increasingly secular society, church membership no longer provided the discipline to bind people together into cohesive social groups. Well-integrated neighborhoods with long histories and strong identities had given way after World War II to faceless suburbs. Corporate and professional elites tended to be highly mobile, relocating whenever a pay raise was offered. The new American community had become fifty suburban homes and a 7-11 convenience store. New organizations, especially business and government bureaucracies, had assumed power in the United States, but those were hardly places where most Americans could feel comfortable and in control. Blessed with money but deprived of community in the 1970s and 1980s, Americans began to use sports to rebuild their sense of community and fitness to define individual happiness and individual pleasure, creating a culture of competitive narcissism supported by a host of therapeutic panaceas, such as EST, psychotherapy, Scientology, and strenuous exercise.

For individuals, families, groups, and communities, sports had become a new cultural currency, a common ground upon which a diverse people could express their values and needs. Unlike European society, where such traditional institutions as the church, the aristocracy, and the monarchy had maintained order through established authority, America had been settled by lower-class working people and small farmers. The traditional institutions anchoring European society were absent. Without those same moorings, America had always confronted the centrifugal forces of individualism, capitalism, Protestantism, and ethnicity, using the culture of opportunity to stave off social disintegration. Social mobility, the westward movement, the abundance of land, and ruralism helped stabilize a highly complex society.

But in the twentieth century, when industrialization, urbanization, and the disappearance of the frontier changed the definitions of opportunity and progress, the values of individualism, community, and competition had to find new modes of expression, and sports became a prominent one. At the local, regional, and national levels, sports evolved into one of the most powerful expressions of identity. Outside observers marveled, for example, at the "religion" of high school football in the more than eleven hundred independent school districts of Texas. When viewed simply as sport, of course, the obsession with football seems absurd, but when viewed in terms of community identity, it becomes more understandable. In hundreds of rural areas, where scattered farms surround tiny county seats, the local high school, with its arbitrarily drawn district lines, was the central focus of community identity. For hundreds of small Texas towns—and rural areas throughout much of the rest of the country —high school athletics was literally the cement of community life.

It wasn't just high school sports which provided new identities in the United States. After World War II, social and economic pressures worked against the nuclear family. More and more women were working outside the home; more and more men were working at job sites long commutes from the suburbs; and divorce rates were way up. Childhood play became less spontaneous and more organized as schools, government, and communities assumed roles once played by the family. The most obvious consequence was the appearance of organized youth sports. Little League grew by leaps and bounds beginning in the 1950s; child's play, once the domain of the home and immediate neighborhood, became a spectator sport complete with uniforms, umpires, scoreboards, leagues, play-offs, drafts, and championships. By the 1980s, Little League was competing for time with Pop Warner football, Little Dribblers basketball, soccer, and swimming, with organized competition beginning in some sports at the age of three. In 1987 sports sociologists estimated that thirty million children under sixteen years of age were competing in organized sports.

Sports functioned as identity on the regional level as well. In an age when television, movies, and mass culture threatened regional distinctiveness, sports emerged as the single most powerful symbol of localism and community loyalty. That was obviously true of high school and college sports, but even in professional sports, when ownership shifted away from local businesses and entrepreneurs to conglomerates and national corporations, the regional identity of teams remained critically important to gate receipts and television revenues. The rivalries between the Chicago Bears and the Green Bay Packers, or the Boston Red Sox and the New York Yankees, or the Boston Celtics and the Los Angeles Lakers, filled stadiums, arenas, and living rooms with fans desperate for the home team to win. Five hundred years ago, European cities dedicated all their surplus capital over the course of 100 to 200 years to build elaborate cathedrals to God. In the United States during the 1970s and 1980s, the modern equivalent of the medieval cathedral was the domed stadium. For sports, not for God, American communities would sell bonds and mortgage themselves for the next generation.

Even on the national level, sports competition

reflected and promoted American nationalism. Sports was a mirror of federalism, at once local in its community loyalties but national in its collective forms. The 1984 Olympic Games in Los Angeles did not just expose a rising tide of patriotism and national pride; they became a major force in stimulating a new American nationalism. Unlike the recent Olympic Games in Montreal, Moscow, and Seoul, the Los Angeles Games did not accumulate billion-dollar deficits and require the resources of national governments to prop them up. In 1984 "free enterprise capitalism" organized and conducted the Games, used existing facilities, and turned a profit. The Los Angeles Coliseum was filled with flag-waving Americans cheering every native athlete winning a medal. On television back home, Europeans watched the proceedings with astonishment and not a little fear, worrying about the burst of American patriotism, nationalism, and even chauvinism. Nearly a decade after the debacle in Vietnam, American pride and optimism was on the rebound, and the 1984 Olympic Games was center stage for the resurrection of the American sense of mission.

Modern sports in the United States also provided a sense of identity cutting across class, racial, and ethnic lines. In penitentiaries throughout the country, intense struggles were waged every evening over television and radio programming, black convicts wanting to watch soul stations and black sit-coms and whites demanding MTV or white sit-coms. But there was no trouble or debate on Sunday afternoon or Monday nights during the fall. It was football, only football, and blacks and whites watched the programs with equal enthusiasm. On Monday evenings in the fall, whether in the poorest ghetto tenement of the South Side of Chicago to the most tastefully appointed living room in the Lake Forest suburbs, televisions were tuned on to football, and discussions at work the next morning revolved around the game, who won and who lost and why.

For ethnic minorities and immigrants, sports similarly became a way of identifying with the new society, a powerful form of acculturation. During the 1980s, for example, Los Angeles became the second largest Mexican city in the world, behind only Mexico City in Spanish-speaking population and larger now than Guadalajara in terms of Mexican residents. At Dodger Stadium in Los Angeles, Mexicans and Mexican Americans became an increasingly large part of the evening box office, helping to sustain Dodger attendance at its three million-plus levels each year. In September 1986, when Dodger pitcher Fernando Valenzuela won his twentieth game of the season, the Spanish cable network SIN broke into its regular programming nationwide for live interviews. The fact that sports was making its way to the headlines and front pages of major newspapers was no accident in the United States. It had become, indeed, a new cultural currency in modern America, a way

10

to interpret change and express traditional values.

Women, too, used sports as a vehicle in their drive for equality and identity. The development of women's and men's sports in America has varied considerably. From the first, men's sports have emphasized fierce competition and the ruthless pursuit of expertise. Early male and female physical educators, however, believed women were uncompetitive and decided that women's sports should promote a woman's physical and mental qualities and thus make her more attractive to men. They also believed that sports and exercise should sublimate female sexual drives. As renowned nineteenth-century physical educator Dudley A. Sargent noted, "No one seems to realize that there is a time in the life of a girl when it is better for her and for the community to be something of a boy rather than too much of a girl."

But tomboyish behavior had to stop short of abrasive competition. Lucille Eaton Hill, director of physical training at Wellesley College, urged women to "avoid the evils which are so apparent . . . in the conduct of athletics for men." She and her fellow female physical educators encouraged widespread participation rather than narrow specialization. In short, women left spectator and professional sports to the men. Indeed, not until 1924 were women allowed to compete in Olympic track and field events, and even then on a limited basis.

During the 1920s the tennis careers of Suzanne

Lenglen and Helen Wills were used to demonstrate the proper and improper pursuit of victory by
athletic women. Tennis, for the great French
champion Lenglen, was not only a way of life: it
was life. Her only object on a tennis court was
to win, and between 1919 and 1926, when she
turned professional, Lenglen lost only two sets of
singles and won 269 of 270 matches. But at what
cost? Bulimic in her eating habits and subject to
dramatic swings in emotions, she suffered several
nervous breakdowns and lived in fear of losing.
In addition, male critics noted that, far from keeping her looking young, tennis cruelly aged
Lenglen. Journalist Al Laney remarked that by the
mid-1920s Lenglen looked thirty years older than
she actually was and that her complexion had
turned dull and colorless. Her friend Ted Tinling
agreed that before she turned twenty-five, "her
face and expression had already the traces of deep
emotional experiences far beyond the normal for
her age."

In contrast, Helen Wills was a champion of
great physical beauty. Before Wills, Americans
tended to agree with journalist Paul Gallico that
"pretty girls" did not excel in sports and that outstanding female athletes were simply compensat-
ing for their lack of beauty. Summarizing this
school of thought, Larry Engelmann observed:
"Athletics was their way of getting attention. If
Suzanne Lenglen were really beautiful, for instance, she wouldn't be running around like crazy
on the tennis courts of Europe. She would have

been quietly at home, happily married. Athletics proved a refuge and a last chance for the desperate female ugly duckling."

Yet Wills was beautiful, and she was great, winning every set of singles competition she played between 1927 and 1933. Journalists explained Wills' success and beauty by stressing the fact that tennis was only a game for her, not a way of life and certainly not life itself. Losses did not worry her. She slways appeared composed. "My father, a doctor," she explained, "always told me not to wince or screw up my face while I was playing. He said it would put lines on my face." And no victory was worth a line.

Women were not fully emancipated from the older ideal until the 1970s, when they asserted their right to be as ruthless and competitive in athletics as men. Tennis champion Billy Jean King symbolized on the court as well as off this new attitude. Like Lenglen, she single-mindedly pursued victory. And she was no more concerned with sweating and grimacing than Pete Rose. Unlike Wills, King was not interested in art or starting a family. When asked why she was not at home, she replied, "Why don't you ask Rod Laver why he isn't at home?" It was as eloquent a statement of athletic liberation as could by asked for.

To develop fully as an athlete, King had to earn money. Along with Gladys Heldman and Philip Morris Tobacco Company, King helped to organize the Virginia Slims women's tennis circuit in 1971. That year she became the first female athlete to earn $100,000 in a single year. More importantly, she labored to get women players a bigger share of the prize money at the major championships. In the early 1970s women's purses at Wimbledon and the U.S. Open were about 10 percent of the men's. By the mid-1980s the prize money split was equal. As if to punctuate the point that women's tennis had arrived, King defeated the former Wimbledon triple-crown champion (1939) Bobby Riggs 6–4, 6–3, 6–3, in a highly publicized match in the Houston Astrodome in 1973.

Even more important than King for the future of women's athletics was Title IX of the 1972 Educational Amendments Act. It outlawed sexual discrimination by school districts or colleges and universities which received federal aid. Certainly, athletic budgets in high schools and universities are not equally divided between male and female athletics. But women have made significant gains. Before Title IX less than 1 percent of athletic budgets went to women's sports. By the 1980s that figure had increased to over 10 percent. No longer is there a serious argument over the road women's sports should travel. Instead, the battle is over what portion of the pie they should receive.

But it wasn't just countries, cities, colleges, small towns, high schools, and ethnic groups which turned to sports in the 1980s as the most powerful way of defining their values. The most extraordinary development in contemporary popular culture was the extent to which individuals turned to athletics, exercise, and body images as a way of finding meaning in an increasingly dislocated society. In the mid-1980s, a Louis Harris poll indicated that 96 percent of all Americans found something about their bodies that they didn't like and would change if they could. Harris said that the "rampant obsessions of both men and women about their looks have produced an obvious boon for the cosmetics industry, plastic surgery, diet doctors, fitness and shape advisers, fat farms, and exercise clubs." The cult of fitness and the cult of individual happiness went hand in hand. Politicians used international sports at the Olympic level to confirm the superiority of various political systems or prove the equality of their Third World cultures; they mustered professional sports to project the quality of life in major American cities; collegiate sports touted the virtues of different universities; and in the 1970s and 1980s, millions of Americans embraced the cult of fitness to discover the meaning of life, retreating into the fantasy that they are how they look.

# TENNIS

# MICHAEL MEWSHAW

## Wimbledon

*A behind-the-scenes look at Wimbledon, the name of both the most famous tennis court and tournament in the world. Despite the well-known traditions and royal patronage—and the desire of every aspiring tennis player to appear in the finals on Centre Court— Michael Mewshaw calls attention to some less well-known facts about the tournament and its managers —especially about those privileged to be members of the private club that manages Wimbledon, and the advantages they enjoy from their membership. Mewshaw suggests that some of the great profits from the tournament should be used to improve tennis all over England rather than to subsidize the wealthy members of an exclusive private club.*

A lofty fortress of tradition, the All England Lawn Tennis and Croquet Club changes at glacial speed. But the public's perception of it changes slower still, since most journalists, like those generals who are always fighting the previous war, persist in filing reports which have little to do with the realities of Wimbledon and even less with the way contemporary players regard the place. Instead, year after year they churn out stories based upon earlier stories, strumming the same dreamy, euphonious tunes, harking back to a halcyon age which reached its highest literary expression in a 1971 piece by John McPhee entitled "Centre Court."

Strawberries in Devonshire cream, the steeple of St. Mary's Church, royalty, fulsome praise— "This is the greatest tournament in the world"— and the obligatory reference to the fragment from Kipling inscribed over the arch leading to Centre Court—"If you can meet with triumph and disaster and treat those two imposters the same"— McPhee's article contains every building block of the basic Wimbledon story. Less gifted authors have had no compunctions about cannibalizing it for a few sentences, and those utterly lacking professional integrity have ripped off whole paragraphs, reshuffled the elements, and published them as their own.

The All England Club is "ordered within ten acres," McPhee wrote, "and all paths eventually lead to the high front façade of the Centre Court, the name of which, like the name Wimbledon itself, is synecdochic. 'Centre Court' refers not only to the *ne plus ultra* tennis lawn but also to the entire stadium that surrounds it. A three-story dodecagon with a roof that shelters most of its seats, it resembles an Elizabethan theater. Its exterior walls are alive with ivy, and in planter boxes on a balcony above its principal doorway are rows of pink and blue hydrangeas. . . . In their pastel

20

efflorescence the hydrangeas appear to be geraniums that have escalated socially."

If run as an account of the 1982 Wimbledon, McPhee's piece would probably strike most readers as essentially accurate. While the names of the players might be wrong, the tone is right, is timeless. A few details might sound anachronistic, but then a large measure of Wimbledon's presumed charm is its antiquated atmosphere.

"Wimbledon is uniquely considerate toward players," McPhee maintained, "going to great lengths to treat them as if they were plenipotentiaries from their respective nations and not gifted gibbons, which is at times their status elsewhere." He praised the Players' Tea Room: "Hot meals are served there, to players only—a consideration absent in all other places where they play." And he extolled the lavishness of the locker room: "The gentlemen's dressing room is *sui generis* in the sportive world, with five trainer-masseurs in full-time attendance."

For tennis writers and fans the world over, not to mention for the 375 members of the All England Club, these lines possess the resonance of the Talmud. They are true, they are eternal, and any contradiction or doubt amounts to heresy. But in fact Wimbledon is no longer unique and, compared to almost any tournament on the Grand Prix or WCT circuit, it is neither particularly considerate nor opulent.

From Hong Kong to Houston, from Monte Carlo to Mexico City, players receive royal treatment in the form of free limousines, free meals and discounted accommodations, free baby-sitters, abundant free tickets to the tournament, plenty of practice courts, elaborate programs of entertainment for their wives and girlfriends, around-the-clock trainers, masseurs, and doctors, and attentive tournament directors, hostesses, and gofers who dote on the stars and provide whatever they ask for. In some cases this means supplying dope and girls, and in almost every instance it entails the payment of illegal guarantees.

But Wimbledon doesn't need to pay appearance money, and it is less likely to arrange sex or score dope for players than it is to pave Centre Court and use it as a parking lot. This partially explains the crescendo of complaints that plagued the All England Club in the past year. Pampered, paid under the table, and protected by compliant umpires, the top players have lost patience with Wimbledon, which prides itself on treating all outsiders with uniform disdain.

It is this uniform disdain which accounts for the rest of the criticism. In matters petty and profound, the All England Club has, until recently, refused to acknowledge that the players had any legitimate gripes. Instead, Wimbledon chose to establish itself, with the abject cooperation of much of the press, as a theme park, something along the lines of Disneyland, in which crowds gather annually to worship the real and imagined virtues of the nation's past.

In that past, things were reputed to be simpler and people knew their place. If, as McPhee wrote, Centre Court resembles an Elizabethan theater, it is important to note, as he does not, that the crowd is segregated according to the Elizabethan concept of the Great Chain of Being, which bears no resemblance at all to the ATP's computerized ranking. At the top looms God, followed by the sovereign members of the royal family, the lords and ladies, the knights, the foot soldiers and yeomen, the good burghers, and finally the groundlings and stinkards who cluster in the standing-room enclosures. There's none of this democratic nonsense about all men being created equal, nor is there any suggestion that talent or financial success will neccessarily allow a man to clamber hand over hand up the Great Chain. It's impossible to buy membership in the All England Club, impossible to buy into the Royal Box, and frequently impossible to buy a ticket without the help of a scalper.

Even having bought a ticket, a man gets no quarantee that he will see any tennis. In a compound designed to accommodate twenty-five thousand spectators, there are frequently in excess of thirty-five thousand souls jostling for space and teetering on tiptoes to catch a glimpse of a court, any court, and many go home having watched little more than the shaggy backs of other people's heads. Those with a ticket to Centre Court are usually better off, but the stadium roof is supported by iron pillars, and the pillars and overhanging eaves ruin the view from an annoying number of seats.

If it should rain and the day's schedule should be curtailed or canceled, that's just another example of the Divinity moving in mysterious ways to test one's mettle. Don't bother asking for a rain-check. Wimbledon, like God, doesn't provide rain-checks or explanations.

To comprehend Wimbledon, one must keep in mind that it is the single Grand Slam event which not only takes place at an exclusive private club, but also covers that club's annual expenses. Essentially, the tournament is a successful fund-raiser—think of it as an alternative to a raffle or bingo—which allows the Club to hold yearly dues down to $17, to serve members subsidized drinks and meals, and to generate over two million dollars in profits. When this became common knowledge after an exposé by the *Observer* in 1981 —naturally, the article wasn't written by a tennis reporter—officers of the All England Club tried to laugh it off, remarking that the meals were really quite bad. But this was small solace to the fan who had to fork over more for one ticket than a Club member had to pay in yearly dues, and it offered no compensation to the kid with a grounds pass who had to shell out almost as much for a hotdog as a member paid for a three-course meal.

The advantages of membership, however, are not limited to the "ridiculously low" dues, as Club Chairman Sir Brian Burnett describes them, nor to subsidized drinks and meals. The most valuable fringe benefit is access to tickets. Each member receives one free Centre Court seat every day of the tournament and has the right to buy two more at a bargain-basement discount. According to the *Observer*, members pay £2 apiece for extra Centre Court tickets,

> which is roughly a quarter of their face value. The benefit to the member, however, is much greater than the difference between the ticket price and subsidized price. A glance at the personal columns of *The Times* any day will produce offers of tickets at £100 or more. Club members are not supposed to sell them, but it is not unusual for some of their tickets to end up by a circuitous route in the hands of touts. . . .
>
> No wonder membership of the Club is prized. Each year, at the cost of £50, members can distribute patronage to friends, relations or business acquaintances worth £2,500. . . . The Wimbledon membership is a self-perpetuating oligarchy; its benefits are roughly the equivalent of inheriting a fortune of £100,000.

These shady practices reveal not only the tendrils of hypocrisy which flourish at Wimbledon along with the ivy and the hydrangeas, they explain why Great Britain has such poor tennis facilities, so few indoor courts, and just one player in the top hundred. The All England Club, along with the Lawn Tennis Association, is supposed to nurture a national training program. But, said the *Observer,* "It is hard to avoid the conclusion that the superb record (of Wimbledon) has been built up over the years on a selfish, overlavish use of resources, some of which could have—and most ordinary players would argue, *should* have—been put to use in improving the woeful standards of British tennis generally."

Despite evidence of its peccability, the All England Club has steadfastly refused to allow international tennis authorities much, if any, influence over the tournament. Nominally part of the Volvo Grand Prix, Wimbledon doesn't consider itself bound by the code of Conduct.

The Club draws up its own list of seeded players, then still clinging to the Great Chain of Being, it assigns men to two different dressing rooms. Dressing Room Number One, close to Centre Court, is reserved for players with established reputations. Dressing Room Number Two, located behind the field courts, is left to "qualifiers and what-have-you," in the words of Leo Turner, the major domo of the dressing rooms. "There's nothing wrong with Number Two, but the players all want to come in here [Number One]. They don't have a locker [in Number Two] so they put their bags under the seat and then they come to me for a towel and I catch them and send them back."

Megawatts of energy are expended each year catching culprits who have failed to stay in their places and chasing them back where they belong. It's as if the Club views its mission as one of behavior modification and feels it has failed unless players, the press, and spectators slip docilely into the slots assigned to them.

For players, this assignment starts with the dressing room and ends with a court, and a man can calibrate precisely how important he is by where he is forced to play. Since 1977 Bjorn Borg hasn't performed anyplace except Centre Court and Court One. Lower-ranked players are relegated to distant, bumpy cow pastures where the crowd presses in on all sides and sets off a din which makes the Italian Open seem reverentially silent.

It isn't just the surface which is superior on the show courts. So is the officiating. Centre Court and Court One receive a full complement of thirteen officials—twelve linesmen and an umpire—and they employ electronic devices for monitoring the service lines. The remaining sixteen courts make do with six linesmen and an umpire—no netcord judge—and these officials are serving an apprenticeship. If they perform well, they may qualify for minor show courts Two, Three, Thirteen, and Fourteen, and after five years they may graduate to Centre Court or Court One.

It would be wrong, however, to conclude that the arrogance of Wimbledon amounts to total intransigence. There were changes in 1982. Prize money increased by eighty-four percent—it is now nearly a million dollars—and the Club was induced by an American television contract to pitch more than a hundred years of tradition out the window and play the men's final on Sunday.

Tradition isn't all it pitched out the window. Jack Yardley, a groundsman for thirty-two years and just two years shy of retirement, was dismissed because of complaints about the grass.

While Yardley was let go after a long tenure, Teddy Tinling was invited back after more than two decades of banishment. Appointed as liaison between the players and the Club, Tinling assumed much the same position he first held fifty years ago and continued to hold until he put a pair of lace-ruffled panties on Gussie Moran.

The Club also announced that ATP trainers could now work at Wimbledon, just as they did at all other Grand Prix tournaments. And seeded players would receive extra tickets, extra time on the practice courts, and the privilege of bringing a coach or friend into the locker room.

Whether these changes would improve the players' obstreperous moods remained to be seen. But John McEnroe promptly expressed an opinion about Teddy Tinling: he "doesn't know his ass from his elbow."

# LARRY ENGELMANN

## The Goddess

*The early training and conditioning of Suzanne Lenglen, a tennis star of the twenties, one of the early darlings of the French press, produced a great tennis player but a weakened inner person, with many illnesses both real and imaginary. Her career was engineered by her father, who devoted himself exclusively to grooming her into a champion player in an era before there were any tennis coaches for women. He modeled his teaching on the way men rather than women were playing the game, and unwittingly revolutionized women's tennis. Suzanne learned to play the game with a fluidity and ease that confounded her opponents and the press. But her parents had put enormous pressures on Suzanne to succeed, and she never recovered from the psychic damage that their endless criticisms had caused.*

Everything, from the weather to the Americans, vexed and distressed the French in the first weeks of 1926. The glory that had accompanied victory in the Great War seemed suddenly remote, and hopes for security and prosperity were grudgingly abridged. Yet there remained in the midst of this plague of troubles one shining symbol of the indomitable spirit of France. That luminous symbol and unfailing inspiration was Suzanne Lenglen, acclaimed by all of her countrymen as "The Goddess."

She was not a child of any royal family. She inherited no regal empire, no palace, no uniformed armies, no official titles, no scepter, no great seal of state. Yet from 1919 until 1927 Suzanne Lenglen enjoyed all of the influence, prestige, and popularity previously the exclusive realm of the most esteemed hereditary rulers. She radiated an unparalleled imperiousness and was the dazzling cynosure of whatever domain she occupied at a given moment. Every European nation saw evidence of her majesty and appeal. She was greeted everywhere by masses of awed and adoring fans. She traveled exclusively by chauffeured limousine or private rail car. She draped herself fittingly in the white ermine of royalty and crowned herself with a unique jeweled bandeau. Her wardrobe was created by France's leading designer, and what she wore set the style for women throughout the Western world. What she said, did, ate, how she felt, and where she lived were all reported in painstaking and adoring detail in the newspapers. She was the best known and most admired woman in Europe—perhaps in the world. To see her was the rage. To speak with her—the exchange of only a word—set one apart. To France she was a national heroine, as great as Joan of Arc. And when people spoke of her, more often than not they used one of her mythic appellations rather than her name. She was "la belle Suzanne," "notre gracieuse championne," "The Maid Marvel," "The Little Sorceress," and "The Queen." But the deific reference to Suzanne as "The Goddess" perhaps best expressed the feelings of France.

Suzanne Lenglen rose to prominence initially by her extraordinary athletic skill at tennis. But it would by an error simply to say that Suzanne "played" tennis. Others played tennis. Suzanne Lenglen performed tennis. She danced tennis. She celebrated tennis. She laughed and she sang tennis. And there were times when Suzanne suffered tennis. But because she was so unlike any other tennis player in the world, no one ever said that this goddess played tennis. For to say such a thing might bring a comparison with other players, and that would by to miss completely her singular virtuosity and spell.

Lenglen's career was a grimly and gloriously national affair in France. It was a brave journalist indeed who dared to write one word of criticism concerning her activities. Reports of her contests printed in French newspapers were always adulatory. When she lost a game or played an extended set—a rare occurrence—reporters explained faithfully why such an outrageous thing had happened. A close contest in doubles was invariably the fault of her partner. In singles she might lose a game or two because she was preoccupied by a concern for the health of her father or her dog.

And whenever some journalist did make a rare

error in judgment and published something even slightly unflattering about the Goddess, he was immediately denounced by other journalists and his story passionately refuted. Such a newsman was ridiculed not simply as a fool but as an enemy of Suzanne Lenglen, of sport, and of France. Consequently, French newspapers served almost exclusively as a public relations firm for the Goddess. Journalists were reduced to silence or sycophancy. Suzanne's publicity, American correspondents found, was "publicity gone mad," and many of them wondered how the laudatory Lenglen stories could be printed year after year and still retain any credibility with the public. "One would have thought Lenglen would have stopped this kind of thing long ago," one of them complained.

But Lenglen did not stop it. For more than a decade, from 1914 until 1926, she encouraged it and abetted those who composed the fables. Indeed, she lived in ecstatic symbiosis with her nation's newsmen, providing pleasant and often dramatic materials for inquiring reporters and then basking in the public attention that followed the publication of such accounts. Few editors could resist describing in colorful detail her most recent athletic contests or alleged romantic liaisons. Flattering photographs appeared weekly in the rotogravure sections of the Sunday papers. In Suzanne Lenglen journalists had at last stumbled upon a subject commensurate with their capacity for hyperbole.

Lenglen mesmerized not just journalists but almost everyone who watched her. Tennis star René Lacoste remembered first falling under her spell in 1921. In the spring of that year young Lacoste traveled with his parents to Saint-Cloud. After promising to return in a few minutes, Lacoste was permitted to enter the Stade Français to watch part of the final match for the World Hard Court Championship between Suzanne Lenglen and the American champion, Molla Mallory. Lacoste, a perceptive student of tennis, kept a detailed notebook in which he analyzed the strengths and weaknesses of various leading players, information he used to improve his own performance. Perhaps there was something he could learn by watching Lenglen. "At first," Lacoste said of his initial glimpse of the French woman, "I was disappointed, as were most of those who saw her for the first time after having heard so much about her." He expected to see a woman execute extraordinary tennis strokes. But Suzanne did not. He found "she played with marvelous ease the simplest strokes in the world. It was only after several games that I understood what harmony was concealed by her simplicity, what wonderful mental and physical balance was hidden by the facility of her play." Lacoste was spellbound by her simple perfection. In his head he had a vague notion of the way the game should by played. But not until he watched Suzanne did Lacoste see the ideal made real. "I had promised to stay a few minutes," he recalled, "but I remained there a long time without being able to depart, looking at this admirable spectacle with wide-open eyes."

Grantland Rice watched the same match at Saint-Cloud and was hardly less restrained in his enthusiasm for the Maid Marvel: "An amazingly symmetrical figure, replete with grace and litheness, arrayed in a white silk dress that barely flutters below the knees. White silk stockings and white shoes. Above this background of white, hair as black as a raven's wing, bound with a brilliant orange band. Perfectly molded arms, bare and brown from many suns—the entire effect being one of extreme vividness—an effect immediately to catch and hold the eye." But even this description, Rice readily confessed, failed to do the Goddess justice. Her movement, her deific grace, the ineffable wonder of her, defied description. Rice watched her "astounding mid-air fluttering, as of some brilliantly colored bird, with the orange band flashing like a flame of yellow fire," and he could only think that "Solomon meeting the Queen of Sheba beat us to it with the proper phrase—'The better half has never been told.' "

A writer for the *New York Times,* seeing her in 1921 for the first time, concluded simply that Lenglen was "one of the most wonderful machines that have ever been created out of a woman's body."

On the pink clay courts of the Riviera and the indoor hard wood surfaces of Paris, Lenglen's performances were graceful enough to be set to music, even were music themselves. Her game was not just serve and volley and forehand and backhand, but rather toccata and cadenza and sometimes, during long rallies, rhapsody. She appeared to play as well as many men but she played with a poetry of motion, a fluency, a bravura, that no male or female had previously even attempted. She reduced the intensity and intricacy of athletics to simplicity and then rechoreographed them so that the prosaic basics of play were surprisingly transformed. And what made all of this even more extraordinary was that she made it appear so easy. While those across the net from her scrambled frantically and huffed and puffed, working themselves to exhaustion, the goddess moved with seeming effortlessness and efficiency like a beautiful gliding bird in flight.

There was a fabled quality to the rise of Suzanne Lenglen. And nearly every Frenchman could provide in precise and painstaking detail stories of her childhood, training, and career whether they actually happened or not. Even Suzanne and her parents had trouble keeping their stories straight on how she had trained, how she had won, and how difficult this or that contest had been. There was unanimous agreement, however, on one central aspect of her career. Although all of France now claimed her, "notre Suzanne" was really the result of the dream of one man, Charles Lenglen. He was Suzanne's father, teacher, trainer, adviser, coach, agent, manager, protector, mentor, and at times even her tormentor.

When asked, Papa Lenglen, a heavyset bear of a man, usually began his somber version of the creation of the goddess with a prophetic mystical incident that took place during a vaudeville performance in the Casino Municipal de Nice in 1912. Among the entertainers during that evening, Papa remembered, was a hypnotist accompanied by a medium who served as his subject. The couple performed demonstrations of mental telepathy, thought-reading, and fortune-telling. The medium, with her eyes blind-folded, said she would answer any question in the mind of any person in the audience. Papa Lenglen concentrated on the question, "Will my daughter one day become champion of France?" Within a few seconds the medium answered, "Better than that—better than that." The success of Suzanne was then something foretold, Papa insisted. But he also knew of the enormous and trying effort and the painful dedication that went into making that which was foretold and destined into actual fact.

Suzanne Rachel Flore Lenglen was born in Compiègne, France, on May 24, 1899. The Lenglen family claimed to be of Franco-Flemish origins, but even this was uncertain. American journalists described Suzanne as a "Provencal type intermingled with a Semitic strain." Papa Lenglen, a businessman of some means, managed the omnibus concession he had inherited from his father. The enterprise prospered, and soon after

Suzanne's birth Papa sold it and moved with his wife, Anais, and their daughter to a rustic villa in Maretz-sur-Matz near Compiègne. There the Lenglens enjoyed a life of pleasant leisure, dividing their time between the new home in the Oise and a small vacation villa in Nice.

At an early age Suzanne demonstrated unusual athletic ability. She was a large-boned and strong girl with superb coordination. At eight she was an accomplished cyclist and a strong swimmer. She could run faster, jump higher, and throw a ball farther than boys her age. And while the family wintered in Nice, Suzanne developed a passion for diabolo, a game that became the rage among European children early in the century. In diabolo, a spinning top is balanced and manipulated on a string held between two sticks. Talented diabolo players, like little Suzanne, could throw the top high into the air and then catch it on the string, or with another player could throw the top back and forth and play what was called "diabolo tennis." In Nice, Suzanne played the game daily on the Promenade des Anglais and became so skillful at it and displayed such unusual panache that crowds of tourists would gather to watch. In time she became such a leading attraction on the street that people asked at what hour the little girl would perform. When she arrived there was applause from those who have gathered to watch. Years later, in recounting the important influences in Suzanne's life, Papa attributed her poise before large crowds to her early experience playing diabolo before the adoring tourists of Nice.

Suzanne studied at the Institute Massena in Nice, where among her courses was one in classic Greek dance. Later, when her movements in tennis were described as like those of a dancer, it was rumored that she had studied with the Ballet Russe de Monte Carlo. But she had not. The single dance course at the Institute was the basis for the grace of movement she so expertly transferred to endeavors in other areas.

While on the Riviera, Papa Lenglen had the opportunity to watch some of the world's best tennis players. Competitors from America, the British Empire, and the Continent began their annual campaigns each winter in the club tournaments on the Riviera. From there they moved on to Saint-Cloud for the World Hard Court Championships in the spring and then to Wimbledon for the World Championships in June. Papa had batted tennis balls around for recreation but was never an accomplished player. He became instead an interested and well-informed observer of the game. He was fascinated by the tactics and maneuvers of tennis, and he was especially impressed by the deference paid to the men and women accomplished in the sport, who were treated like aristocrats. They were housed and fed in the grand hotels and the finest restaurants, escorted back and forth between tournaments by limousine, lionized by the society of sybarites who ranged the Riviera, and invited to party and play with statesmen, monarchs, titled aristocrats, and wealthy industrialists. They were welcomed aboard the most expensive yachts and were pointed out on the street. Dressed in their spotless tennis whites, they were a little like demi-gods cavorting in play beside this azure sea. (Years later, Jack Kramer wrote of men's tennis attire: "If you never saw tennis players in their long white flannels, I cannot begin to exlain to you how majestic they appeared. . . . Tennis clothes were a rare elegance that could transform a man.") Papa envied them. He had a restless passion for fame, and he would have liked to enter the select sporting coterie of the Riviera. Too far past his prime to join that select brotherhood, he watched and fantasized instead.

In time Suzanne come to share Papa's interest in tennis. She expressed a desire to learn the game after seeing her parents play a set on the lawn of their Martez-sur-Marz villa. Papa later remembered the fateful day—in June, 1910—when he presented his daughter with her first tennis racket. It was an inexpensive instrument that he had purchased in a toy shop in Compiegne. He expected his daughter to amuse herself with it for a time and then tire of tennis.

Papa patiently outlined a tennis court on the lawn where Suzanne played with friends and seemed to enjoy the exercise. She did not tire of the game, and within a month Papa noticed that she had learned to handle her racket quite well, striking the ball with unusual dexterity. So Papa

39

purchased another one from a manufacturer in Paris, a racket that was light and properly balanced for a youngster of Suzanne's stature. To get a better idea of her capabilities, Papa played against Suzanne on the family lawn and was pleasantly surprised. "Even at that youthful age," he later recalled, "she showed signs of her developing genius for tactical execution."

Papa next concocted a special backboard for Suzanne to hit against, a board with warps and cracks in it so the ball came off in surprising ways unless it hit certain small even spots. He painted targets on the even areas. Suzanne thrashed away energetically at the board, memorizing its surface geography and eventually mastering it so she could play steadily against the board, smacking back the ball again and again and again to precisely the same spot.

Three months after Suzanne began to play, Papa took her to see a friend, Dr. Cizelly, who lived near Chantilly. Cizelly was a tennis enthusiast and the owner of a good clay court on which Suzanne played her first set on a hard surface before a gallery. She was skilled enough for Dr. Cizelly to suggest she be entered in a local tournament. Suzanne competed in the event, won four rounds, and captured second place.

Papa was encouraged enough to start giving Suzanne some serious tennis instruction. But what should he teach her? And how? With only a few teaching professionals available on the Continent most tennis players taught themselves the game through a slow process of observation and imitation. So Papa began observing in order to teach Suzanne to imitate.

On the Riviera that winter he studied the tennis of the Englishwomen. Their game was played over an extended period of time and consisted of ground strokes and slow tactical maneuvering from the baseline. The game was extremely civilized and unhurried and depended more than anything else upon patience and success at meticulous placement. After a few weeks Papa gave up teaching such play to Suzanne. It was undramatic and tedious and dreadfully boring, and it was totally unsuited for a girl so filled with enthusiasm and energy.

Papa turned then to the game of the men who astounded him "by the remarkable superiority of their methods." "Why, then, should not women adopt the masculine method? It seemed to me that with a well-directed course of training any woman could by taught the game as it was played by the men, although naturally she would be unable to play with the same degree of force."

And so Papa studied more closely the ground strokes and styles and strategies of the all-court game of the leading male players. He visited the courts of the various Riviera clubs more frequently and with a new purpose, and he watched and listened and questioned the players and took careful mental notes. Then he taught Suzanne the strongest features of each player: the forehand of this one, the backhand of that one, and the services of three or four others. He experimented in order to see exactly how much of the men's game a young woman might learn. Without actually intending to do so, he revolutionized women's tennis.

As Suzanne's tennis skills improved, Papa's aspirations increased. The fame and attention and deference he has bestowed upon tennis players on the Riviera might some day be his through Suzanne. His daughter could accomplish things that no woman had ever before imagined possible. Old assumptions concerning the physical strength, ability, fragility, speed, and expertise of women had never really been tested, Papa believed. Need anatomy actually be destiny? What were the real limitations for a woman athlete? Papa set out to discover for himself. There was no feminine model he could hold up as an inspiration for Suzanne, no woman who stood high above the common crowd of competitors in sport. Papa had only a dream to guide him in his efforts. He dreamed of something entirely new in women's sports—the perfect union of athletics and art. He dreamed of a woman who was the master of every stroke and tactic of the men's all-court game, but a woman who played that game better than any man and who played it with the effortless physical grace and ease of an accomplished dancer.

In late fall 1910, when the Lenglens took up their seasonal residence on the Riviera, Papa applied for the admission of Suzanne to the prestigious Nice Tennis Club, to which he already belonged. The Nice Club was one of the princial sites for winter tournaments on the Riviera, and the best male and female players in the world played on the club's clay courts. Children had not previously been allowed on the courts, but now, by special dispensation, Suzanne was granted limited access.

Papa practiced with Suzanne at the Nice Club, and in a short time his training methods became legendary. Suzanne practiced a single stroke from a set position on the court hour after hour while Papa or a club professional hit balls to her. After Papa sensed that the mechanics of the stroke had been mastered, control and placement became the goal. Papa placed a handkerchief on the court across the net from Suzanne, and the youngster aimed her shots at the small silk target. Gradually, no matter what the bound or speed or angle of the shot, Suzanne could return the ball to the target. Then Papa decreased the size of the target, folding and refolding the handkerchief, and eventually he replaced it with a coin. To the delight and disbelief of observers, Suzanne was soon capable of striking a coin anywhere on the court. On occasion she could hit a coin five times in a row while moving about the court and keeping the ball in play. Some days Papa divided the inner fringe of the court into squares like a chessboard. Suzanne then practiced striking certain squares in sequence from various positions across the net. The drill was repeated again and

43

again, Suzanne returning up to three hundred shots in a row without a break.

Photographer Jacques Henri Lartigue watched Papa training Suzanne, and he recorded in his journal, "Father Lenglen is very severe and it is easy to see he would really like his daughter to be a boy. Mother Lenglen, with her huge eyes and friendly smile, apparently feels differently. She would much prefer it if her daughter would just play and amuse herself like all the other young girls around here. But Suzanne wants to be a champion and that's why she spends every free moment hitting balls into the small square which have been marked out for her on the tennis court."

Papa prescribed an equally rigorous system of physical conditioning off the court. Conditioning was imperative, he insisted, because fully half of tennis was footwork and speed. So Suzanne swam, ran sprints, and jumped rope every day. Eventually these exercises brought her fame in athletic activities other than tennis. By 1919 she was the high jump champion among French women with a leap of four feet six inches—a mark within four inches of the world record for women at the time. She could jump over the tennis net from a standing position while keeping her feet together. She could run the eighty-meter dash in less than eleven seconds. This was all accomplished at a time when few women athletes trained strenuously. Typical of the conventional wisdom of the day was the attitude of Molla Mallory, a former singles champion of Norway who dominated the women's singles competition in America for nearly a decade after 1914. Mallory, a chain smoker and enthusiastic party-goer, affirmed, "I held that too serious training took more out of a girl nervously than she gained physically."

On Sunday afternoons Papa packed up the entire family and drove to tournaments at the various Riviera clubs. Suzanne watched and listened while Papa analyzed the strengths and weaknesses of each player. This was followed by a post-match discussion between father and daughter with detailed questions about the mobility and strokes of this or that player. Then back to the Nice courts and the handkerchiefs and coins and chessboard squares and dreams.

Papa did not work alone in developing Suzanne's tennis skills. He unabashedly solicited the best male players on the Riviera to practice with his daughter. His cry, *"Voulez-vous jouer avec ma fille?"* (Will you play with my daughter?) became a familiar appeal to many Riviera tennis regulars who took time to rally with the little girl and stayed to answer her father's endless questions.

Alvardo Rice, secretary of the Nice Tennis Club, also took an interest in Suzanne's athletic progress and found accomplished male players to hit with the eager little girl. He also served as Papa's assistant in training and conditioning Suzanne. Finally, the resident professional of the Nice Tennis Club, J. Negro, worked regularly with her. Because of his uncanny ball control, Negro was a particularly valuable addition to the

Lenglen team. Negro's game was full of tricks and surprises, spins and slices. One amazed spectator concluded of Negro's abilities: "If you told me he could make the ball sit up and beg, I wouldn't be the least bit surprised." Negro was nothing less than a sorcerer of tennis, and little Suzanne became his studious apprentice.

Papa insisted that Suzanne master every maneuver and every shot, that there not be even a hint of a weakness in any part of her game. When a difficult stroke troubled the little girl, Papa worked on it with her for days or weeks, analyzing and practicing until the problem was solved. Late in her career Suzanne recalled that during those early training days on the Riviera the backhand return straight down the line rather than cross court had once given her real problems. She practiced the shot over and over again, but just could not execute it effectively. She telegraphed the shot or hit it long or patted it back weakly. She started to avoid the shot, to play around it, but Papa refused to let her. She must not just learn the shot, he insisted, she must perfect it! Suzanne resorted to tantrums and tears to resist, but Papa prevailed. Suzanne learned it and practiced it until it became one of the many deadly strokes in her arsenal. The shot was particularly effective when Suzanne fired it from a half volley. Eventually she could announce with confidence: "A favorite shot of mine is the backhand drive down the line."

On occasion Papa told the truth about Suzanne's strenuous training. "It was necessary for my daughter to do an enormous amount of work before she could show any appreciable results in playing with masculine methods," he wrote in 1926. "She had need of all her tenacity of purpose and all the help given her by her comrades at the Nice Club." At other times, however, he dismissed the time and effort that went into the making of his little athletic virtuoso and stressed instead Suzanne's natural genius and his own constant concern for his daughter's physical and emotional health. He said Suzanne had practiced on the courts of the Nice Club for just one hour each day. Such testimony, no doubt, was intended to enhance the myth of Suzanne by attributing her skills to nature rather than to hard work—a champion born, not made. God provided the raw skills, Papa merely polished them. But far too many had watched as Papa's little girl practiced to exhaustion to give credence to such stuff.

Many of those who watched Suzanne's practice sessions expressed dismay at the way Papa and Mama Lenglen callously utilized emotion to keep their daughter practicing and working and running hour after hour and day after day. When Suzanne did well, when she learned a stroke or maneuver quickly and correctly, Papa and Mama were happy and proud and expressed their approval and affection loudly. When Suzanne had trouble with a shot or was slow on getting into position or made unforced errors, Papa and Mama were quick to express their impatience and disgust with unrestrained volume. In the early days of her training, Suzanne's mistakes were punished by Papa's withholding a treat from her, such as jam with her tea. She was rewarded by treats also, just as a trainer might reward a dancing dog or a horn-playing seal. Papa quickly discovered much more severe and emotionally destructive ways to motivate his little girl. He assaulted and battered the child's self-esteem, ridiculed her in front of spectators, and reduced her to tears and hysterics. Following pandemics of deprecation he embraced and comforted her and sent her back onto the court for another try at winning his love by doing exactly what was expected of her. When Suzanne erred, Mama too openly expressed her dissatisfaction, hissing, "Stupid girl! Keep your eye on the ball!"

Love—the offering or the withholding of it—became the whip Papa snapped. Papa stressed the importance of practice and perfection. Suzanne was not working for herself alone, but for the family. When she failed, she failed Papa or Mama. When she failed, she did not deserve their love and affection or should she expect it. And so Papa advised, directed, teased, criticized, cajoled, denounced, decried, praised and condemned his little girl without ever seeming to be really aware of the pulverizing emotional effect of his methods. His critical, unforgiving eye followed her every move, missing no mistake. And while Suzanne's tennis skills flowered, her emotional growth was stunted. She became athletically formidable and emotionally tattered.

It was ironic that long after Suzanne Lenglen was almost universally acknowledged as the avatar of tennis perfection, she still lacked normal self-confidence. She remained morbidly afraid of failure. She trumpeted self-assurance but there was a parchment-thin quality to that assurance. Just beneath the surface of her certitude was a fear of failing that stemmed not from reality but from childhood conditioning. The person who doubted Suzanne most was Suzanne. At any moment she might become the terrified child clutching for the daddy who might not be there. Her emotional structure was neither strong nor resilient, but a crystal web easily fractured. And time after time the servomechanism that made her nerves and muscles work in harmony went crazy for no good reason.

Papa and Mama Lenglen kept up their criticism at courtside throughout Suzanne's amateur career. Englishman Ted Tinling, who officiated some of Suzanne's matches on the Riviera, recalled that "Papa and Mama Lenglen chattered incessantly on the bench below me," during one of Suzanne's matches. "At that age I spoke better French than English," Tinling wrote, "and my thoughts wandered repeatedly as I overheard, fascinated, their running commentary on Suzanne's every movement. 'She's not arching her back on her serve today,' from Papa Lenglen. 'I liked last year's cardigans without sleeves much better,' from Mama."

For many spectators this was but one part of

the unusual ambience created by the presence of the Langlens. Mama provided yet another daft aspect by her very physiognomy. Mama had such an acute astigmatism, according to Tinling, "that both eyes looked outward in opposite directions, saving her the need to turn her head when following Suzanne's shots during the million hours she spent clucking over her daughter from the sidelines."

For Suzanne there was but one escape from the rigid exhausting routine and the endless ridicule —a flight into illness. Early in her career she learned of the temporary respite to be gained over Papa and Mama through sickness or collapse. Only when she was clearly ailing did she receive rewards of sweet, unsolicited parental affection. As a result, from an early age, Suzanne enjoyed poor health. Only through illness could she slip away from the insistent tyranny of Papa, the tedious practice drills, and the tournaments.

By the early 1920s Suzanne was clearly neurasthenic. And when her physical health really did deteriorate, it became impossible for fans or officials to distinguish between her idiopathic behavior and more serious maladies. At times this led to cruelly unfair criticism of her behavior on and off the tennis courts, which only deepened her fears and uncertainties.

Papa cautiously managed Suzanne's career the way one might guide a promising young boxer up through the ranks of more experienced competitors. She was entered in selected local tournaments, where she won more than she lost. But, win or lose, she always learned. She won the regional championship of Picardy in singles and in doubles in 1912 and went on to win several other local championships. She maintained at the time certain disconcerting childish mannerisms. At the Picardy championships, for example, one of her opponents refused for a while to play against a child who spent her time off the court not in watching other matches or practicing ground strokes but in galloping around on the lawns attracting birds by imitating their calls.

In 1913 Suzanne Lenglen was the surprise winner of the club championship of the Nice Tennis Club. She was then selected as the representative of the club in a match against the Italian Bordighera Club. In Italy, Mama Lenglen was greeted as the representative of the Nice Club and was directed to the dressing room. To the disbelief of the tournament officials, the diminutive Suzanne was then introduced as the actual French competitor; then to their dismay and delight, she won match after match. By the end of the summer of 1913, English travelers were returning from the Riviera with incredible stories about the young tennis thaumaturge they had watched shellac veteran players on the French and Italian clay.

In early 1914 Papa entered Suzanne in the Carlton Club tournament in Cannes for her first real test against top women's competition. She breezed through to the finals, where she outlasted Mrs. R. J. Winch, a ranking English player and a Wimbledon veteran. Lenglen and her partner, the legendary Anthony Wilding, took the mixed doubles title in the tournament.

During the course of her long three-set match against Mrs. Winch, an incident occurred that Papa was fond of describing. At the beginning of the final set Suzanne seemed exhausted, and she told Papa that she could not continue. It was not the first time that the little girl would ask her Papa to allow her to leave the court. And it was not the first time that he absolutely refused. Instead of providing permission to default, Papa provided Suzanne with stern words of warning and encouragement and reminded her that her opponent was also tired. According to Papa, Suzanne concluded before returning to the court: "Then it is not good tennis, it is courage that will win this match." That was the true spirit of Suzanne, Papa pointed out. Courage. And in the end Suzanne's superior courage had indeed brought her the victory. She was not just the best tennis player in the world, she was also the most courageous.

The fall of Mrs. Winch to the little French girl caused a flurry of excitement in tennis circles both on the Continent and in England. The directors of the Carlton Club frankly admitted that they believed Suzanne Lenglen had faced an impossible task in her fight against Mrs. Winch. But Suzanne was now making a habit of winning impossible contests. And all of France was beginning to take notice.

Following her surprising Riviera victory, Suzanne Langlen traveled to Saint-Cloud for the World Hard Court Championships at the Stade Français. She celebrated her fifteenth birthday at the tournament. Many spectators who now got their first glimpse of the rising star were enthralled by her. Suzanne seemed to stand no taller than her tennis racket, yet she managed to win match after match. And after each victory the crowds delighted in seeing the talented child skip excitedly into the proud embrace of her Papa. English correspondent A. Wallis Myers noticed that during each match Papa and Mama Lenglen sustained Suzanne "by communicating their own partisanship to her youthful spirit." Myers also found that Suzanne's movement across the court was already extraordinarily fluid. She was, he wrote, "a child of the bounding stride who defied ordinary mobility." At Saint-Cloud, Suzanne won world titles in singles and doubles and placed second with her partner in mixed doubles. After that it was clear that she was fast becoming the most popular sports personality in France. To the public she now became the amazing "Bébé Peugot." She was, others suggested, the reincarnation of the fifteenth-century Lady Margot, who came to Paris from the country of Hainault in 1427, and who was a master of *jeu de paume,* a primitive form of tennis, which she played far better than any man. Her reputation for skill in the sport was so great, in fact, that she was invited to play before the royal court of Scotland. There, thanks to her exceptional control and versatility in stroke production, she handily defeated every one of her male opponents. At the time of her visit to Scotland, Margot was but fifteen. Now at the age of fifteen it seemed that Suzanne might match Margot's feat by crossing the English Channel to challenge the best English tennis players at Wimbledon.

But Papa Lenglen refused. Suzanne was not ready yet for the fast grass courts of England, he believed. Wimbledon would have to wait one more year. Papa had seen Dorothea Lambert Chambers, winner of six Wimbledon singles titles, when she played on the Riviera. She was a big, powerful, and tireless woman and a superb court tactician, a master of the backcourt game. This year she would be seeking her seventh Wimbledon singles title, and surely she would overpower Papa Lenglen's little girl. This was not Suzanne's year. She needed more practice and more experience. To push her at this time against a woman so clearly her superior on grass might do irreparable damage to her frail self-confidence and jeopardize her future.

At Wimbledon that year the indomitable Mrs. Lambert Chambers won her seventh singles title, just as Papa expected. Then, even before summer's end, the Great War began in Europe, and Papa's plans for Suzanne's athletic triumphs were postponed indefinitely. The international tournaments at Saint-Cloud and Wimbledon were suspended from 1915 through 1918. These were good years in Suzanne's development, years when she had the stamina and the youthful energy and desire to play and to win. Her health was never better. Later, although they seldom discussed it with others, the Lenglens realized that the wartime hiatus had robbed Suzanne of the chance to capture several national and international titles. In the absence of the big tournaments, however, there was little that Suzanne could do but practice and wait and dream and regret.

In these years legends concerning Suzanne's dedication to France were formulated by the Lenglens for later distribution. One account of the Lenglens' life during the war years indicated that even the Germans recognized and admired Bébé Peugot. During the German invasion of the Oise, Suzanne left the family home and wandered curiously into the street. A German officer stopped and saluted her. "You are little Suzanne, unless I am mistaken," he said in halting French. After Suzanne confirmed her identity, the officer warned, "I beg you to leave immediately while there is time." And so Suzanne hurried home with the alarm. Her trophies were buried to keep them from falling into enemy hands, and the Lenglens retreated to their villa on the Riviera for the duration of the war.

Later, by way of emphasizing Suzanne's patriotic fervor, Mama and Papa insisted that during the war years Suzanne, like all good daughters of France, had been very concerned with the military situation. She played tennis, they "admitted," perhaps only a dozen times between 1914 and 1918, but she spent most of the time during those years knitting socks or rolling bandages for the soldiers.

There was, of course, disagreement with this account. Observers on the Riviera noticed that Suzanne appeared to practice continually during the war years with a routine even more rigorous than before. From early morning until late afternoon she was seen drilling and practicing her strokes and footwork on the courts of the Nice Tennis Club. The war years on the Riviera provided her with an unusual advantage. Soldiers from Australia, England, America, and the Continent convalesced there, and among them were were some of the premier players of the world, many of whom played in exhibition matches for the Red Cross. Included among the exhibition players were Richard Norris Williams, the American singles champion, and Clarence "Peck" Griffin, the national doubles champion.

Suzanne watched the servicemen's tournaments and played in some of the exhibition matches with the American and English players. All of those who hit with her were impressed by her precocious expertise, and they returned to their native countries with still more stories of the Riviera darling who danced her way through matches, who kept the ball in play indefinitely until her opponent made an error, the little girl who understood all of the fine points of the game, whose mind comprehended every nuance of strategy and tactics, who was court-wise as no other woman, who hit the ball and covered the court like a man, and whose father was always at court-side encouraging, beseeching, cajoling, and criticizing her. Griffin and Williams were so struck by the young prodigy that they returned to America saying they believed she might beat several of the men ranked among America's top ten players.

By the end of summer 1925 Lenglen had established a record of dominance in tennis unequaled in that or any other sport. In seven years she had defaulted in one match and suffered what most Frenchmen now considered a technical loss. With the single exception of the tragic interlude at Forest Hills, Lenglen had not lost a match in singles competition in seven years of tournament play. In those seven years she had lost only two sets in singles. At Wimbledon she had played ninety-two matches in three categories and had won eighty-nine. She had also won fifteen World Hard Court Championships, fifteen French National Championships, six Wimbledon singles titles, and two Olympic gold medals.

The effect of all of this on France was to give an enormous boost to national pride. Suzanne Lenglen was unquestionably the great national heroine now. Indeed, some Frenchmen said she was even greater than Joan of Arc. Writing in *Le Journal,* Clement Vautel announced that "an Englishman told me, 'The two greatest French women are Joan of Arc and Suzanne.' I replied, 'You burned the former, but you have not yet beaten the latter,' " Vautel's pride was indicative of the national sentiment that surrounded Suzanne Lenglen. They had not beaten her. They would never beat her! Every Frenchman knew that. And Vautel, along with the overwhelming majority of his countrymen, believed that the Americans had utilized deception and a base conspiracy to confuse and humiliate her when she was not well. What happened in America had nothing whatever to do with Lenglen's greatness but very much to do with the hypocritical American spirit. It was typical of the kind of behavior the French were beginning to expect more and more from their former ally, thanks to the highly impassioned controversy over the repayment of war debts. Could a nation that insisted on bleeding France nearly to death during her financial crisis be expected not to take advantage of the single most glorious symbol of French courage? The Americans! Their greed blinded them to true beauty.

By 1925 Lenglen's fame had spread far beyond the sporting world. She was the first female athlete to be acknowledged as a celebrity outside her particular sport. People who cared little for tennis or who knew nothing of the game now applauded her struggles and triumphs because they were beautiful allegories of France's struggles and triumphs. The masses scrambled to see her. In unison they chanted her name in order to be recognized as part of the great civilization that produced such a wonderful woman.

But it was not just the common crowd that bowed down to the Goddess now. The great and the near great also sang hosannas. A visit by celebrities to the Riviera without an audience with Suzanne was like a visit to Rome without an audience with the Pope. Prosperous industrialists, war profiteers, politicians, writers, movie stars, maharajahs, kings, ex-kings, and pretenders competed for her attention. King Gustav V of Sweden was an unabashed admirer, as was ex-king Manuel of Portugal. Douglas Fairbanks and Mary Pickford visited the Lenglen villa, as did Rudolph Valentino, Georges Carpentier, and scores of lesser lights.

What did Suzanne Lenglen think of the crowds in the streets and in the galleries and the wealthy camp followers who sought her company? She believed that some were in love with her, "others are content with good friendship, while a large percentage are attracted by the reflected glory which comes to them from the association with so famous a personage. They like the limelight even when not directed full upon themselves." She wrote somewhat wistfully that she distributed her attentions and smiles "with royal impartiality." "It is what is expected by the public," she believed, and so she had to make some return for the flattery and the adulation showered upon her.

Of herself, Lenglen revealed that she was

"human enough to react joyfully to this new atmosphere." She "enjoyed the interest in people's eyes, the new respect in their voices." She found that it was thrilling to find herself "in the very warm center of things instead of standing outside in the cold circumference; to have her opinion asked, her advice taken; to hear the language of compliment instead of disdain; to feel that wherever she went she made a stir."

Lenglen intimated that she had made an indelible mark in two kingdoms—beauty and sport. Yet anyone who saw her realized that such a conviction was based largely upon illusion. No matter how enchanting her performances on the courts of Europe, no one ever made the mistake of saying Suzanne Lenglen was a beauty. To do so was merely to demonstrate an extraordinary capacity for self-delusion.

Suzanne Lenglen stood about five and a half feet tall. She was a muscular, large-boned girl with gray eyes, raven hair, and a sharp, birdlike profile. She had an unusually long nose and large irregular teeth that protruded unhandsomely from her mouth when she smiled. Paul Gallico recalled that she had "a hatchet face and a hook nose"; while Hazel Wightman, a lifelong friend of Suzanne, described her by simply saying, "She was so homely —you can't imagine a homelier face." Bill Tilden summed up her appearance charitably by observing, "Heaven knows no one could call her beautiful."

Yet despite her physiognomy, she had a rather

attractive and healthy demeanor in the early 1920s. Because she eschewed the traditional long-sleeved blouse and wide-brimmed hat of the other players, her face and arms were deeply tanned. But the pressure of practice and of play gradually eroded her physical health as well as her emotional stability. By the mid-1920s, when she stood at the pennacle of her career, she looked thirty years older than her actual age. There were deep dark circles under her eyes and her skin was wrinkled and creased. The constant exposure to the sun caused her complexion to deteriorate rapidly. She found it necessary to wear ever heavier layers of powder and makeup. Al Laney noticed in the mid-1920s that she had a dull, almost sallow, colorless skin. Under the powder her face appeared puffed, her eyes were rheumy and conveyed the deep inner loneliness of a woman who had a awareness of the inadequacies of athletic genius before the tireless assaults of time.

Ted Tinling, a close friend of the Lenglen family, attributed her premature physical and emotional deterioration to Papa, who "drove her relentlessly toward the goal of absolute supremacy, which was compulsive to both their egos. To maintain this," Tinling wrote, "Suzanne began very early to deprive herself of all the joys of a normal existence." To maintain her athletic supremacy she realized, Tinling found, that there would have to be "the total sacrifice of all natural life." Consequently, even before she turned twenty-five, "her face and expression had already

61

the traces of deep emotional experiences far beyond the normal for her age."

And yet nearly everyone who watched her perform pirouettes on the tennis court remarked that her lack of physical beauty was largely overcome by her grace and poise and movement. There was a remarkable transformation in Suzanne when she stepped onto the court, as though the area within the chalked rectangles was an enchanted kingdom in which the ugly duckling became, for a time, a beautiful swan, or, as one writer referred to her, "an insouciant butterfly." Scores of observers commented on this very fact—the impact of the kinetic upon the aesthetic in the metamorphosis of the mortal Suzanne into the Great Lenglen, the Goddess. Paul Gallico found that "she dressed divinely and her ugliness became almost an asset." It was the movement that held the spectator in thrall, that satisfied the lust of the eye, and for a while disguised her lack of beauty. Suzanne communicated a singular *joi de vivre,* a bubbling *bonhomie* on grass or clay when things went her way, and they almost always went her way. In a world recovering from the horrors of a world war, this gliding goddess by her every move compellingly and enticingly proclaimed, "Behold, I'm absolutely wonderful, come have a look." And the whole world did.

Accurately describing her motion was difficult and tested the rehetorical capabilities of countless spectators. C. C. Pyle, the hard-boiled American promoter, searched for the right words to describe her graceful glissades. "Why, if she were merely to rise from this chair and walk over to the door—it would be, well, it would be like a seagull leaving a wave." Perhaps it was the peculiar slant of the Riviera sunshine, or maybe the effect of ingesting champagne in the casinos in the early afternoon, or both, but the adoring crowds who watched Suzanne in competition in Nice and Cannes every spring suggested that she appeared to glide above the clay, suspended like a beautiful bird in flight. She swooped after the ball, now a floating seagull and then in an instant a falcon diving with deadly speed for the kill. And between points she pranced around on her toes—on her toes—reminding spectators of a prima donna positioning herself for a dance. To many people seeing her for the first time, this seemed a distracting and unneccessary affectation. But Suzanne believed it important never to let her heels touch the court, to be prepared to leap for the ball at any moment and to be, as she once described it, "like a cat walking on hot bricks." Tennis was, after all, a performing art when executed by the Great Lenglen.

A. Wallis Myers felt that the English grass "permitted the best expression of a refined art" when Suzanne played tennis. "Fluency of footwork, at which the French excel, reveled in the lighter and easier tread, the softer carpet for swift toe work. The delicate volley, the application of check or slice, the strokes that satisfied finesse rather than force—these were better displayed on green and yielding turf." England, he felt, provided the Goddess with a better stage than did France.

Even when Lenglen bent down to pick up a ball, her movement was lithe and lambent and memorable. Her turns were not prosaic mechanical maneuvers, they were poetic pirouettes. And all of this was accentuated by her adoption of a dancer's gown for tennis. Her costumes were all of light silk, and she seldom wore a slip under them. Consequently, there was an additional titillating appeal to her movement, for when she leaped high on the court, with the sunlight behind her, her clothing became transparent and the "naughty old gentlemen" at courtside got a delicious peak at the outlines of the body beneath the silk. Sometimes, Ted Tinling recalled, spectators got more than a peak at the outlines. "When she was in flowing stride," Tinling recalled of Suzanne on the Riviera, "it wasn't unusual for one of Suzanne's breasts to pop out."

She was simply incomparable, a singular, odd, suspended phantom of delight, a lovely, haunting apparition who startled the hearts of all who watched her. But neither the costume nor the grace of Suzanne Lenglen made her tennis extraordinary. Those were simply frills. It was rather her absolute mastery of the fundamentals of the game that produced her singular virtuosity. She played a basically simple and crisply efficient game. Young Helen Wills concluded that "the printed word can hardly convey an idea of her efficiency on the court. When you saw her play you

64

did not know how good she was because it looked so easy. It was only from the other side of the net that you realized how really good she was. Her control and delicacy of placement will probably never be equalled."

On the court, Lenglen's primary concern was ball control rather than speed, even though she was capable of hitting consistently with the deceptive power of most male players. Most of her opponents commented on the softness of the drives as well as on the height at which they passed above the net—always about one meter. Papa had drilled into Suzanne the importance of keeping the ball in play by clearing the net. If the ball were hit over the net, even if it were hit hard enough to fall beyond the baseline, there was still the chance that the opponent might play it. But a ball hit into the net was always a lost point. Thus Papa taught Suzanne to observe a "margin of safety" in clearing the net and keeping the ball in play. When she failed to clear the net Papa ridiculed her mercilessly. She learned to remember and regret every netted ball she hit. Sportwriter Al Laney spoke with her during a 1924 Riviera tournament and was impressed by the few times she netted the ball—four times in four matches. When he mentioned that fact to Suzanne, she replied condescendingly, "But of course, my little one. . . . I have been careless this week, *n'est ce pas?*"

Because of that margin of safety, it seemed that Suzanne Lenglen would be vulnerable to a serve and volley player, an easy victim to the player who could rush the net and cut off those enticingly high returns. That was inevitable a miscalculation of many challengers. As if by mental telepathy, she seemed able to anticipate such a move on the part of any opponent. Her sense of anticipation was extraordinarily fine and, when an opponent moved toward the net to volley, her passing shots —perfectly disguised—were almost always winners.

Mary K. Browne pointed out an uncanny aspect of Lenglen's play. From the other side of the net, Browne noticed, "some of the balls hit by Suzanne came so slowly that they seemed to float over the net. But as you approached them with confidence to kill them, something seemed to go wrong. The returns went into the net or floated back beyond the baseline. She seemed so vulnerable," Browne observed, because of that margin of safety. Yet she was invulnerable. She knew when you were coming in to volley—she read your mind. And when you went for the score off a volley she knew just where you would hit it and she had it back at you instantly. Against Lenglen the serve-and-volley game was not only ineffective, it could be suicidal.

The constant pressure of staying at the top of the tennis world, competing in all of the major European tournaments and facing challenger after challenger, as well as accommodating legions of journalists and dignitaries, gradually took its toll on Suzanne Lenglen. Consequently, her attitude toward competition and crowds changed. She became more moody and petulant as the years passed. Her refusal in 1920 to obey the dictum of the French Tennis Federation was merely a first act of rebellion. Such episodes became common, and her mercurial temperament became legend. Americans never really appreciated her behavior, but she dismissed it all and concluded that the Americans were simply incapable of comprehending the fiery Latin spirit. Her apologists explained that the Goddess had the soul of an artist. And such a soul could never be confined within the rules of a game or the chalk lines of a tennis court. It bubbled over and defied convention on the court and off. She just found it impossible to emulate the studied insouciance of Anglo-Saxon phlegm that English and American audiences seemed to value so highly. And so she regularly indulged herself with explosive emotional displays when things did not go as planned. And, extraordinary as it seems, the French crowds favored the Maid Marvel during such exhibitions and seemed to symapathize completely with her frustration.

When Suzanne Lenglen disagreed with a line call, she glared at the linesman or snapped at him between points or stopped and stamped her foot on the ground. When her partner failed to play up to expectations, Lenglen defaulted and left him on the court alone. Following a questionable line call made against her during a Riviera match in 1925, she threw down her racket in protest. The referee then declared a foot fault against her as a penalty. That only enraged the Goddess more, and she loudly cursed the linesman was hard of hearing. She screamed that his hearing was not at issue. It was his vision she questioned. Was he blind? The match was delayed still further while Lenglen had her complaints written down for the offending linesmen and the tournament officials. This was done with mock dignity, and when the linesman was finally shown her written indictment—he could see well enough to read— he left the match.

Suzanne Lenglen was indulged in such behavior because both she and the officials realized that the crowds had come to see the Goddess perform and not to watch linesmen make questionable calls. Such calls merely interfered with the show. And given the choice between Lenglen performing and a linesman making calls, both crowd and officials sided with her. The presence of the linesman was simply an inconvenient and sometimes obtrusive formality when Suzanne Lenglen played before a French gallery.

During an exhibition match in Austria in 1925, Lenglen was paired with one of her favorite doubles partners, Count Ludwig Salm Von Hoogstraten, the most temperamental of the male players on the Continent. But she outdid even the temperamental Count when it came to emotional pyrotechnics. When he played poorly and missed a shot, she hurled her racket into the net, glared at her partner for several seconds, and then stomped off the court. Her exit was accompanied by sympathetic applause. She refused to return to the court despite earnest apologies from her partner and pathetic pleas from tournament officials. After several hours a default was announced.

Behind Lenglen's explosive displays of temperament was an awareness of certain unpleasant realities. Time did not pass her by. Her dominance in tennis could not last forever. Sooner or later on some sunny afternoon it would all end, probably without warning. Some young upstart would come along to unseat the Goddess, and her time in the sun would be over. But not quite yet. Not quite yet.

She continued to defend her titles successfully as her health deteriorated. Her flights into illness were now often the real thing. She suffered from two types of jaundice and from pernicious anemia. She caught colds more easily. And she taxed her fragile constitution by overeating for weeks at a time and then going on severe starvation diets. At times she seemed to be bulimic. Helen Wills noticed that Suzanne Lenglen dieted so severely at times that she ran out of energy on the tennis court. In late 1924 she suffered from a severely strained tendon that made her movement on the court during the next year extremely painful. She had always been high strung and extended herself time and again to the outermost limits of her physical and nervous capabilities. At times she crossed those limits. By the mid-1920s she experienced regular hysterical fits of crying followed by uncontrollable laughter and then the meaningless babble of logorrhea. She fluctuated between emotional highs and lows. She suffered several nervous breakdowns, or, as they were referred to by her closest friends, *crises de nerfs*. Before important matches she became withdrawn and sullen and then, at times, hysterical. Off the court and on, she was playing against herself.

Lenglen's severe physical and emotional problems in the mid-1920s were exacerbated both by the French financial crisis and by Papa's lingering serious illness. Just when she began thinking of retirement and rest, playing and winning became increasingly important. It was a final cruel irony in her career. The family fortune began to slip away. Lenglen recalled, "Our money began to decrease in value and its buying power began to grow smaller and smaller. My father began to find that the very comfortable income which we had once enjoyed, although unchanged in size, had considerably decreased in value. Luxuries which we had once enjoyed gave way to mere comforts." Financial solvency depended more and more upon Suzanne.

Beginning in 1926, there was a renewed earnestness to her play and even more grimness about winning. There was something far more important at stake in the play than a simple game of tennis. People continued to watch her win and marveled at her skill and analyzed her tactics but they could never know what it all meant to her. They saw the show, the facade. Only a few knew of the emotional storm within.

It was tragic for the Lenglen family, also, that Suzanne had been unsuccessful in establishing herself either in a comfortable marriage or in a financially rewarding career ourside sport. After amateur tennis, what would the world hold for her besides memories? Tennis was her life. She could never support herself as a novelist or as a professional journalist—as a writer she was a good tennis player. And although she had been a close associate of royalty and aristocracy for years, and although there had been scores of suitors and dozens of delicious rumors concerning romance and marriage, no man ever requested the privilege of sweeping her off to a comfortable country estate. Her closest friends and confidantes, after Mama and Papa, were all women. When she took a brief rest away from home and vacationed in Switzerland or Italy or Spain, she was accompanied by female companions. That fact, too, became a source of intriguing rumor. And some of Suzanne's fellow players insisted that she was in fact interested in men only because of her overwhelming dedication to Mama and Papa and their desire for respectability. Part of the emotional storm that unsettled her may have been due not simply to her inability to find a husband, but to her actual lack of interest in finding one.

And so Papa's little girl never found that shining prince who might love her and support her and make her happy and bring security and financial stability to the family. There remained but one man in Suzanne Lenglen's life—her Papa. Now Papa's health was failing, and there was no man to take his place. He still sat beside the courts every day, the shell of the man he once was, wrapped in blankets, pale, watching his daughter. She had become his dream girl, the ideal he had once envisioned. . . .

# FRANK DEFORD

## "I'll Play My Own Sweet Game"

*The first American to win the Wimbledon Men's singles championship was Bill Tilden. And Centre Court at Wimbledon was the scene of Tilden's dramatic breakthrough as the world champion. Though he had previously made it as far as the finals, he had never won a major tournament until that moment in July 1920 when he came into his own as a player. Older at twenty-seven than most players when he won his first championship, Tilden went on to become almost unbeatable for the next decade. As described by sports writer Frank Deford, Tilden projected the image of a confident and quintessentially masculine athlete, but he was in fact a homosexual and always a lonely man who died penniless and forgotten in walk-up room near Hollywood.*

With any artist who attains the ultimate in his craft, there must be one moment, an instant, when genius is first realized, when a confluence of God's natural gifts at last swirl together with the full powers of endeavor and devotion in the man to bear him to greatness. Virtually always, of course, that moment cannot be perceived, and it passes unnoticed, but with Big Bill Tilden it was isolated, forever frozen in time,. He knew precisely when he had arrived, and, thoughtfully, he revealed it.

This happened on Centre Court at Wimbledon in 1920. Tilden was already twenty-seven, and although he had never won a major championship, he had reached the finals. It was his first trip abroad, and to his delight the British, unlike his own countrymen, had taken to him right away. Americans always only grudgingly granted Tilden recognition, never mind respect, largely because they were emotionally hung up on Big Bill's main rival, Bill Johnston, who was affectionately known as Little Bill, or even, in the soupiest moments, Wee Willie Winkie. Johnston was five feet eight, a wonderful cute doll-person from the California middle class, and all Americans (Tilden prominently included) were absolutely nuts about him: The little underdog with the big heart who cut larger fellows down to size.

By contrast, at six feet one-and-a-half inches tall, 155 pounds, angular and overbearing, a Philadelphia patrician of intellectual pretension, Big Bill was the perfect foil for Little Bill, and the great American villain. Until 1920 he had also cooperated by remaining a loser with a healthy reputation for choking in important matches. The year before, in the finals at Forest Hills, Johnston had defeated Tilden in straight sets, and so it was assumed that Wimbledon would serve as the stage where Johnston, the American champion, would

74

duel Gerald Patterson, the Wimbledon defender, for the undisputed championship of the world.

Unfortunately for hopes for this classic confrontation, Johnston was waylaid in an early round by a steady English player named J. C. Parke. Not until the next day, when Tilden routed Parke, avenging Little Bill's defeat, did Big Bill move front and center as Patterson's most conspicuous challenger. Of course, from the moment Tilden strode upon their grass that summer, the British had been enchanted with him—his game, his manner, his idiosyncrasies: "This smiling youth, so different from other Americans." A woolly blue sweater Tilden wore seems to have positively enthralled the entire nation, and the *London Times* exclaimed that "his jumpers are the topic of the tea-table."

While little Johnston struck the British as just that, a pleasant little sort, the lean giant caused them admiration and wonder: "Of great stature, he is loosely built with slender hips and very broad shoulders . . . in figure, an ideal lawn tennis player." His game they found so arresting— "There is no stroke Mr. Tilden cannot do at full speed, and his is undoubtedly the fastest serve seen"—that one of the more poetic observers even rhapsodized, "His silhouette as he prepares to serve suggests an Egyptian pyramid king about to administer punishment."

Seeing Tilden for the first time, unprepared for that sight, was obviously a striking experience. Not so much in what exactly they said but in their evident astonishment and determined hyperbolic reach, do the British of 1920 best intimate what an extraordinary presence Big Bill Tilden must have been. Yet perhaps even more important, the British understood immediately that here was a different sort of athletic temperament. The Americans were not to fathom this in Tilden for years, if indeed many of them ever did. But Tilden had played only a handful of matches in England that summer before he was assessed perfectly in the sporting press: "He gives the impression that he regards lawn tennis as a game—a game which enables him to do fascinating things, but still a game. . . . When he has something in hand he indulges his taste for the varied at the expense of the commercial."

Pleased at the attention given him, even more gratified that his playing philosophy was appreciated, Tilden grew assured, and, boldly and not without some conceit, he began to enunciate his theories of the game. When not at the courts or attending the theater, he spent all his time writing in his hotel room, and within three weeks he had completed his first book, *The Art of Tennis.* "The primary object in match tennis is to break up the other man's game" was, significantly, the point he most emphasized.

Patterson, meanwhile, remained quite confident. An Australian, the nephew of the great opera star Nellie Melba, he was not only the defending Wimbledon champion but star of the team which held the Davis Cup. He was at his peak and generally recognized above Johnston as the ranking player in the world. At Wimbledon Patterson had only to bide his time scouting the opposition and practice at his leisure, for in those days the defender did not play in the regular tournament but was obliged only to meet the All Comers winner in a special Challenge Round.

Patterson's supremacy seemed all the more obvious after Tilden appeared to struggle in the All Comers final against the Japanese, Zenzo Shimizu. In each set Tilden fell far behind: 1–4 in the first, 2–4 in the second, 2–5 in the third. He won 6–4, 6–4, 13–11. Nobody realized it at the time, but it was one of Tilden's amusements, a favor to the crowd, to give lesser opponents a head start. Tilden had whipped Shimizu 6–1, 6–1 in a preliminary tournament the week before Wimbledon, and he certainly had no intention of cheating his Centre Court fans with that same sort of lopsided display. In the final set Big Bill tested himself and kept things going, largely just by hitting backhands and nothing much else.

"The player owes the gallery as much as an actor owes the audience," he wrote once; and Paul Galico summed it up: "To his opponents it was a contest; with Tilden it was an expression of his own tremendous and overweening ego, coupled with feminine vanity." Big Bill never really creamed anybody unless he hated them or was in a particular hurry to get somewhere else.

Certainly he was not ever anxious to hastily depart Centre Court at Wimbledon, and he returned for the championship against Patterson on Saturday, July 3. Big Bill found this date especially felicitous; and obsessive patriot, he noted that, for an American, July 3 was the next best thing to July 4. He further buttressed this omen by somehow obtaining a four-leaf clover that he was assured had once grown under the chair that Abraham Lincoln used to sit in on the White House lawn. And so, with that talisman safely ensconced in his pocket, he set out to become the first American ever to win the Wimbledon Men's championship.

Patterson had a strong serve and forehand, but his weakness was an odd corkscrew backhand that he hit sort of inside out. And so, curiously it seemed, Tilden began by playing to Patterson's powerful forehand. The champion ran off the first four games with dispatch and won the set 6–2. But then, as Tilden changed sides for the first time in the second set, he spotted a good friend, the actress Peggy Wood, sitting in the first row with a ticket he had provided her, and he looked straight at Miss Wood, and with a reassuring nod, that kind delivered with lips screwed up in smug confidence, he signaled to her that all was quite well, that it was in the bag, that finally, at the age of twenty-seven, he was about to become the champion of the world.

Miss Wood, of course, had no notion that she would be used as a conduit for history; nor, for that matter, could she understand Tilden's cockiness. He had lost the first set 6–2; he was getting clobbered by the best player in the world. But down the five full decades, and more, that have passed, she cannot forget that expression of his, nor what followed. "Immediately," she says, as if magic were involved, "Bill proceeded to play."

In that instant he had solved Patterson's forehand, and the champion, his strength ravaged, had nothing but his weakness to fall back upon. *The primary object in match tennis is to break up the other man's game.* "A subtle change came over Patterson's game," the *Guardian* correspondent wrote in some evident confusion. "Things that looked easy went out, volleys that ought to have been crisply negotiated ended up in the net." Tilden swept the next three sets at his convenience, losing only nine games, and toward the end it was noted for the record that "the Philadelphian made rather an exhibition of his opponent."

Big Bill did not lose another match of any significance anywhere in the world until a knee injury cost him a victory more than six years later. Playing for himself, for his country, for posterity, he was invincible. No man ever bestrode his sport as Tilden did for those years. It was not just that he could not he beaten, it was nearly as if he had invented the sport he conquered. Babe Ruth, Jack Dempsey, Red Grange and the other fabled American sweat lords of the times stood at the head of more popular games, but Tilden simply was tennis in the public mind: *Tilden and tennis,* it was said, in that order. He ruled the game as much by force of his curious, contradictory, often abrasive personality as by his proficiancy. But he was not merely eccentric. He was the greatest irony in sport: to a game that then suffered a "fairy" reputation, Tilden gave a lithe, swashbuckling, athletic image—although he was in fact a homosexual, the only great male athlete we know to have been one.

Alone in the world of athletics, nearly friendless and, it seems, even ashamed of himself, there was seldom any joy for the man, even amidst his greatest tennis triumphs. It's quite likely that in his whole life Tilden never spent a night alone with an adult, man or woman. And his every day was shadowed by the bizarre and melancholy circumstances surrounding a childhood he tried to forget; certainly it is no coincidence that he did not blossom as a champion until just after he discarded the name of his youth.

He had been born on February 10, 1893, and christened William Tatem Tilden Jr., which he came to hate because everyone called him Junior or June. Finally, arbitrarily, around the time of his twenty-fifth birthday, he changed the Junior to the Second, II. That onus officially disposed of, June became Bill and then, even better, Big Bill.

He had been introduced to tennis early. It was an upper-class game, and the family he was born into was rich, of ascending social prominence, and even greater civic presence. The family mansion, Overleigh, was located in the wealthy Germantown section of Philadelphia, only a block or so from the Germantown Cricket Club. The Tildens belonged, of course, and the club was indeed to be the site of many Big Bill triumphs, but the family summered at a fashionable Catskill resort, Onteora, and it was there that young June learned the game of tennis, in the last year of the nineteenth century.

The first clear vision of him as a player does not arise, however, until about a decade later, when Tilden was playing, with little distinction, for the team at his small private school, Germantown Academy. This day he was struggling on the court, slugging everything, all cannonballs, when Frank Deacon, one of his younger friends, came by. Even then, as a schoolboy, Tilden was always closest to children years younger than he. At the end of a point, which, typically, Tilden had violently overplayed, hitting way out, Deacon hollered to him in encouragement, "Hey, June, take it easy."

Tilden stopped dead, and with what became a characteristic gesture, he swirled to face the boy, placing his hands on his hips and glaring at him. "Deacon," he snapped, "I'll play my own sweet game."

And so he did, every day of his life. He was the proudest of men and the saddest, pitifully alone and shy, but never so happy as when he brought his armful of rackets into the limelight or walked into a crowded room and contentiously took it over. George Lott, a Davis Cup colleague and a man who actively disliked Tilden, was nonetheless this mesmerized by him: "When he came into the room it was like a bolt of electricity hit the place. Immediately, there was a feeling of awe, as though you were in the presence of royalty. You knew you were in contact with greatness, even if only remotely. The atmosphere became charged, and there was almost a sensation of lightness when he left. You felt completely dominated and breathed a sigh of relief for not having ventured an opinion of any sort."

Tilden himself said, "I can stand crowds only when I am working in front of them, but then I love them." Obviously the crowds and the game were his sex. For a large part of his life, the glory years, all the evidence suggests that he was primarily asexual; it was not until he began to fade as a player and there were not enough crowds to play to that his homosexual proclivities really took over. But ahh, when he was king, he would often appear to trap himself in defeat, as he had against Shimizu, so that he could play the better role, prolonging his afternoon as the cynosure in the sun, prancing and stalking upon his chalked stage, staring at officials, fuming at the crowd, now toying with his opponent, then saluting him grandly, spinning, floating, jumping, playing his own sweet game, reveling in the game.

And yet, for all these excesses of drama and melodrama, his passion for competition was itself even superseded by another higher sense: Sportsmanship. Tilden was utterly scrupulous, obsessed with honor, and he would throw points (albeit with grandeur. Pharisee more than Samaritan) if he felt that a linesman had cheated his opponent. Big Bill was the magistrate of every match he played, and the critic as well. "Peach!" he would cry in delight, lauding any opponent who beat him with a good shot. And, if inspired or mad enough at the crowd or at his rival, he would serve out the match by somehow holding five balls in one huge hand and then tossing four of them up, one after another, and pounding out four cannonball aces—bam, bam, bam, bam; 15–30–40–game— then throwing the fifth ball away with disdain. That was the style to it. Only the consummate showman would think of the extra ball as the closing fillip to the act.

"He is an artist," Franklin P. Adams wrote at Big Bill's peak. "He is more of an artist than nine-tenths of the artists I know. It is the beauty of the game that Tilden loves; it is the chase always, rather than the quarry."

Further, even more unlike almost all great champions in every sport, whose brilliance is early recognized, early achieved, Tilden was required to make himself great. Very nearly he created himself. Only a few years before he became champion of the world, he could not make the college varsity at the University of Pennsylvania. He taught himself, inspired himself, fashioning a whole new level for the game in the bargain.

Withal, it is probable that the very fact that he was homosexual was largely responsible for the real success he achieved in tennis; he had none elsewhere. Urbane, well-read, a master bridge player, a connoisseur of fine music, he held pretensions to writing and acting as well as tennis, but these gossamer vanities only cost him great amounts of stature and money, and even held him up to mockery. For all his intelligence, tennis was the only venture that June Tilden could ever succeed at, until the day he died in his cramped walk-up room near Hollywood and Vine, where he lived out his tragedy, a penniless ex-con, scorned or forgotten, alone as always, and desperately in need of love from a world that had tolerated him only for its amusement. "He felt things so very deeply," Peggy Wood says. "He was not a frivolous person, and yet, I never saw him with anybody who could have been his confidant. How must it be like that? There must have been so many things deep within him that he could never talk about. I suppose he died of a broken heart." It seems he did.

To the end, in the good times and the bad, he searched for one thing above all: A son. He could not have one, as he made himself a great player to honor the dead mother he worshipped. But the boys he found, whom he loved and taught, would grow up and put away childish things, which is what any game is, what tennis is, and ultimately, what Big Bill Tilden was. He was the child of his own dreams, always, until the day he died, age sixty, his bags packed, ready once again to leave for a tennis tournament.

# HERBERT WARREN WIND

## About Chris Evert

*Remaining calm, coming from behind in a crucial match, Chris Evert first made her mark in women's tennis at her debut in the 1971 U. S. Open at age sixteen. Carefully trained by her father, tennis pro Jimmy Evert, who stressed the basics until they became second nature, Chris achieved a mastery of her game that enabled her to sustain a memorable career. She held her own against an array of worthy opponents: Margaret Court, Billie Jean King, Evonne Goolagong, Martina Navratilova. A canny, resourceful player, she was noted for her fierce concentration, her two-handed backhand, her intelligence in psyching herself during matches, and her unfailing sportsmanship. Herbert Warren Wind reviews her career and gives us insights into her earthbound sense of self.*

The United States has never before had a sports heroine quite like Chris Evert Lloyd. A number of appealing and able women golfers, tennis players, skaters, skiers, swimmers, divers, gymnasts, and even a few women track stars have captured the country's imagination from time to time, but certainly not to the same degree Evert Lloyd has. Tennis is probably the sport in which women can display their athletic skill to best advantage, but none of our earlier tennis champions established as fervent and enduring a rapprochement with the American public as Evert Lloyd has. Helen Wills, perhaps our greatest woman tennis player, was too remote and queenly. Alice Marble, a tomboy who used to shag fly balls in the outfield during the San Francisco Seals' practice sessions, was a gifted all-court player and a delight to watch, but her career at the top—from 1936 through 1940— was delayed by a siege of serious illness and cut short by the outbreak of war. Maureen Connolly, the best of the many fine American players who came to the forefront after the Second World War, was sixteen in 1951, when she won the first of her three straight United States championships. She went on to win the Wimbledon championship in 1952, 1953, and 1954, the French championship in 1953 and 1954, and the Australian championship in 1953; that year, she became the first woman to bring off the Grand Slam—winning all four major championships. Connolly was still in her teens in 1954, when, in the period between the end of Wimbledon and the start of our championships, she had the misfortune to break her leg severely in a riding accident and was forced to retire from tennis. (The record book in which I happened to look up the years when Connolly won her championships, the 1983 edition of the "World of Tennis," noted that she hit her ground strokes "with remorseless accuracy," a phrase that goes right to the heart of the matter.) Mention must certainly be made of Billie Jean King, one of the leaders in the formation of the women's professional tour in 1970, and the holder of the all-time record of twenty victories at Wimbledon, which she set between 1961 and 1979: six in the women's singles, ten in the women's doubles, and four in the mixed doubles. She won our singles four times, in 1967, 1971, 1972, and 1974, and carried off the Australian singles in 1968 and the French singles in 1972. She will be remembered also for the shellacking she gave Bobby Riggs, 6–4, 6–3, 6–3, when they met in the garishly promoted "battle of the sexes," in 1973, before more than thirty thousand people in the Houston Astrodome.

What is it about Chris Evert Lloyd that makes her so special? To begin with, there is her awesome record. In the four major championships, she has amassed a total of eighteen singles victories: seven in the French Open, in 1974, 1975, 1979, 1980, 1983, 1985, and 1986; six in the United States Open, in 1975, 1976, 1977, 1978, 1980, and 1982; three at Wimbledon, in 1974, 1976, and 1981; and two in the Australian Open, in 1982 and 1984. Over the last thirteen years, she has won at least one major title each year—a feat that no other tennis player, man or woman, has accomplished. She made her first appearance in our national championship in 1971, when she was sixteen. After a smashing debut, she grew up in public, as it were, with a following as ardent and loyal as a film star's in the golden age of motion pictures. Her fans liked many things about her besides how well she played tennis. She was pretty and feminine—a blondish young lady, five feet six, with attractive legs. On the court, she rarely questioned a call, and even when she was off form and struggling, her respect for the game of tennis took precedence over her frustration. In an age when outstanding players of both sexes were abusing the officials in several languages, she had the character to place sportsmanship above triumph and disaster. "Those two impostors," as Kipling called them, can be only too real for tennis players or other athletes caught in long, gruelling encounters that they feel they can pull out if only they can be patient, clear of mind, and able to concentrate on making the right shots. In modern times, few other champions in head-to-head sports have stayed at the top as long as Evert Lloyd. Her fans have seen her change from a cool, precise teen-ager, who wore her hair in a ponytail, into a somewhat heavier young woman who used a bit too much mascara, and next, in her middle twenties, into a married woman—Mrs. John Lloyd—who, trim as a whistle, moved faster and seemed better-looking than ever. Those who got to know her fairly well were seldom disappointed. They found her to be extremely intelligent— something they had suspected from the way she spoke at presentation ceremonies and during television interviews—and to have a bright sense of humor, and exceptional closeness to her family, a strong streak of independence, the gift of fastidiousness, a fondness for old friends, and an inherent honesty about herself. Evert Lloyd still plays tournament tennis at the relatively advanced age of thirty-one, because, demanding as it is, she likes to play tournament tennis.

The roots of the Evert family are in the farming village of Grosbous, in Luxembourg. Near the end of the nineteenth century, Christine Evert's great-grandfather John Evert and his family came to this country and bought some land at the western rim of Chicago, near Evanston. He sold it at a handsome profit and went into banking, but he was hit hard by the stock-market crash of 1929 and the Great Depression. His son Charles, who worked for a florist, had four sons, the third of whom was James Andrew Evert, Chris's father. The family's home was across the street from the Chicago Town and Tennis Club, but the Everts could not afford membership. At the age of eleven, Jimmy Evert became the ball boy for the club professional, George O'Connell. During the winter, after school was over he made the long trip across the city to the Southside Armory, where O'Connell taught during the off-season. There, too, he served as ball boy for O'Connell, and at the end of the last lesson of the day O'Connell showed his gratitude by working with young Evert on his game. Evert went on to attend the University of Notre Dame on a tennis scholarship. In his junior year, 1947, he was the captain of the Notre Dame team. At the end of the spring term that year, the team went on a long tournament-a-week tour that took it to Chicago, Tulsa, Los Angeles (where the national intercollegiate championship was played on the courts of the University of California, Los Angeles), Salt Lake City, Tacoma, Seattle, Vancouver, and Milwaukee. The team's week in Vancouver coincided with the playing of the Canadian championship, and Evert won it. This was undoubtedly the high point of his tournament career, although in 1942, one of five years he played in the United States championship, at Forest Hills, he reached the round of sixteen, and then lost a four-set match to Frederick R. (Ted) Schroeder, Jr., who went on to win the title. In 1948, Evert became the tennis supervisor for the city of Fort Lauderdale, Florida. Four years later, he married Colette Thompson, of New Rochell, New York, the youngest of twelve children of Joseph and Marie Thompson. From an office at 236 Water Street in downtown Manhattan, Thompson ran the family shellfish business. Working out of Greenport, at the tip of the North Fork of Long Island, the captain and crew of the company's boat grew and harvested oysters in Greenport and were then transported at express speed to the Grand Central Oyster Bar and other New York restaurants that prided themselves on providing their patrons with oysters that had been out of the sea less than twenty-four hours.

James and Colette Evert had five children—

James Andrew, Jr., Christine, Jeanne, John and Clare. Both parents believed in hard work, high standards, and old-fashioned values. Jimmy Evert was at the courts from eight in the morning until six, and sometimes eight, in the evening, seven days a week. In 1958, the city built Holiday Park, a large recreation complex, and Evert was put in charge of its tennis facilities. As the number of courts at Holiday Park grew from eight to twenty during the tennis boom of the nineteen-sixties, two instructors were added to his staff. (Evert required his assistants to be as dedicated to their work as he was, and one of them with a sense of humor gave the boss the nickname of Lash.) Mrs. Evert was no less industrious. She prepared breakfast for the family; helped to serve lunch in the cafeteria at St. Anthony's School, which the Evert children attended before they moved on to St. Thomas Aquinas High School; cooked dinner for her husband and herself; and was so capable and well organized with her housework and laundry that she never felt burdened and found plenty of time for her children. When the Evert children were five and a half or six, their father began teaching them tennis, because the game had been a source of great pleasure for him, and he wanted his children to enjoy it, too.

James Jr., who is called Drew, and is now thirty-three, went to Auburn University on a tennis scholarship, and he is currently the director of tennis at the Boar's Head Sports Club, in Charlottesville, Virginia. Jeanne, twenty-eight, is the director of tennis at the Stonebridge Golf and Country Club, in Boca Raton, Florida—her husband, Brahm Dubin, is the club's director of operations—and, until recently, when she and her husband adopted a baby boy, she also supervised the Woman's International Tennis Association camps for young players, which are held in Miami. John, twenty-five, attended Vanderbilt University on a tennis scholarship, and now supervises some of the players under contract to the International Management Group—he looks after the interests of Mary Joe Fernandez, an up-and-coming fifteen-year-old tournament player from Miami, and Leo Lavalle, a young Mexican, who was the best junior player in the world last year. Clare, the youngest child, is nineteen, and is a student at Southern Methodist University, in Dallas. She began college last year on a tennis scholarship but, in her second semester, she stopped playing tennis to concentrate on her studies. She is planning to rejoin the tennis team. "Clare is the most outgoing child in our family," Chris recently told some friends. "Each successive child in our family has been more outgoing."

Jimmy Evert started teaching Chris (or Chrissie) how to play tennis in the summer of 1960, when she was five and a half. He had her stand, holding her racquet, at the service line, twenty-one feet from the net, while he stood at net on the other side of the court, close to a shopping cart filled with about a hundred and fifty tennis balls. He would take a ball and toss it over the net toward Chris, and she would try to hit it on the first bounce and send it back to him. She had good natural physical coordination, and it wasn't long before she began hitting a high percentage of her shots back over the net. Her father then began hitting balls to her at the service line with his racquet, and as he gradually moved farther back from the net and toward the baseline on his side of the court, so did she on her side. Even as a young child, Chris had exceptional concentration, and she quickly learned to hit the ball smoothly and accurately over the net from the baseline. Her father believes that a player learns to play good strokes by executing the fundamentals, and as he hit the ball over the net he would call out at regular intervals, "Racquet back! Turn sidewise! Watch the ball! Follow through!" As for serving, he didn't teach Chris, or any of his children, a power serve or a serve requiring a fairly intricate technique. The important thing, he told them time and time again, was to get from seventy to eighty per cent of their first serves in, with some pace on the ball, and, of course, the deeper the serve the better. During his rallies with Chris and the others, he stressed such essentials as anticipation and speed of movement, for they give a player sufficient time to set up properly for playing deep attacking shots and also for maneuvering an opponent from side to side, and so gaining control of the rallies. In a relatively short time, Chris was far enough advanced to play with the other young players who regularly used the Holiday Park courts. Her standard procedure was to go directly to Holiday Park after school was over, at three o'clock, and play and practice about two hours each day. On weekends, she played and practiced four or five hours each day. Her frequent lessons with her father continued long after she had finished high school, had turned pro in December of 1972, on her eighteenth birthday, and had earned an international reputation. These days, he prefers to attend her practice sessions with Dennis Ralston, her coach, or with her husband, John, one of the outstanding British players in the last fifteen years, who has been ranked as high as twenty-fourth in the world on the Tennis Players Association computer. After thirty-eight years, Jimmy Evert is still the tennis supervisor at Holiday Park, and he still believes firmly that proper execution of the fundamentals is the key to developing a good tennis game.

As a slim, small-boned young girl, Chris Evert was an instinctive baseliner, as are the large majority of people who grow up on composition-clay courts. The tennis ball digs into a clay court and takes a slow bounce, which gives a player more time to set up with good balance on his or her ground strokes. (Players who grow up on cement courts, on which the bounce is fast and high, or on grass courts, which produce a fast, skidding bounce, are much more likely to become serv-

and-volley artists.) Chris, however, did one thing that was different from what most young players do, irrespective of the surface on which they were brought up. As a very young girl, she didn't have the strength to control her racquet firmly with her right hand when she was hitting a backhand shot, and she began to use both hands on her backhand. When she was about nine, her father asked her to try hitting her backhand with one hand again. She did, but while she still got the ball back regularly, her shots were not hit as solidly. Perceiving this, he told her to stick with her two-handed backhand. When she emerged as a star in 1971, her two-handed backhand was what fascinated most people. It really wasn't a revolutionary stroke. Vivian McGrath, who played on the Australian Davis Cup team before the Second World War, used a two-handed backhand, and so did Jan Lehane, a postwar Australian woman player. So did such first-class players as Bjorn Borg and Jimmy Conners. For Chris, however, the two-handed backhand became one of her most potent attacking weapons, since it enabled her to disguise whether she was going down the line or cross-court.

In the middle nineteen-sixties, tennis was enjoying a tremendous boom in this country, and, in fact, around the world. In Florida, many boys and girls were working diligently on their games in the hope that they might be able to make a career in tennis. Chris Evert was not the only girl in Fort Lauderdale who was thinking in these terms. Her best friend, Laurie Fleming, had the same aspiration. (The two sometimes communicated in a secret code, the "iv" language, which was spoken and understood only by the regulars at Holiday Park. It was a simple enough code: you simply inserted "iv" in every word, so that "holding service," for example, came out as "holivding servivice.") In the beginning, Chris had worked hard at tennis because of the pleasure she knew this gave her father. After a while, she realized that she was pursuing tennis so intensely because of the pleasure that she was deriving from playing the game increasingly well. In 1966, she entered her first national championship, the United States Girls' 12 championship—open to girls twelve and under—which was held that year at the Chattanooga Tennis Club, in Tennessee. She was defeated in the final round by Christine (Plums) Bartkowicz, the younger sister of Jane (Peaches) Bartkowicz. The sisters had been taught the game by Jean Hoxie, an outstanding instructor, at her tennis camp in Hamtramck, Michigan, an extensive municipal enclave that is surrounded by the city of Detroit. In 1968, when she was thirteen, Chris won her first national title, the United States Girls' 14 singles championship. (Laurie Fleming won this event in 1969, and Jeanne Evert won it in 1971.) In 1970, when Chris was fifteen, she won the United States Girls' 16 championship. (Once again, her successor the following summer was Laurie Fleming.)

Only people with a deep interest in tennis know which players are coming to the front in the junior ranks. The first time that the average tennis fan heard of Chris Evert was when she defeated Margaret Smith Court in a women's tour tournament at the Olde Providence Racquet Club, in Charlotte, North Carolina, in September, 1970, two weeks after Court, a formidable Australian, won our national women's championship and became the first woman player to equal Maureen Connolly's feat of sweeping the four major championships in a single year. The director of the Charlotte tournament had invited Chris and her friend Laurie Fleming to fill out the field in an invitational event he was running at the club. Laurie gave a good account of herself against Virginia Wade, of England, before going down, 7—5, 6–3. Chris surprised everyone by the ease with which she won her match against Françoise Durr, a French professional: the score was 6–1, 6–0. She went on from there to beat Court, 7–6, 7–6, by playing nerveless baseline tennis and frequently passing Court when she came to the net to volley. Today, Chris remembers her meeting with Court as the most exciting and most enjoyable match she has ever played—she had no idea at the time that her game had advanced to the point where she could even stay on the court with a player of Court's stature, let alone defeat her. When the match was over, she ran to the nearest telephone and called her father, at his office in Holiday Park. He was thrilled by the news, and gasped, "Let me get up off the floor." The next day, he and Mrs. Evert flew to Charlotte to watch the final. Chris played Nancy Richey, a resolute baseliner from Texas, and was swept away, 6–4, 6–1. Richey won their next four matches as well. "Nancy was a very difficult opponent for me," Chris said not long ago. "She did the same things I did, but she did them better."

In 1971, Chris Evert's progress continued. In the Masters tournament, in St. Petersburg, Florida, she again defeated Durr, and then met Billie Jean King in the semifinal. They split the first two sets, 6–7 and 6–3. Then King informed the umpire that her legs were cramping and that she would not be able to continue the match. In the final, Evert defeated Julie Heldman, another high-ranked player, 6–1, 6–2. That summer, after winning the U.S. 16s, Chris played sensational tennis in the annual Wightman Cup match between the United States and Great Britain, which was held at the Harold T. Clark Courts, in Cleveland Heights. She raced through Wade, the No. 1 British player, 6–1, 6–1, in less than forty minutes, and defeated Winnie Shaw, a young Scottish player, 6–0, 6–4. Then, in the week before the U.S. Open, she won the Eastern Grass Courts championship at the Orange Lawn Tennis Club, in South Orange, New Jersey, defeating Helen Gourlay, of Australia, in the final. By this time, American tennis fans realized that Evert was a player of considerable promise, to say the least, but they did not expect her to play a prominent role in the U.S. Open, at Forest Hills, the home of our national championships from 1915 until 1978. Few players in our championships have made as spectacular a debut, and seldom have the championships needed the arrival of a new star as desperately as they did that summer. Rod Laver and Ken Rosewall, two of the top five players in the world, were not on hand, and the women's field was also weak. Margaret Court, the holder, was home in Australia awaiting the birth of her first child, and Evonne Goolagong, the young Australian who had captivated the galleries in winning Wimbledon early that summer, had been persuaded by her coach, Vic Edwards, to pass up Forest Hills. A dull fortnight was in prospect.

Sensing a great desire among tennis fans to see Evert in action, the tournament director of the championships scheduled her first-round match with Edda Buding, an experienced German player, for the stadium at Forest Hills, which seated about fourteen thousand people. Evert dispatched Buding quickly, 6–1, 6–0. In the second round, she met the fourth-ranked player in the country, Mary Ann Eisel, a hard hitter with a fine serve-and-volley game. Eisel took the first set, 6–4. In the second set, she broke Evert's serve in the eleventh game and, at 6–5, served for the set and match. She collected the first three points, to move to triple-match point. Then it happened: Evert played a sequence of points which those who saw it will never forget. Eisel, serving into the ad court at 40–0, got in a good first serve. Evert pasted the ball down the line for a perfect placement with her two-handed backhand. At 40–15, serving into the deuce court, Eisel did not get her first serve in. Evert moved in a stop or two to play the second serve, and cracked a crosscourt forehand at a severe angle for another perfect placement. On the next point, Eisel double-faulted. Deuce. Eisel went to match point for the fourth time when Evert was long with a backhand, but Evert, showing no sign of strain, got back to deuce by driving a forehand at Eisel's feet as she was coming in to volley. On the next point, Eisel got in a good first serve to Evert's backhand in the deuce court, and when Evert netted her return Eisel went to match point for the fifth time. Serving into the ad court, Eisel decided not to follow her serve into net but to stay at the baseline. She lost the point, however, when she hit a backhand wide. Deuce again. Eisel moved to match point for the sixth time, but the pressure of the situation was obviously getting to her. She lost the point when she hit a loose forehand volley into the alley. Deuce again. Eisel lost the next point when she netted a backhand volley. Evert, now at game point for the first time, took advantage of a short approach shot by Eisel to pass her with a cross-court forehand. That made it 6–6 in games and called for a tiebreaker—in those days, a sudden-death, nine-point tiebreaker. The picture of imperturbability, Evert served the first two points, won them, and ultimately carried off the tiebreaker, five points to one. This gave her the second set, and, with Eisel's confidence now in tatters, there was never any doubt that Evert would win the third set. She did, 6–1.

In the third round, Evert met Durr. In order to give Evert the minimal amount of angle on her gound strokes, Durr played her down the middle of the court. These tactics helped her to win the first set, 6–2, but Evert then took command of the match and won the next two sets easily, 6–2, 6–3. Her quarter-final match against Lesley Hunt, a young Australian, followed much the same pattern. Evert again started slowly, but after dropping the first set, 6–4, she won the sext two sets, 6–2 and 6–3. She had now reached the semi-finals and would be facing the first-seeded player, Billie Jean King. This was a match that everyone wanted to see, because King had been one of the top players among American women for a decade and would certainly be at her combative best against the seemingly imperturbable teen-age challenger. The horse-shoe stadium was packed when they met on a hot, humid afternoon. Evert, serving the first game, lost the first three points, but she collected herself and took the next five to hold service. She seemed more relaxed than King did. King, after losing the first two points on her serve, won the next four in a row for the game. Each player held serve in the next two games—deuced games that featured long exchanges. Each also held serve in the fifth and sixth games, but King, who was now coming to net more frequently than she had been earlier, held her serve at love, twice winning points on volleys and twice forcing Evert to hit hurried forehands out of court. By far the best woman volleyer of this period, King now took charge of the match. She won the next three games to capture the first set, 6–3. She ran off the first three games of the second set, keeping Evert from finding her best timing on her ground strokes by changing the spin and speed of her own ground strokes and also by feeding Evert chips and dinks on her returns of service. King kept her serve deep, volleyed impeccably, and walked through the second set, 6–2. The confrontation that everybody had looked forward to with such eagerness was over almost before it had taken shape. King had blunted Evert's best weapons by coming up with one of the shrewdest performances of her career. She went on to win the final from Rosemary Casals in straight sets. Evert returned to St. Thomas Aquinas High School a national figure. Tennis enthusiasts and Americans in general liked everything about this disciplined, fresh-faced girl. What they particularly remembered was those two brave returns of serve for outright placements in the twelfth game of the second set, which had kept the Eisel match alive. A great many sixteen-year-old athletes prove to be nine days' wonders, but most followers of tennis felt that they would be seeing a lot more of Evert.

Evert came along nicely the next few years. Early in 1972, she defeated King, 6–1, 6–0, on composition clay in the Women's International tournament, in Fort Lauderdale, but a month later, playing on an indoor carpet in the quarter-finals of the T-Bar-M tournament, in Dallas, King, a ferocious competitor, came back after losing the first set and trailing 1–3 in the second to pull out the match, 6–7, 6–3, 7–5. The winner of three Wimbledon singles titles and one United States singles title in the late nineteen-sixties, King probably reached her peak years in the early nineteen-seventies. She won on grass at Wimbledon in 1972, 1973, and 1975; on clay in 1972 in the French Open, at Stade Roland Garros, in Auteuil, outside Paris; and on grass at Forest Hills in 1971, 1972, and 1974. In the 1973 Wimbledon final, King defeated Evert, 6–0, 7–5—a score well worth noting, since it marks one of the few times in which a player has ever rolled over Evert so decisively in a single set. In the Wimbledon semi-finals two years later, King, after droppping the first set to Evert and losing her serve early in the third set, came back to win, 2–6, 6–2, 6–3. From that point on, however, Evert, the classic baseliner, dominated her meetings with King, the classic forecount specialist. In 1977, for example, when they met in the quarter-finals at Wimbledon, Evert won as easily as the score of the match,

6–1, 6–2, suggests. The way she played the opening point was an indication of her complete control of the tactical plan she had divised for the match: King served; Evert made a good return; King, ever the net rusher, came into the forecourt behind a rather deep approach shot; and Evert popped a backhand lob into the deserted backcourt. In the quarter-finals of the U.S. Open later that year—Forest Hills had switched in 1975 from grass to Har-Tru, a slow, claylike surface—Evert played outstanding tennis in beating King, 6–2, 6–0. By this time, King was in her thirties, and Evert, still improving, was on her way to setting a career head-to-head record against King of nineteen victories and seven defeats. King, however, made one gallant last stand. When they met in the semis at Wimbledon in 1982, King, who was then thirty-eight, pushed her old adversary to three sets before succumbing, 7–6, 2–6, 6–3.

The first of the long series of matches between Evert and Goolagong was their meeting in the semifinals of the Wimbledon championship in 1972. A graceful, remarkably pleasant athlete from the wheat fields of Australia, Goolagong, three and a half years older than Evert, was an all-court player. While they had an instinctive liking for each other, they were too different to be good friends. "Evonne was happy and relaxed day after day," Evert Lloyd recalled recently. "She'd forget the score in a game we were playing, but that wouldn't bother her. She was a very nice and kind person." Goolagong had a good, fast first serve, a cream puff of a second serve, and a superb natural backhand, with which she could bring off everything from a low half-volley to an overhead smash—a rare stroke. A frequent tactic of hers against Evert, as against other opponents, was to chip a low backhand shot to her backhand, come into the front court behind it, and volley the return to the open side of the court. The way Evert and everyone else played Goolagong was to put pressure on her unreliable forehand. In 1971, on her first trip to Winbledon, Goolagong's forehand had stood up well when she defeated Court in the final, 6–4, 6–1. In her semifinal match with Evert the next year, Evert took the first set and also led 3–0 in the second, but Goolagong persevered and turned it around, 4–6, 6–3, 6–4. This greatly pleased the English "mums," the proper middle-aged women who rarely miss a day's play at Wimbledon, and who make it clear by their applause and general support which women players they regard as "the right sort." At the start, they didn't care much for Evert. The way she went about her matches was much too businesslike and serious. The kind of player they like is one who has a capable game but who smiles after making a stupid error and is essentially a jolly, hearty sort of girl.

The mums may have been right, in a way. An Evert match has a different atmosphere and mood from most others. When she walks out onto the

court with her opponent, she pleasantly acknowl-
edges the gallery's applause, but her mind is already running through and checking off the list
of offensive patterns she has decided on for that
match. During the warmup, one notices the solid
contact she makes with the ball from the very beginning of the exchanges. Her exceptional hand-
and-eye coordination enables her to arrive at the
ball with her racquet already back in position, and
as she steps into her shot she watches the ball onto
the racquet.

During the last sixteen years, there have been
many larger and taller women than Evert in tennis, but few have hit the ball so hard and so deep
so consistently. During both the warm-up and the
match itself, she reminds one of a frontiersman
sighting down the barrel of his rifle at a distant
object when she fastens her eye on the approaching ball for what seems like several full seconds
before hitting it in the center of her racquet and
drilling it back over the net. Some friends of mine
used to wonder how she could concentrate so long
on staring the ball into her racquet and manage
at the same time to watch where her opponent
was moving. They finally agreed that a top-class
player can tell from an opponent's first few steps
after she hits the ball what she will be doing, and
they came to believe that there is also a kind of
instinctive sense, which operates even when a
player's mind is fixed on the ball and which in-
forms her where her opponent is. Apart from
these matters, an Evert match has a certain crisp-

ness and dispatch. There is no need to plant a "Positively No Loitering" sign on the court. She brooks no nonsense. She wants to get on with the game. Helen Wills used to specialize in drubbing the hapless players she met in the early rounds of a tournament, 6–0, 6–0. Chris is much the same: get the match over and get on to the next thing.

The Ice Maiden—a nickname Evert was given early in her career, because she went about matters on the court so coolly and efficiently, and with barely a change of expression—later developed some of the frailties of other human beings, but this didn't appear to alter her attitude during her matches. Virginia Wade, in a well-remembered interview she gave on the opening day of the 1975 U.S. Open (she was wittily frank about the idiosyncrasies on court of the top women players), stated that Evert hides her feelings very successfully during a match, and that only if one scrutinizes her when a close line call goes against her can one detect that she lifts a shoulder a little and turns it with just a suspicion of pique as she walks back to the baseline to play the next point. In any event, Evert hates to lose. She loves to play tennis well. She appreciates that she has been relatively free from injuries. She has a winning attitude. She said not long ago, "I go on the court thinking I can win my match. Why, exactly? Because of all of the balls I've hit all my life. I believe I can get one more ball back over the net than my opponent."

Evert Lloyd's chief current rival, Navratilova, is hardly a recent one. In 1973, when she was sixteen, two years younger and an inch and a half taller than Evert, Navratilova, a rangy left-hander, first played her, in a tournament in Akron. Evert was the winner, 7–6, 6–3. It was evident those many years ago that Navratilova, who then weighed at least twenty pounds more than she does today, was an extraordinary athlete. She later faced Evert in the final of the 1975 French championship—Evert won in three sets—and that season they also met in the semifinals of the U.S. Open, and Evert won, 6–4, 6–4. (A brief digression: it should be mentioned that Navratilova has a number of talents besides her athletic prowess. For example, I know of no one who has picked up English as quickly as she did. Many months before her defection from her native Czechoslovakia, in September of 1975, she was speaking English so idiomatically and with such a breezy delivery that one would have thought she was born in Fort Worth, where she now makes her home.) Not only is Navratilova's rivalry with Evert Lloyd among the longest and most intense in the history of sports but, more often than not, the quality of the tennis in their matches has been something to behold. Evert Lloyd dominated the early years. In April of 1981, after a 6–0, 6–0 victory over Navratilova in the Amelia Island tournament, in Florida, she felt that for sheer command of technique this was the high point of her career, and today she sees no reason to alter that opinion.

As recently as late 1982, when she defeated Navratilova to win her first Australian Open championship, Evert Lloyd held a thirty-to-eighteen edge in the number of matches won in their head-to-head competition. However, beginning just after the 1981 U.S. Open and continuing throughout 1982, with the considerable assistance of what the press referred to as "Team Navratilova"—a group that included her personal tennis professional, Renée Richards; her physical-training coach, Nancy Lieberman; and her dietitian, Dr. Robert Haas—Navratilova worked to really get in shape, and began to fulfill her potential as a tennis player. She increased both her speed and her agility, corrected her one glaring weakness of stroke by developing a reliable topspin backhand, devised a better second serve, and, recognizing how much her tennis had improved, added one more ingredient—confidence. By early 1983, some old tennis hands were wondering if any woman had ever played the game as completely and as well as Navratilova. From December, 1982, through 1984, for example, she put together a string of thirteen consecutive victories in her matches against Evert Lloyd. (Two of them came in the final of the U.S. Open, and another in the final of Wimbledon. Between 1978 and 1986, incidentally, Navratilova has won

Wimbledon a record-tying seven times.) This tremendous run of head-to-head wins came to an end early in 1985, when Evert Lloyd stopped her, 6–2, 6–4, in a match played on a cement court in Key Biscayne, Florida. While Navratilova has continued to play absolutely glittering tennis, Evert Lloyd has beaten her twice more in the last two years, both times in the final of the French Open, on the slow red clay of Stade Roland Garros. She has had to come up with heroic performances to do this, because she could easily have lost both matches.

On the eve of the 1986 U.S. Open, Navratilova led her ancient rivalry with Evert Lloyd thirty-seven matches to thirty-three. Austin is the only other Evert Lloyd rival who has been able to win the majority of their matches—she won nine and lost eight. Evert Lloyd's head-to-head statistics against her other principal foes go like this: nine wins and four losses against Court; six and five against Nancy Richey; nineteen and six against Hana Mandlikova; seventeen and three against Andrea Jaeger; and twenty-five and thirteen against Evonne Goolagong Cawley. Her last loss to the attractive Australian was a painful one. It occurred in the Wimbledon final in 1980. Cawley hadn't won any tournaments that year, and her form was so spotty that few people at Wimbledon considered her a serious contender. She started playing beautiful tennis in her first match, kept in that groove round after round, and, to everyone's surprise, upset Austin in the semifinals, 6–3, 0–6, 6–4. In the other semifinal, Evert Lloyd, to her great joy, defeated Navratilova, 4–6, 6–4, 6–2. Navratilova's serve-and-volley game is at its fiercest on the fast grass courts at Wimbledon, and she had defeated Evert Lloyd in their two previous encounters there, in the finals in 1978 and 1979. In her elation on the evening after her victory over Navratilova, Evert Lloyd allowed herself a pleasant, relaxed dinner, instead of starting to key herself up for the next day's match with Cawley. In the final, she lost the first set, 6–1, before she began to appreciate the high quality of the tennis that Cawley was playing, and the seriousness of her own position. She got down to work immediately. It was a little too late. Cawley held on long enough to take the second set, 7–6, in a tiebreaker, and Evert Lloyd had lost a golden opportunity.

Evert Lloyd has been on the go for sixteen years now, and the pattern of returning to Fort Lauderdale after a tournament and leaving for another tournament a bit later has become second nature to her. This summer, for example, she flew back to Fort Lauderdale for a breather after Wimbledon, and was off some two weeks later to the Federation Cup tournament, the annual competition between national women's teams, which was held this year in Prague.

111

There is a good deal to Chris Evert Lloyd, and much of it doesn't catch the eye. I had the pleasure of a good, long conversation with her this summer at her family's home after she returned to Fort Lauderdale from Prague, and I learned a lot about her. Here are her views on a variety of subjects:

On the reasons she became so good a player as a young girl: "First of all, there was the sound method that my father's lessons instilled in me. Another big reason was that I always had Laurie Fleming, my best friend, right at my heels. She was an excellent player. It's funny, but early in my career the people I most didn't want to lose to were my best friend and my sister Jeanne. They were threats to me, because I was emotionally involved with them."

On how calm and nerveless she appeared to be when she first played against the big stars in important tournaments: "I *was* very confident. I never let emotion get involved. I was very mental in my approach to tennis, very machinelike, as they used to say. I had such concentration then that I came across to the galleries as being as cool as a cucumber. I was. I could concentrate on a tennis court better than anyplace else."

On not turning professional too early: "I think that a young girl is much better off if she graduates from high school and if she also waits until she's eighteen before turning pro. In my own case, those weren't my decisions but my parents'. Thank heaven they decided that way."

On her first intimations that she could become a tennis champion: "I would watch the U.S. Open on TV every year, and I never thought it would have a bearing on my life. I was never one of those kids who thought, I want to play Wimbledon, or, Someday I ought to be No. 1 in the world. It wasn't until I was fifteen and I beat Margaret Court, and later played good matches against Billie Jean, Frankie Durr, and Nancy Richey, that I started to say to myself, 'Hey, I'm giving these women who are among the big stars in the world all they can handle!' When I was sixteen and had won the national 18s and had been named to the Wightman Cup team, the U.S.T.A. gave me a form to fill out for the U.S. Open. I didn't know if I was going to play in it or not. Maybe I was too young. For another thing, school was starting, and I had to get back."

On what she remembers about her match with Mary Ann Eisel in the 1971 U.S. Open: "Not very much. She overpowered me. She had a classic serve-and-volley game. I felt very loose. The only thing I remember clearly—I remember saying it to the press—is that in the twelfth game of the second set the tennis ball seemed to be a lot bigger, and that I could do whatever I wanted to with the ball when I was down those match points. I don't remember the nine-point tiebreaker. I'll tell you what I remember—my match with Billie Jean in the semifinals. She just gave me a lot of junk—chips, dinks, and all that stuff."

On what now comes first to mind when she recalls her matches with Goolagong: "Evonne played such flowing tennis. It was hard, when you played her—you wanted to watch her and not the ball."

On what she remembers about her match in the semifinals on the 1980 U.S. Open with Tracy Austin, who had beaten her in straight sets in the final of the championship the year before and had defeated her the four times they met afterward: "That match was really strange, because I felt that I was ready and that I was playing well. I was really eager. At the start of the match, she was up 4–love in about five minutes. I thought, Hey, I'd better figure this out. I don't think I'm playing this badly. What's happening here? I still felt that I was hitting the ball well. So I said to myself, 'Just hang in there.' I lost that set, 6–4. I was unlucky to lose it, because at 5–4 and 30–all she just hit one of those no-brainers—an unbelievable shot. So after that I said, 'Fine. You came close.' Then I won the next two sets easily. I just did everything right ... I think that Tracy and I were probably more intense than any two rivals I know of, because we were so alike."

Her reflections on her match with Navratilova in the Amelia Island tournament in 1981, when she won 6–0, 6–0: "I played very well, and Martina was not playing well. She had her mind on about five hundred other things. Every player has certain matches in which they're in the zone, as we call it. In those matches, we feel that whatever we do it's going to work, it's going to be a great shot, and we'll be able to keep concentrating the whole way through. That was one of those matches."

Her thoughts on her return of service and her volley: "I'm aware that my return of service is one of the best. That's because I have a target. The same is true of my passing shots. If I'm playing a serve-and-volleyer, I know I have two targets—I can play down the line or crosscourt. I know I can be accurate. I think that this has somthing to do with having been brought up on clay, where you simply learn accuracy."

On her gradual acceptance by the English mums: "They started to like me after I had lost a couple of times and they saw I was human. They saw I didn't rant or rave in defeat. Of course, after I married John I instantly became one of their favorites."

On keeping in shape: "As you get older, it takes longer to recuperate. If I have a good, tough match, the next day I feel it. And if you lay off, it takes twice as long to get back. If I have a week off and I don't want to hit the ball, I'll still probably go to the gym and work out, or I'll go for runs."

On getting up, mentally and emotionally, for a match: "I have to spend a quiet evening the night before. I like to stay quiet and collect my thoughts, and talk a little bit with John or Dennis about strategy, but basically to stay very quiet and store up my energy."

On her victories over Navratilova in the French Open in 1985 and 1986: "It's only against her that at times I haven't been confident and attacking, because she nearly always takes it away from me. She's always moving the whole time. Every other player I can attack, but Martina has always been a little tougher for me. In the finals of the French the last two years, I wasn't confident when I walked onto the court. But when you've been drummed thirteen times in a row—I've never been beaten like that by anyone else, and naturally Martina has a psychological edge on me. In the final of the French this year, I learned a good lesson. At 3–all in the third, most of the time Martina would have pulled out the march, but I pulled it out. I learned that I should feel a little more confident against her. It's very tough. You can't bluff confidence. I had to play myself into the match. Then I found out that she was missing a few more shots than usual, and I felt I was hitting the ball well. People say about Martina to me, 'Of course, if she's up four games to love, she's going to hit winning passing shots off her backhand. If you get her into a 4–all situation, where there's a little pressure, then those are the shots that break down.'"

On sportsmanship: "Tennis is not worth making a scene ever—being vulgar or throwing your racquet. It's a game. It's not worth it. You hurt the game. I wish I could say that the reason I try

116

not to make scenes is the effect it would have on young kids. But the reason I don't act up is that it's not in me to show that part of myself. Maybe it's because I'm essentially a private person when it comes to my emotions. I choose to play tennis a certain way. I don't wear my heart on my sleeve. If I had been brought up a different way, or if I had different parents, maybe I would be different in expressing myself."

On what has had the most impact on her during the fifteen years her tennis travels have taken her to many foreign lands, and, in the process, she has met so many diverse people, been to so many different homes, seen some of the wonders of the ancient world, and experienced some of the wonders of the present world: "It's been going to certain places, like Prague, where we went for the Federation Cup matches this summer. Or East Berlin, where I went for a day last summer. And the times I've gone to Johannesburg, in South Africa. It's like—Well, little kids should always have to go to the hospital once in a while, to see how other people live and to see how lucky and fortunate they are. That's the comparison I would make with people who aren't able to see how the other half lives. How lucky I feel just to have the freedom and the choices that I have! The people in those countries are not happy. The prejudices people have, like in South Africa—that hit me harder, because there are black players on the tennis tour. You've seen the emergence of the blacks in America. And the prejudices have really gone down. In East Berlin, nobody smiles. People who are walking are gloomy, they're dreary. It's so depressing. Maybe it's not depressing to them, in the sense that they don't know they're missing out on anything—they don't know anything else. Do you know what living in those countries does? It kills your spirit."

# MIKE LUPICA

# Advantage, Mr. McEnroe?

*Without a doubt, John McEnroe has made his name in tennis both as a consummate player and as an intolerable poor sport, prone to throwing embarrassing tantrums whenever he decides an official has made a questionable call. In this interview with Mike Lupica, McEnroe makes efforts to understand his notorious behavior, now that he had reached the age of twenty-eight, married glamorous movie star Tatum O'Neal, and had become a father. In this close look into the private world of a champion player, the reader detects some of the immaturity of the past as well as McEnroe's awareness that the great days of tennis will end soon and he must find some new occupation to fill the rest of his life—although nothing will replace the excitement of being Number One in tennis. But for now, McEnroe is dreaming of a comeback.*

"Watch this." John McEnroe says.

It is 9:30 in the morning at the McEnroe condominium at Turnberry Isle, one of those instant prestige addresses north of Miami where you don't have to worry much about bumping into the Golden Girls. McEnroe is in the baby's room with Estella, the nanny, and Tatum O'Neal, wife and mother.

Estella has just finished changing Kevin Jack McEnroe, nine months old. The boy already looks like his mama, the kid she was in *Paper Moon*. McEnroe says, "I think the only thing he's got from me so far is his hairline."

He takes Kevin out of Estella's arms and gives him to Tatum. "Anyway, watch this."

Tatum, already pregnant with the next one, smiles, takes the boy, and steps back. Kevin McEnroe shrieks and tries to leap into his father's arms.

"You're not a mommy's boy at all, are you, Kevin?" McEnroe says, grabbing the boy and holding him over his head. "You're a daddy's boy all the way, aren't you?"

McEnroe hands the baby back to Estella and heads upstairs, which looks like a lot of places where he has stashed his life over the last ten years. There are boots and discarded jeans over there, and a pile of rackets on the couch, and an electric guitar, and *The Miami Herald* opened to a story about the rock group Genesis, and a battered Chicago Bears cap. Next to the front door is a big black equipment bag, filled with sneakers and sweats and more rackets.

Tatum O'Neal apologizes for the mess. "He still never takes his bag away from the door. I think it's a pretty old habit. But he's not going to make any more quick exits. The boy's in love."

McEnroe is sorting through rackets. He is

dressed in white shorts and a Lakers T-shirt and some new Nikes with flaps over the top. As usual, he looks like everything is on backward.

He is getting ready to practice with Jimmy Connors, who is playing in a tournament over in Key Biscayne. The two to them once nearly came to blows during a changeover at Wimbledon. That day Connors told McEnroe, "Next time, I'll let my son play you, you're about the same age." McEnroe said of Connors last July, "I don't think I could ever be that phony."

Now it's like they starred together in *Platoon*. Everybody gets older, even Jimbo and Johnny Mac. McEnroe, who can do everything to a tennis ball except make it recite the Pledge of Allegiance, at twenty-eight has become what Connors eventually became after his fall from number one: guy fighting to fool everybody and get back to the top.

And he would very much like to do that this year. Or next.

"Don't want to keep Jimbo waiting." McEnroe says, and kisses his wife on the cheek.

"Oh, honey," he calls to Tatum as he goes out the door, "you think maybe you could whip me up some pancakes when I get back?"

He came along in 1977, an eighteen year old, a nobody, with a headband and a bad temper and a left-handed tennis game so big it filled up that first Wimbledon until Connors finally stopped him in the semifinals. They couldn't even pronounce his name that year, but he spit and sassed his way out of the qualifying rounds and then won five matches in the main draw.

"Mc-EN-roe," the umpires kept calling him. "*Please* play, Mr. Mc-EN-roe."

Ten years and $10 million in prize money later, he's an American icon. You misbehave now in sports, you're acting like McEnroe. Who do you think you are, *McEnroe?* Illie Nastase was bad, Jimmy Connors—believe me—has always been much, much worse out there than people think. But McEnroe, especially to the casual fan, just walked in and retired the trophy. And he's had some run. Reggie Jackson became an elder states-man after he left the Yankees, like he was running for Cosby or something. Ali got old, Jim Mc-Mahon was a flash-in-the-pan, one big bang.

Always there was John McEnroe. It figured he would end up in Malibu, and at Lakers games with Jack Nicholson. Even marrying a movie star made sense. John McEnroe invented the Brat Pack. He was the first one, way back in 1977, when Sean Penn was collecting baseball cards, or burning them, whatever he did. Nastase had come before, and so had Connors, but McEnroe was different, going where no man had gone before. It was tennis in a leather jacket. Nobody as good had ever been as bad.

Right away, he was better than everybody ex-cept Bjorn Borg. At Wimbledon in 1980, they played the most famous tennis match ever, five sets. 8–6 in the fifth, the whole thing elevated into legend by that 18–16, twenty-two minute, fourth-set tie breaker, during which McEnroe fought off five championship points.

Borg won the match, extending his streak of Wimbledon titles to five. But McEnroe came back to Wimbledon the next year and beat Borg in the final. Two months later, he beat Borg again, in the final of the U.S. Open; this time. McEnroe messed the Swede up. At twenty-two, McEnroe was number one, and Borg didn't want to play anymore. Borg skipped the postmatch press conference, got into a courtesy car, drove away, and never really came back.

McEnroe had lost his worthiest adversary. Tennis had lost its greatest rivalry. It was like Frazier bailing out on Ali.

After Borg left, McEnroe stayed number one in 1982 and 1983 and 1984. He may have missed the Swede and pined away, but he kept going. Rackets were broken, matches were interrupted, suspensions were earned, fines were paid, there was an ongoing war with Wimbledon and the British press and still photographers the world over. He once threw sawdust at a U.S. Open fan. He berated a female reporter in Canada to a fare-thee-well.

He has never exactly been thrilled by that shotgun mike CBS keeps near the court at the U.S. Open.

If you were in the one-hundredth row of the stands at one of his matches and you crossed your legs and scratched your nose, it sent him into a tailspin. "Don't you know I see *everything?*" he snapped once to a friend at the U.S. Open, explaining why he got so distracted by some obnoxious fans during one of his matches.

This ump was an incompetent fool. That one—or was it the same one?—was the pits of the world. He basically got away with all of it. Borg was gone. He was the only game in town. McEnroe was a Beastie Boy swinging a Dunlop, getting bigger and bigger, making one fortune after another.

Then in 1986, it all came apart. When that happens, especially in tennis, it happens fast. If you don't believe it, ask Borg. I think he turned thirty the other day.

McEnroe was embarrassed in a first-round match at the Nabisco Masters tournament by someone named Brad Gilbert. McEnroe either looked washed up or just old that night, depending on how you were rooting. The next week, he announced he was taking a sabbatical. It was a beauty. Tatum had the baby. They got married. They went to his house in Malibu. In no particular order.

McEnroe came back last August, getting to the final of a tournament in Stratton Mountain, Vermont, where he faced Boris Becker. McEnroe had match points, was undone by a bad call on one of them, yelled some at the German kid, lost. But it was luminous tennis. Borg-McEnroe comparisons were irresistible; tennis needed a new rivalry and the fans and the writers take anything in the neighborhood.

McEnroe says, "Me and Becker could be something, but he's not Borg, okay?" Then he mocks the little boogie Becker does after a winning shot, pumping his arms, wiggling his knees Charleston-style. "It's not like *that* makes you an interesting person, if you know what I mean." he says.

The Stratton match had filled him with the old bravado. Even though he lost, he wasn't intimidated by Becker's two straight Wimbledons. "It looked like coming back was going to be easier than I'd thought," he says.

It wasn't. He lost in the first round of the Open to Paul Annacone, the greatest player in the history of Southampton, New York. While on sabbatical McEnroe had promised better behavior and he was true to his word, but it was like some pilot light had gone off, and his game with it. McEnroe lacked power, his volleys had lost their teeth. He was a step slow all day long. McEnroe appeared burned out, just as he had against Brad Gilbert in January. He played like a Smurf on the court where he'd won four singles titles. All of a sudden, at twenty-seven, he looked like a former number one trying to hang on.

Then McEnroe and doubles partner Peter Fleming were defaulted for showing up late to the National Tennis Center after getting stuck in traffic. So his whole Open lasted the couple of hours it had taken Annacone to dispatch him. McEnroe, who treasured his Open championships the most because he'd been raised ten minutes away in

Douglaston, Queens, had been run out of the tournament as if he were a scalper.

"If I ever get to be number one again," McEnroe says, "it will be because of the moment when they told me to get lost from the Open."

We are in a Philadelphia hotel room, in town for the Ebel U.S. Pro Indoor Championships, his first tournament of the new year. McEnroe, ranked fifteenth in the world, has won his second-round match over Mel Purcell. He lies on his belly in front of the television set, remote-control in his hand, white sweat pants pulled down to his knees, ice pack attached to bare buttocks.

It was McEnroe who brought up the subject of number one.

"You want to be number one in the world again?"

McEnroe says, "I'd like to be, but I don't have to be. It's not like I'm going to bag it if I don't make it back to number one *this* year. I'm not like all those jerks out there who think my biological clock is ticking or something. I just want to get back into the top five, and see what I need from there. But "—he shifts slightly on the floor—"like I said, if I do get back to number one, it'll be because of what happened at the Open. I mean, I sat in the house for a week after that. I was *steaming*. I just kept saying, 'Can you *believe* this shit?' All those guys who wanted to get even with me all those years were starting to get even. Tiriac was right."

Tiriac is Ion Tiriac, the bearish Romanian

126

coach who made champions out of Nastase and Guillermo Vilas and now plays Colonel Tom to Becker's Elvis. McEnroe is referring to a comment Tiriac made at the Open last year, before McEnroe lost to Annacone, before the default.

Tiriac was standing outside the trainer's room, waiting for Becker to change. McEnroe happened to be there, looking skittish, a New York Islanders cap on his head, telling well-wishers. "I got a feeling it's going to get worse before it gets better."

Tiriac said to whoever cared to listen: "You know what is going to be the toughest thing for him now? He is going to start getting the Nastase treatment. All those years when Nastase was best player, they have to put up with all his bull-shit. But they all wait. Then comes the day when Nastase isn't Nastase anymore. And all the ones who wait are ready. Doesn't matter who they are. Umpires, linesmen, officials, other players. Is all the same. They say to him. Fuck *you* now. You piss on us all these years? Okay, now we piss on you. McEnroe is going to get the Nastase treatment, wait and see please."

Couple of days later came the default. McEnroe knew what everybody else knew: if he were still number one, they would have waited until Christmas for him to show up for a first-round doubles match.

McEnroe uses the remote control on the television set, switching from the Joan Rivers show to a Philadelphia Flyers hockey game.

"I've never been defaulted out of a match in

127

my life," he says. "No one knew what to say to me for a week. Well. I knew what to say: Screw it. I'm going back to being John McEnroe."

By the end of '86, John McEnroe had won three tournaments, beaten Lendl once, and been fined and suspended.

Girl meets boy.

Tatum O'Neal says. "So this girlfriend of mine says, 'John McEnroe's coming up to the party later, do you want to meet him?' I thought, 'Why not?' "

Her husband is practicing with Connors. She is sitting on the sofa, wearing a white WORLD TEAM CUP, DUSSELDORF T-shirt over a long white linen skirt. She looks younger than twenty-three, fair and freckled, softer and sweeter than she is in photographs. She is about three months pregnant. Estella has put Kevin down for the rest of the morning. A powerboat cruises past outside the dining-room window. Tatum O'Neal—Ryan's daughter, Griffin's sister, Farrah's whatever—sips coffee.

"John hates caffeine," she says. "I love caffeine."

The party was in early October 1984, at a record producer's home in Los Angeles. McEnroe does show up, as advertised. He is with Vitas Gerulaitis. John and Tatum are introduced.

"The next thing I know, he comes over and sits down right next to me. I mean, *right next to me.* I thought, 'Oh my God.' " They chat. They hit it off, she thinks. There is another party the next day, at the home of Alana Stewart. She was married to George Hamilton and Rod Stewart. John and Tatum chat a little more. They discover they are both going to be in New York later in the month.

"He calls me up in New York. It's like October 27 or 28. He says, 'You want to see my new apartment?' Sure. And John took me to this place on Central Park—this quadruplex—and I promise you, I couldn't believe my eyes. I said, 'How old are you? Twenty-six? Twenty-seven? And this place is *yours?*' It just kept going up and up and up. I was overwhelmed. I'd seen nice places before in my life. But this was the nicest place I'd ever seen.

"There is also some chemistry going on. I can feel it. But about 11:00, I left. Then I had to go back to Los Angeles. Then I went to Las Vegas, where my dad was making a movie. John was off playing a tournament in Stockholm, and he misbehaved. One morning my father shoved the newspaper in my face with the stories about John and said, 'Look at this! How can you *like* this guy?' Uh, thanks, Dad."

I say, "Things different now between John and your dad?"

Tatum O'Neal smiles brilliantly and delivers the line like the kid who won the Oscar.

"Oh yes," she says brightly. "They're much, *much* worse."

McEnroe used to tell his friends he'd never

marry an actress, he'd never move to L.A., and he'd never have a kid before he was thirty. But you can't stop love. "I know he wasn't marrying Farrah at her peak, or Madonna," Tatum says. "I'm not the paparazzi queen of the moment, okay? John McEnroe didn't marry the 'It' girl of the year. But I know what it's like to be inside that bubble and be young. Maybe he wanted someone a little more like him."

It isn't Joe and Marilyn, myth on myth. Nothing is ever going to be. It isn't even Sean and Madonna, but no doubt John and Tatum take the silver medal as the paparazzi pair skaters of the moment.

McEnroe says, "Let me put it this way: being with Tatum took me to a whole new plane. Until I met her, I'd never been in the *National Enquirer*."

They spent most of their time in Malibu. The photographers hid in garages across the street or camped on the sidewalk. McEnroe would go to the grocery store, and he would be followed. He'd be shooting a Frisbee around with Ahmad Rashad, the NBC Sports commentator, on the beach, and they would discover a photographer from a British tabloid had screwed himself into the sand. When McEnroe took the sabbatical, there was a day when a Brit Journalist—a lot of them think investigative reporting is remembering the limerick from the men's-room wall—rang the doorbell and said to Tatum. Excuse me, ma'am, isn't your husband in rehab at such-and-such?

McEnroe denies that he was in rehab anyplace,

though rumors were very much in the air while he was away. Somebody knew somebody who had been with McEnroe at this hospital—we got that sort of call at the paper where I work. Another guy called up and talked about this treatment program in New Jersey or that one in L.A.

McEnroe says, "It's a lie. Anybody who knows me knows that I'm honest. I'm the worst liar in the world. I don't do that stuff. I wasn't in rehab. But all of a sudden that was the story on me. Even people I thought were friends didn't believe me when I denied it.

"I was going to Lakers games all the time. I was at concerts. I was in the public eye. But it made a good story, so no one wanted to check anything."

As it was, the thing he needed was rehab from tennis.

"At the end of 1985," McEnroe says, "I wasn't playing well to begin with, and then it seemed like all this stuff with Tatum and me just kept piling up. The combination did it to me. I knew I had to dig myself out of this hole I'd gotten myself into." At the Australian Open in December of '85, there came the day when McEnroe suddenly found his hands around the throat of a reporter. Only a warning from a bellhop kept the picture out of newspapers the world over. He lost to the immortal Slobodan Zivojinovic at the Australian Open—"First match I ever felt like I tanked in my life"—and then lost to Gilbert in New York a month later, and beat it.

In their Turnberry living room—they also own an estate in Cove Neck, Long Island—Tatum O'Neal says. "I think John is coming to the realization that it's just not a big deal anymore with the photographers. It's happened to Frank Sinatra his whole career. It happens to everyone in these businesses if they're any good." She giggles. "Well, not Lendl. The point is, after all these years, I'm used to it. It's my life, *our* life, and after a while you just say to yourself, 'My life is more important than all that.' One night we were out with Sean Penn and I started talking to Sean about it, because of all the problems he's had. And John just gave me this look. Like, 'Couldn't we be talking about something more important with Sean?' "

She says they forged their relationship during his six months away from tennis. Kevin was born in May. They were married in August on Long Island. Tatum was Ryan's daughter and now she was McEnroe's wife.

McEnroe: "Let's face it, it stinks being married to a professional athlete."

It was as if more tumult had been added to the tumultuous life of Tatum O'Neal. Her parents, Ryan O'Neal and former actress Joanna Moore, were divorced when she was a child. Her brother Griffin has had well-publicized drug problems and was cited last year for criminal negligence in the boating death of director Francis Ford Coppola's son. Ryan O'Neal has sired a child out of wedlock with actress Farrah Fawcett, who was

Farrah Fawcett-Majors when she was married to the Six Million Dollar Man.

McEnroe: "It's a credit to Tatum how well she's turned out, considering."

Tatum herself says, "I look at the upbringing John's had and the family situation he came out of—how *normal* it all is—and I think how lucky he is."

She disappears into the kitchen and comes back with more coffee. She goes to the door and gives a listen for Kevin. Then she sits down and primly rearranges her skirt as she crosses her legs on the coffee table.

"I didn't realize how much support he was going to need from me." she says. "It took me a long time to adjust to that. Sometimes I find myself saying, 'Look, John, I don't know how to be a wife.' But I chose. I chose John. And eventually, I think I can be everything I want to be— support system, actress, wife, mother.

"I've learned patience. I let a lot of things go by. I wasn't used to that, I've got a hell of an Irish temper. You know, let's get everything out in the open and deal with it right now. We have some beautiful fights. He gets so angry with me, and he finally says, 'you know who you are? The female John McEnroe! And you know what else? You've got all his worst qualities.' "

John McEnroe says, "Are you kidding? When I was eighteen years old and starting out, I would have been thrilled to have the career I've had. You know, three Wimbledons, four U.S. Opens, the Davis Cup."

That was then, this is now.

"I felt he was going to be the greatest player of all time," says Bud Collins, *Boston Globe* columnist and NBC broadcaster. "He had everything. Genius. Artistry. And that serve. I thought he'd go past Roy Emerson and have the most grand-slam singles titles ever {Emerson had twelve}. Then he couldn't handle it, I guess. Plus, he was never in shape to begin with. I still love watching the kid play. I can see him winning another Wimbledon, or Open, maybe even the French if he ever works at it. But I honestly don't feel he's been true to his talent."

In what was supposed to be his prime, McEnroe didn't push himself. But then again he never did. Tennis always came so easily to him. From the time he was a kid at the Port Washington Tennis Academy on Long Island, he got special treatment from his coaches: even the late Harry Hopman, the legendary Aussie taskmaster, was soft on Junior.

If he did not abuse his talent, perhaps he took it for granted. Other players, such as Lendl, were torturing themselves on Nautilus machines and retaining conditioning coaches. McEnroe played his guitar and acted like a rock star. When he found out that Lendl was on the Robert Haas Eat-to-Win Diet McEnroe joked, "I'm on the Häagen-Dazs diet." While Tiriac had Becker running up mountains in Germany, McEnroe was running around the country on his "Tennis Over America" tour, making big bucks in meaningless exhibition matches.

McEnroe, blessed with the skills of a champion, has always had the disposition of an artist: just put up the net and let's do it.

And when he was young, McEnroe did it to Borg, he did it to them all. Punch them out with the serve, get to the net in an eye-blink, then drop one of those volleys on the other side, the ball dying like a pillow hitting a mattress. In the long rallies, he would hit one ball with top spin, slice the next one, hit the next flat, start the whole program over again.

"A nick here, a nick there," Arthur Ashe says, "and pretty soon you're bleeding to death."

One night he was talking about Becker's serve, the best he's ever seen. "Did Tiriac teach it to him?" McEnroe spits out some club sandwich and continues, "You're born with something like that. Becker just understands things that champions are supposed to understand."

McEnroe always hated practice. Instead he played doubles with Fleming to hone his game, smooth out the rough patches. He jokes about his work habits. That night in Philly, he put ice to his fanny, ice to his shoulder, he attached this elastic thing to his ankles and edged slowly across the room, he did sit-ups, he did curls. At one point during our conversation I said, "How old are you now?" and McEnroe said, "Twenty-eight. Which means twenty-eight years of not being in shape."

Last summer, on the verge of the comeback from the sabbatical, McEnroe decided to change all that. He cooled his longtime coaching relationship (if not his friendship) with Tony Palafox and hired a combination Zen master and drill instructor named Paul Cohen. There was yoga in the morning, brutal workouts in the afternoon. He ended up with perfect muscle tone but no upper-body power. Now he's dumped Cohen and gone back to Palafox, who is more like a graduate assistant than a teacher. He lets McEnroe be McEnroe.

"I made some mistakes in the last couple of years." McEnroe says, "and they set me back." McEnroe believes that the biggest mistake he ever made was in not winning the 1984 French Open final when he had it in his grasp.

"You know," he says, "if I'd won that French, it might have changed the way everybody looks at my career."

No American male had won the French Open on the red clay of Roland Garros Stadium in twenty-nine years. In 1984, the final was against Lendl. McEnroe led two sets to none. Then he led two sets to one.

"Two sets to one, 4–3 in games, 40–30 on my serve," he will say whenever the subject comes up, like he's reciting a grocery list. "Five points from the match."

Lendl broke McEnroe's serve, eventually broke his back. The heat got to McEnroe. Lendl got to McEnroe, photographers got to McEnroe, he tried to whack an NBC hand-held camera. Lendl won the fourth set, the fifth set, the title. McEnroe didn't have the French. Lendl wasn't a choker anymore. McEnroe would win the U.S. Open later that year. It was his last grand-slam championship. He was twenty-five years old. "I choked that French Open," he says.

For years, Lendl chased McEnroe. Now McEnroe chases him. It is not a buddy movie.

"The guy hasn't been good for tennis," McEnroe says. "He's been so selfish. And he's certainly not the kind of guy who brings out the best in others. He's hurt the popularity of the game so much. Borg was different. Borg gave this feeling to people. Borg became this huge celebrity without saying a *thing*. It's hard to say nothing and turn out as big as he did."

It was the best tennis show of all. There had never been quite the collision of excellence that Borg and McEnroe brought to their battles in the late '70s and early '80s. It was McEnroe's fire, Borg's ice. Net versus baseline. Righty, lefty. McEnroe would hit a big hook serve, take Borg into the flower boxes, and Borg would somehow punch a two-fisted backhand down the line for a winner. Borg would hit what was a sure passing shot against anyone else in the world, and McEnroe would dive and spit back a winning volley.

"The only way you could win a point," McEnroe said after the Wimbledon final in 1980, "was to hit a winner.

"Borg's a legend. I'm not kidding you, I still miss Borg. It took me a long time to get over his leaving like that. All of a sudden, he just bagged it, like, poof, he was gone. I thought, 'Wait a minute, we were just getting started, this was just getting interesting.' It affected me for a whole year. Then by the time I got my act together, there were Lendl and Jimbo ready to pounce. See, Borg never considered one thing: that I could screw up."

Between the Philadelphia tournament and the vacation at Turnberry, McEnroe had some wisdom teeth pulled, lost a match to Johan Kriek in Memphis, and played an exhibition match with Bjorn Borg in Toronto. Over the last few years, they've done this several times, like some rock 'n' roll revival. In Toronto, McEnroe asked Borg what he thought he, Mac, should do.

" 'Retire,' " McEnroe says, laughing.

"I gotta believe I can do it again," he says. "I think it took guts to walk away the way I did. Nobody ever did that. I think that's going to pay some dividends along the way somewhere. I'm not going to panic if I lose some matches. Everybody panics so fast. I'm going to be around for awhile."

Courtesy car in Philadelphia. Tony Palafox is in the front seat of the van. In the back, McEnroe is talking excitedly about the Giants winning the Super Bowl, asking questions about all the Mets' off-season problems, announcing that all New Yorkers had to begin rooting for the New York Rangers, give New York a triple. McEnroe may

138

be a Lakers fan, but he is still happiest at Madison Square Garden and Shea Stadium, drinking beers with his old Douglaston pals, watching the teams he grew up with.

He is asked what the biggest public misconception about him is.

He says, "That I'm not a nice person. Because I am. I'm just not nice 100 percent of the time. But I'll tell you this: I make a lot more people happy than not."

You know all the bad parts. What you don't know: McEnroe is smart, funny, honest, an intensely loyal friend. When rich young American players couldn't be bothered, he played Davis Cup, made it mean something again in the United States. Of course, this doesn't justify anything. Just balances out the scales, maybe more than you thought. He's no punk.

"Nobody ever talks about South Africa," says his father. "Chris Evert, Miss Perfect, took the money and went down there. Jack Nicklaus went down there and played golf. They offered John $1 million just to go down to Sun City and *lose* one match and go home. Then they offered him $5 million for five years if he'd come down. And my son stood up and said no. People can think what they want about him. But principles are high up on his list of priorities. My wife and I are thrilled at the way he's turned out."

John McEnroe Sr. is a balding, ruddy-faced Irishman every bit as tough as his kid. You want to mix it up with Junior, you have to get by the old man first. He grew up on Seventy-ninth Street and Third Avenue in Manhattan, when, as he likes to say, "Third Avenue was still Third Avenue, not some fashionable part of the Upper East Side." He came out of Fordham Law and was a successful member of Paul, Weiss, Rifkind, Wharton and Garrison, a prestigious New York law firm, before his kid ever sneered at his first Wimbledon umpire. Ultimately, you want to set up anything important, business-wise, with John McEnroe Jr., you deal with John McEnroe Sr. And his presence in the stands has become a tennis fixture: the camera eventually finds him, squinting underneath a floppy white hat or some network's baseball cap, trying to be cool and Big Daddy-like while his son is doing something terribly embarrassing in a big match.

"He wasn't a fighter as a kid," the father says. "The only fistfight I can ever remember was when he was defending his brother Mark against this kid who was three years bigger than Mark at the time. And that time, I told him he did the right thing, defending his brother." There is still some Third Avenue there; it almost comes out "brudder."

The father laughs.

"Of course, he was always a hooter and howler on the tennis court," he says. "Except when he was first starting out. The kids were calling their own lines then, so he had nobody to argue with. So John spent a lot of time yelling at himself. But that was John. Playing Ping-Pong with his brothers, he tried to beat you. Pickup basket-ball with his friends, same thing. John *always* wanted to win."

Kay McEnroe, the mother, says, "The signs were always there. Even if he didn't get the best mark in Latin, in grammar school, he'd be *furious*. One time he got 94 and his friend got 98, and there was just no speaking to him."

Kay McEnroe is a tall, attractive, silver-haired woman who looks more like an ex-Vogue model than the ex-nurse whom her husband met a long time ago, while she was working at Lenox Hill Hospital. She is a lady, polite to the point of courtly, extremely close to her son, quite different from the rough-and-tumble of both father and son. She is also the quiet steel of the McEnroe family, even if she's not out in front running interference. To this day, when there is some sort of nontennis problem, John likes to run it by his mother.

"With John, I know I'll hear about it," she says. "My other boys (Patrick and Mark), they're more quiet. John's always been different. I expect I'll be mother to him for quite a while. He's always been very complicated, and I don't think that will ever change. But of the three boys, he's the one who never misses my birthday or Mother's Day."

The son's tennis always made the mother nervous, at whatever level it was being played. So did the sound and the fury when the ball the son thought was out was called in.

Kay McEnroe says, "My first reaction is that

I'd like him to be quiet. The moment it happens, I think, 'Oh my God.' First and foremost, he's my child. and I don't want anything to pain my children, whatever the circumstances. So I'm thinking, 'John, don't do that, it will only upset you.' " She giggles. "One time, oh, a long time ago, I said. 'Honey, don't worry, the next one will go your way.' And John looked me right in the eye and said, 'Mother, that's bullshit.' "

The father sighs when you bring up "pits of the world" and so forth.

"It goes back to what I said about principles," he says. "John always thinks he's right."

A lot of what has happened to John McEnroe Jr. he did to himself. He never knew when to fold his hand. But he has come to understand—he says—that it doesn't matter anymore whether or not he was right about every single line call that took place since Wimbledon of '77.

McEnroe on McEnroe: "The way I'm thinking now is this—'What satisfaction is there in making someone feel bad, even if you're right?' Also, I don't want to go down in history as being Nasty Jr., or whatever. When you get to the stage where I am now—husband, father, twenty-eight years old—the whole thing just gets to sound like sour grapes.

"I don't know. After a while, when I'd get the bad call, what happened next was almost like an addiction. I mean, I'd feel my feet moving toward the chair before I'd even think about going over there. And so now I'm stuck with the rep, I understand that. I might only do something once or twice a match, but that's all people want to remember. The thing I hate is that people think it's an act. It's not an act. It was never an act. It's just something that became part of me that I'm trying to recover from because there are more important things to get on with."

Once John McEnroe Sr. and his wife were the ones who had to sit and watch when the fireworks came. Now it is Tatum who must sit there with the stiff upper lip, smiling bravely.

"I just think, 'John, get back into the game,'" Tatum says. " 'Forget about that point, get on to the next one.' He's come to know how proud I am of him when he *doesn't* do those things."

Tatum O'Neal, Kevin's mom, shrugs her shoulders, like she's trying to shake off the whole subject.

She says, "Mostly I think all that crap is a waste of time."

Addiction or just plain crap, take your pick. Bad behavior apparently doesn't go away just because John McEnroe says it will. In April, he lost to Miroslav Mecir in the finals of the WCT Finals in Dallas. Early in the match, McEnroe snarled at the chair umpire, "You're going to be hearing from me all day, and there's nothing you can do about it."

In the third set he threatened to walk out of the match. Later, after yet another call that seemed to cause him physical pain. McEnroe screamed,

"It's a goddamn conspiracy." Good intentions are very nice, but it may be that if you are born round, you don't die square.

Tatum O'Neal says, "Watch it. Honey. Hot plate."

She sets the plate of hot pancakes down on the coffee table in front of her husband. As McEnroe attacks his lunch with fury—at that first Wimbledon in '77, one writer described his "eating the traditional strawberries and cream without benefit of the traditonal spoon"—he talks about something interesting that happened during his six months off.

They missed him.

The crowds missed him. So did the nabobs of the sport who sometimes thought of him as acid rain. Suddenly, there were no heroes out there, anti or otherwise. Lendl, on the court, has the personality of an IBM home computer. ("What's the matter?" McEnroe asks sarcastically. "Do you like a robot being number one?") Becker, for all his screaming youth, really does have a personality that ends with scraped knees. Connors hasn't won a tournament of any kind since the first Reagan administration; all of his competitive qualities are still admirable, but he's an opening act now. By the middle of April, Tim Mayotte would be the only American to have won a Grand Prix tournament anywhere on the planet in 1987.

*Tim Mayotte?*

Borg and McEnroe played twenty-two minutes of tie breaker once at Wimbledon that was more gripping than anything that has happened in tennis the last couple of years.

So all of a sudden they missed Junior. Without him, the game lay in state. And wasn't nobody coming along. It's like parents who spend all those years telling the kids to keep the noise down, then go crazy with the quiet when they go off to college. All the ones who scorned McEnroe suddenly were dying of heartbreak when he went away.

He says, "I'm losing this match to (Johan) Kriek in Memphis a few weeks ago and, like, they *love* me. I'm thinking, 'Why couldn't it be like this eight or nine years ago?' "

A few minutes before he came back from practice for some of Tatum's flapjacks, she was saying, "Right now he's in good shape. He understands it's going to take some time to get into great shape. and when he gets into great shape, he knows he'll be able to play the way he wants to play. But God, people are so negative. Ever since he's come back, he's had to take so much crap from so-called friends and contemporaries and people in the press about how the clock is supposedly running on his career."

John walks in as she's speaking, tosses his blue headband and racket on the floor, flops on the couch, unlaces his sneakers, picks up the electric guitar and begins a loud, off-key version of "This Land is Your Land." After a few bars, Tatum disappears into the kitchen, laughing and covering

145

her ears. McEnroe says, "Listen, it's not too late to change my attitude, or my approach, or whatever. I've watched Connors use the crowd, and he's really good at it. I think I can get a big part of the crowd rooting for me. I think they understand that whatever they thought they knew about me, the bottom line is that I'm good for the game. I'm not a robot. It's like this: people either like or don't like what they think they know about you."

He strums a big chord, theatrically, on the guitar.

"I'm happier off the court than I've ever been in my life," he says. "For all the bad stuff that happened last year, it was a *great* year, because it was a family year. Now this year is for me, to start seeing if I can still do it."

A month before, in Philadelphia, I'd asked McEnroe what he thought he'd be doing when he reached forty. He got up and paced the room. He has always been nervous energy, standing up, sitting down, patting his hair, flailing at imaginary ground strokes, shooting imaginary jump shots, like the room is Borg and it's jerking him around.

"The things I'd really like to do aren't realistic," he says. "I'd like to be in a rock 'n' roll band. Or the eleventh man on an NBA team. Or an NBA coach. I used to want to be the twelfth man on an NBA team, but I've upgraded my goals. Hell, I want to get into some games, get some minutes. Or maybe make a movie with Jack (Nicholson, fellow Lakers fan). If Jack called and said, 'John,

I've got to have you in my next movie,' that would by nice. It's also not going to happen."

For now, John McEnroe has to prove that at twenty-eight, he is not an old man in a young man's game. Things happened to him. Borg went away for good. Maybe number one wasn't all McEnroe thought it was going to be. Neither was being famous. He squandered too much of his genius in big-money exhibitions. He made way too much noise about small matters.

A few years ago, when he was still number one, McEnroe was asked what it would take for him to get the crowds on his side. "I'll have to get married, have a kid, and start losing," he said. He was referring to Connors, who was booed off the court at Forest Hills after losing the '77 Open final to Vilas, but who somehow turned it around and became the people's choice, at least in this country.

The remark is mentioned to John McEnroe, who is married, has a kid and, at least for now, is losing more than he ever has (in February, March, and April, McEnroe played four finals, lost four finals).

"I know," McEnroe says. "I know. Weird how things work out, huh?"

He shouts to the kitchen.

"Honey," John McEnroe says, "we got any more of that Aunt Jemima?"

# JIM LOEHR

# The X-Factor Delivers a Championship

*Whether champion athletes are born or bred is a debate that rages on, but here sports psychologist Jim Loehr identifies another component of winning performance—the "X-factor." Referring to an athlete's emotions—the positive feelings that support and enhance an athlete's physical potential or the negative ones that undermine performance—it is often the deciding factor in matches where the players are otherwise equal. Here is the example of twenty-year-old tennis star Gabriela Sabatini who came back after her disappointing performance in 1990 to win the United States Open championship against superstar Steffi Graf. Her success, Loehr explains, was the result of emotional training that helped Sabatini to regain a sense of the challenge and fun of championship tennis. In his prescription not only for the professional but also for the amateur, Loehr outlines the "chemistry of peak performance."*

A young tennis player stares at her coach with empty eyes. Her passionless face tells it all: Why am I here? Where am I going? Is there a future for me? Lost, confused, disconnected from herself

148

and the world around her, she searches for a light out of the darkness. Not in her wildest dream could Gabriela Sabatini forsee that, in only five months, she would emerge from her most frustrating period as a professional to become the 1990 United States Open champion.

No one gave this struggling veteran of 20, who first romanced the professional tennis world as a 14-year-old, any chance against the likes of Graf, Seles, Navratilova and Capriati. All the statistics and logical analysis in the world could never have predicted such an outcome. How did it happen?

Rest assured this great triumph was not the result of luck, fate or idle happenstance. The explanation quite simply was emotional.

It's the X-Factor in sport. The incalculable. It refers to what's happening at the deepest personal level within the athlete, to the private, complex inner world of feelings and emotions. If I have learned anything over the last 15 years as a sports psychologist, it is to respect the powerful role emotion plays in performance.

Make no mistake about it, the fullest expression of genius, talent and potential occurs only when the emotional dimension of the person is healthy, balanced and strong. The right emotions bring energy, sparkle, flow, fight and brilliance. And Sabatini displayed all of these things. To witness this elegant athlete finally break free from the turmoil, the fear, the doubt, the months of agonizing indecisiveness and personal pain was a memorable moment.

To break free was wonderful enough but to do so in the final of a Grand Slam event against the No. 1 player in the world, before millions of fans, was even more satisfying. Speechless she was and speechless she will be for some time, I am sure. Unable to express in words her feeling of joy was not surprising. The astonishing success simply confirmed that the gradual transformation that had occurred deep within her was real and right.

The physical and emotional demands of a sport like tennis are enormous. The glitter, glamour, money and fame conceal undescribable pressures and expectations. Although hard to measure and difficult to define, this X-Factor can never be ignored.

Steffi Graf now understands the downside of the X-Factor. Her world was unjustly ripped apart earlier this year by a scandal that left her dazed, angry, sorrowful and confused. She summed it up to Peter Bodo of Tennis Magazine after her Wimbledon loss to Zina Garrison this year by saying: "These days I am not at my best. I could not fight as usual because of all the turmoil. Tennis is a game won with the head and lately my head has not been in my tennis."

The team that had so consistently and precisely sustained her emotional lifeline was under seige. Tennis is an individual sport but players never make it alone. Behind every great success is a team: parents, coaches, friends and trainers. The team brings wisdom, knowledge and skill, but most importantly, it brings safety.

For Sabatini, this special team—her parents, brother and close friends—jump-started the X-Factor with stronger signals, better communication, clearer messages and more support. As the staleness and fear faded, Sabatini gained renewed hope and eagerness. But it was a new coach that became the strongest beacon.

Carlos Kirmayr, a mellow, sensitive Brazilian, ignited the spirit. His smiling, playful style and his own genuine love for the game was contagious. A sense of challenge, energy and fun gradually replaced Sabatini's doubt.

The world of sport science is gradually closing in on a scientific understanding of the X-Factor, but much is still unknown. What is known is that emotional responses have a clear and verifiable biochemical basis. Stress responses such as fear and anger are rooted in complex biochemical events that profoundly affect physiological and psychological functioning. It is very important to understand that relaxation, recovery, joy and fun are also anchored fundamentally in biochemical events that potentially affect every cell in the body.

The chemistry and the psychophysiology of joy is vastly different from that of fear. As waves of emotion come and go, corresponding changes ripple through the body and actually provide measurable alterations in heart rate, muscle tension, brain wave patterns and blood pressure.

As hormonal levels of such substances as cortisol and epinephrine rise or fall, and as levels of neurotransmitters and neuropeptides such as serotonin, endorphin and dopamine change, the body's potential for peak performance varies accordingly.

There is clearly a chemistry of peak performance. Emotional conflicts, unhappiness, staleness and chronic stress create chronic changes in the physiology that make peak performance impossible. The X-Factor will one day be precisely linked to a specific biochemical-neurochemical foundation.

In the meantime, the X-Factor is real. The emotional world of the athlete must be valued, protected, understood and constantly nourished. Emotional training can connect to the physiology as powerfully as physical training and, if peak performance is the goal, the chemistry of emotion must be right, balanced and strong.

For Sabatini, emotional goals in the form of fun, playfulness, positive energy, personal happiness and relaxation became the highest priority in the total training menu. The result was mental toughness: confident, fighting, focused and fearless in the face of adversity and incomparable pressure.

It is to be hoped that the experience will lead Sabatini to new heights and new personal victories. One thing is certain: she now understands much more about this mysterious and puzzling X-Factor and as a result her future is much brighter.

# BASKETBALL

# DONALD HALL

## Basketball: The Purest Sport of Bodies

*In 1891 James Naismith, a student at the Young Men's Christian Association's Training School in Springfield, Massachusetts, conceived of the game of basketball. Filling in the gap between baseball and football, the game was an instant success. However, those first, clumsy efforts little resembled the gracefully executed game of today. Looking like "minnows in the pond," contemporary players stun the spectator with their sinuous, seemingly gravity-defying moves. As Hall observes, of all the major sports basketball is most suited to the proportions of the television screen and the instant slow-motion replay where the spectator can savor the nuances of this "ferocious ballet." Here the writer celebrates the beauty of contemporary basketball's improvised choreography.*

Professional basketball combines opposites—elegant gymnastics, ferocious ballet, gargantuan delicacy, colossal precision. . . . It is a continuous violent dream of levitating hulks. It is twist and turn, leap and fly, turn and counterturn, flick and respond, confront and evade. It is monstrous, or it would be monstrous if it were not witty.

These athletes show wit in their bodies. Watching their abrupt speed, their instant reversals of direction, I think of minnows in the pond—how the small schools slide swiftly in one direction, then reverse-flip and flash the opposite way. NBA players are quick as minnows, and with an adjustment for size great whales drive down the road. As a ball careens from a rim, huge bodies leap with legs outspread; then two high hands grasp the ball, propel it *instantly* down court to a sprinting guard, and *instantly* seven to ten enormous bodies spin and sprint on the wooden floor, pass, dribble, pass, pass, shoot—block or whoosh. . . .

Then the same bodies flip-flash back to the place they just departed from, fast as an LED display from a punched button—an intricate thrashing, a mercury—sudden pack of leviathans. . . . In all sport, nothing requires more of a body than NBA basketball; nothing so much uses—and celebrates—bodily improvisation, invention, and imagination.

In football they measure forty-yard sprints. Nobody runs forty yards in basketball. Maybe you run the ninety-four feet of the court but more likely you sprint ten feet; then you stop, not on a dime, but on Miss Liberty's torch. In football you run over somebody's face.

When I was growing up, the winter sport was hockey. At high school, hundreds of us would stand outside at 0 degrees Fahrenheit beside a white rink puffing out white air, stamping our painful feet, our toes like frozen fishsticks. On the ice, unhelmeted shoulder-padded thick-socked blocky young men swept up and down, wedded to the moves of a black hard-rubber disk and crushing each other into boards, fighting, crashing, shooting, fighting again. Then we tromped home to unfreeze by the hot-water radiators, red-cheeked and exhausted with cold, exhilarated with pain and crowd-fight.

But basketball was a sweaty half-empty gym on a Friday afternoon, pale white legs clomping down court below billowing gym shorts; it was the two-handed set shot: pause, arch, aim, *grunt*. In the superheated dim gymnasium, twenty-seven friends and relatives watched the desultory to-and-fro of short, slow, awkward players who were eternally pulling up twelve feet from the basket to clatter a heavy brown beachball harmlessly off a white backboard. Always we lost thirty-eight to nineteen.

It was a hockey town, and New England was hockey country.

Meantime, elsewhere—in city park, in crepuscular gymnasiums after school with the heat turned off, or in Indiana farmyards with a basket nailed to the side of a barn—other children practiced other motions . . . and the best of these motions found their showcase, over the decades and for decades ahead, in New England's metropolis, in the leaky old ship of Boston Garden.

When I was at college, I took the subway into Boston to watch college double-headers. My Harvard team was better than the high school I went to . . . but I do not recollect that we were invited to the NIT. I watched Harvard, Boston College, Boston University—and Holy Cross. Of course I remember the astonishment of one young man's innovations: the infant Robert Cousy, who played for Holy Cross, dribbled behind his back and passed with perfect swift accuracy in a direction opposite the place toward which he gazed. Or he faked a pass, put the ball to the floor, and cut past bewildered defenders for an easy and graceful layup. As far as I am concerned, it was Robert Cousy, and not Colonel Naismith, who invented basketball.

One of the extraordinary qualities of basketball is its suddenness of change, in pace and in momentum.

Years ago, when I lived in Michigan, I frequented Cobo Hall when the Detroit Pistons played there. I watched good players on bad teams: great Bob Lanier, Big-Foot with bad knees, enormous and delicate and always hurt; Dave Bing and Chris Ford, who ended their careers with the Celtics. Once I took my young son to see the Detroit Pistons play the Boston Celtics in a play-off game. It was 1968, the first time the poor Pistons made the play-offs. It was Bill Russell's next-to-last year as player-coach of the

Celtics; they went on to beat the Lakers for the championship.

I sat with my boy and his friend David, who was a Celtics fan because he had lived in Boston until he was eight months old, and watched three periods of desultory play. There were good moments from Bing and Lanier, good moments from Havlicek and White—my man Cousy retired in 1963—but Bill Russell looked half asleep even as he blocked shots. In the fourth quarter the Pistons, astonishingly, led—and I entertained notions of an upset. . . .

Then my small charges developed a desire for hot dogs; I dashed out for a few minutes, and as I returned laden, I heard a swelling of wistful applause from the knowledgeable Coba crowd. I looked toward the floor to see Bill Russell floating through the air to sink a basket. In the space of two hot dogs, Boston had gone up by ten points— or rather, not Boston but the usually inoffensive Russell. He had waked up—and when Russell opened his eyes it was over for Detroit. . . .

"Momentum" is a cliche of the football field, but it is a habit of the wooden floor. Basketball is a game not so much of important baskets or of special plays as of violent pendulum swings. One team or another is always on a run, like a madcap gambler throwing a dozen sevens. When the Celtics are down by a dozen points in the second quarter, looking listless, hapless, helpless, we know that suddenly they can become energized—rag dolls wired with springy, reactive power. We know that twelve points down can be six points up with a crazy suddenness.

Sometimes one player does it all by himself. On a night when Cedric Maxwell has twelve thumbs and Kevin McHale three knees, when every pass hits vacant air, when the foul-shooter clanks it off the rim, suddenly Larry Bird (usually it is Larry Bird) grows five inches taller and five seconds faster. With legs outspread he leaps above the rim to take a rebound, pivots, and throws a fastball the length of the court to Gerald Henderson who lays it up. Then as the Knicks (or the Bulls, or the Bullets . . .) go into their half-court offense, he appears to fall asleep. His slack jaw sags and he does his Idiot Thing . . . only to swoop around a guard and steal the ball cleanly, like pluching a sheep-tick off a big dog, then sprint down court and float a layup. Then he steals the inbound pass and, as the power-forward fouls him, falls heavily to the floor; only while he falls, he loops the ball up with his left hand over a high head into the basket—and *impossible* three-point play. Then he fast-breaks with Maxwell and Parish, zapping the ball back and forth, and leaps as if to shoot over an immense center. But, looking straight at the basket, he passes the ball blind to Robert Parish on his left, who stuffs it behind the center's head. . . .

We have just run off nine points.

This is a game you can study on television because

it is small enough to fit in the box; and, through television's slow-motion replay, we study at our leisure the learned body's performances—as when Dr. J. or George Gervin soars from the base line, ball in the right hand, appears to shoot, pauses in midair, and, when a shot-blocker hovers beside him, transfers the ball to the left hand, twists the body, and stuffs the ball through the loop.

It is only two points. If this were gymnastics or diving from the high board at the Olympics, it would be *ten* points.

The Celtics play team ball, passing, seeking the open man when defenders double-team Bird or Parish. The ball moves so rapidly, it is like a pinball machine in which the steel ball gathers speed as it bounces off springs, rioting up and out, down and across. Zany ball, with its own wild life, always like the rabbit seeking its hole.

Or.

The Game.

Slows.

Down.

Despite the twenty-four-second clock, there are passages of sheer stasis. The point guard bounces the ball: once, twice, three times. The guard in front of him is all alert nerves, arms spread and quivering. Will he drive right? Left?

Bounce.

Bounce . . .

Bounce . . . . . .

He goes right NO-he-only-seemed-to-go-right-he-is-left-around-his-man, he rise into the *air* and . . . blocked-by-a-giant-under-hands-to-his-own-giant . . . who backward-stuffs it. BANG.

Oh, my. Basketball is the purest sport of bodies.

# ROBERT LIPSYTE

## Sport of the Seventies: Sly, Midnight Moves

*Six-foot-eight-inch Connie Hawkins was a gifted basketball player from New York City's Bedford-Stuyvesant. His difficult journey from ghetto playground—where basketball is a "macho performing art"—to the university of Iowa and finally as a professional to the Phoenix Sons reflects the experience of many other young players who pour their hopes for escaping poverty and the ghettoes into sports. Robert Lipsyte exposes the high school and college systems that ignore the academic deficiancies of these athletes and then use their basketball talents for the glory and financial gain of the institutions. To attract the best of these players colleges offered scholarships, salaries for nonexistent jobs, apartments, cars, and transportation costs for girlfriends. These perks —sometimes offered surreptitiously for professional teams —culminated in the 1961 college basketball scandals that ended the careers of many promising athletes and nearly destroyed Hawkins's future in basketball.*

New York's most salable human export tradition-
ally has been its annual crop of college-bound basketball players, planted in the ghettoes, nurtured
in the playgounds and community centers, harvested in the high schools, and packaged for distribution throughout the country; rangy Irish
gunners and scrappy Jewish playmakers and, by
the sixties, game-busting black forwards and centers who could do everything with a basketball except read its label.

Products of the "city game," they reappear as
college stars in South Carolina and Tennessee and
West Texas and Wisconsin, often after a year of
"prepping" at one of several small private acad-
emies in the South and West that seem to exist
primarily to sand off the roughest of their streety
ways and teach them to understand, if not speak,
white English. The conventional SportsWorld
wisdom, that most of these young men would
never have a chance to attend college without basketball, is absolutely true. And a condemnation
of the educational system that barely needs comment.

One of the city game's finest products was a
functional illiterate named Connie Hawkins who
was shipped to the University of Iowa in 1960.
He was 18 years old, almost at his full height of
6 feet 8 inches, and gifted with remarkable agility
and body control. He had all the moves. He also
had a general diploma, which was little more than
a certificate of attendance, a kind of honorable
discharge fom high school for those the guidance

counselors have pre-tracked for the city's pool of unskilled labor.

Hawkins has become in recent years a shining star in SportsWorld, another proof of locker-room homilies, You Can't Keep A Good Man Down, or, If You Come to the End of Your Rope, Tie a Knot and Hang On. But for almost the entire sixties Hawkins was a prototype of the Sports-World sacrificial victim, the man left dangling when the going gets tough and the tough get going.

Hawkins attended Boys High in Brooklyn. When the neighborhood, Bedford-Stuyvesant, was white, the school was considered one of the best in the city. It drew future doctors and judges from all the boroughs. It was staffed by vigorous and idealistic young Irish and Jewish teachers eager to provide their younger counterparts with the tools to remake the world.

But by Connie's senior year, 1959-1960—which coincided with my own first year as a reporter, covering high school sports—the student population was more than three-quarters black, and the faculty was middle-aged and unprepared for the area's transition into a filthy, murderous reservation where crime and sports were prestige trades. The only respected badges of young manhood were the colors of a fighting gang and the varsity jacket of a Boys High team. For better or worse, the school's positive image was now based on its leadership in producing future college basketball stars.

165

Hawkins' coach, Mickey Fisher, was internationally recognized—he would abandon his high school team in the middle of Connie's last year to coach the Israeli Olympic team. Fisher was a classic inner-city coach, a white missionary who dedicated his life to saving black boys through sport. At the time, I did not question his role; I just nodded and smiled and took my notes and anticipated my by-lines as Fisher radiated energy and joy even as he complained of his personal sacrifices, his long hours, the occasional ingratitude of the community.

Fisher was relentless in pursuit of college scholarships for his boys, although he often placed them in colleges for which they were academically unsuited, colleges from which he must have known they could never be graduated.

Fisher bought his boys food and socks with his own money. He supervised their studies. He interceded for them with other teachers if their eligibility was in jeopardy. He drilled them constantly in fundamental ball control and team basketball, but he was shrewd enough to allow them an occasional dash of ghetto playground style: Even Fisher's 5-foot 8-inch guards could spring above the rim to smash the ball down through the basket.

A self-styled psychologist, showman, platoon sergeant, Fisher assumed that his culture was superior to his players', that his love was more dependable than what they might find at home, that his way of integrating them into the white middle-class value system with a salable skill was the best way, and the only way.

The terrible presumption of this attitude, so typically SportsWorld, was not really challenged until the late 1960s, when it became a very hot issue involving black student groups and their liberal faculty allies on one side, and traditional athletic departments on the other. Of course, it rarely occurred on campuses where the team was playing well or where the team leaders had professional aspirations. For example, Coach John Wooden of UCLA, who coached some of the hippest black athletes in America, rarely had to take time from winning national championships to put down mutinies against his paternalism.

Had Mickey Fisher lived into the 1970s, when high school athletes were questioning their coaches, he, too, would have escaped rebellion as long as he was sincerely teaching them how to win, how to get into college, how to make out in the world. In his own time, as patient and kindly and perceptive as he was, Fisher would have been aggrieved and resentful if the assertion of black consciousness had disrupted his relationship with his players; after all, he hadn't made the rules, he was just trying to save souls—bullying, cajoling, yelling, even hitting the boys if he felt they needed that kind of physical proof that he really cared about them. It is easier, in retrospect, to criticize the Fishers for the colonial administrators they were than to praise them for the practical way in which they armed a few for battle beyond the ghetto. After all, the Fishers were also trying to survive in SportsWorld.

Fisher's players were hand-picked, scouted since grammar school through community centers, schoolyards, and junior high school tournaments. Connie Hawkins was auditioned for stardom. A veteran starter from "The High" brought Connie around when he was a scrawny ninth-grader. Fisher looked him over with little interest, then asked him to try to touch the metal basket rim. Without a running start, Connie jumped straight up, grabbed, and swung from the rim with both hands. The coach's eyes lighted up. He had found a prime soul to save.

Connie's childhood contained all those neo-Dickensian touches the SportsWorld biographers love: He was the fifth of six children, his father left the family when Connie was 9, about the same time he started scavenging deposit bottles to redeem at the corner candy store where Mrs. Hawkins, who was losing her sight from glaucoma, got her telephone messages.

"Until I got good at basketball," said Connie many years later, "there was nothin' about me I liked, there wasn't a thing I could be proud of. I was kind of quiet and insecure. It didn't seem like I had anything going for me. I was ashamed of the way I looked. We all wore hand-me-downs. But my brothers were short and wide and I was long and skinny, so nothin' fit me right. I didn't feel sharp enough to talk to girls."

Boys High is an exotic outpost and Connie

168

Hawkins an extraordinarily gifted and misused athlete, but the basic lessons of Sports World were here for me to learn in 1959. I failed the course. I went out to Boys High to attract attention within the paper, to practice technique, to test myself against the competition, to prepare for the Big Leagues. And so I saw Mickey Fisher as a kind of social worker in sneakers, a man with a mission to salvage what he could from society's slag heap; and I saw Connie Hawkins as a nice, but dumb, povet with a remarkable talent.

Only Mickey Fisher and the round brown ball would save him from a dull life, perhaps even jail. My own naked ambition could be served with positive stories about this worthy place and its worthy boys, and SportsWorld would applaud us all.

I never really knew Connie Hawkins or understood what happened to him until David Wolf described his rise and fall and rise again, first in *Life* magazine, and later in a rich and rewarding book called *Foul!* In grammar school, wrote Wolf, Connie was truant to avoid continual embarrassment; he was called Long Tall Sally, he looked weak, and was bullied. None of the fighting gangs wanted him. He had huge hands, mugger's hands, it was suggested, but he was too scared to try. His brother branded him a "chickenshit faggot."

Then he found basketball at the community center where his mother worked, and nothing else could ever be so important again. Perhaps because sports is play for most of us, and a relatively

169

brief active career for professionals, the passion to participate is usually treated in a condescending or trivial way. But that moment when a poor, skinny, weak black suddenly realizes he has found the form in which to pour his energies and hopes is certainly as valid and drametic as the pre-seminarian's epiphany or the future revolutionary's click. Then Connie found Fisher.

"Mr. Fisher was a father-type person," said Hawkins. "He treated me like a human being, never made fun of me. He took time to talk about my problems in school—and I had a lot."

Connie became Fisher's property; the inner-city coach has awesome clout—he is pope and police chief—and teachers might mock Connie or ignore him, but they didn't dare damage him.

The head of the English department told Wolf, "I suppose I was so fascinated by Connie's playing that I looked the other way when he didn't come to school or missed some classes. At Boys High, it took a hell of a lot of courage for any teacher to flunk Connie Hawkins. And few did."

Summers were orgies of basketball for Connie. The New York ghetto playgrounds in summer are justly celebrated for basketball as a macho peforming art. Collegians and pros drop back to show off, work out, test the young blood, and serve the SportsWorld Gods of cool, style, and put-down. The individual is supreme: One-on-one, and the winner must do it with moves that can rouse a crowd that has seen the best. Connie perfected fabulous sleights of body, dips, turns, twists, fakes, leaps, that eventually made his name synonymous with the balletic schoolyard style.

There is a mystique about the quality of New York schoolyard basketball that implies that if dope and malnutrition and emotional depression were somehow eradicated, every National Basketball Association team would be starting two blacks from Harlem, two from Bed-Stuy, and one white from Indiana as mix. The "world's greatest player" has always just overdosed. Basketball almost saved him, but . . .

But basketball is a hard drug, too. On the coldest winter's night in any slum playground you will invariably see a boy alone, swimming in an outdoor lamp's eerie yellow pool: He is driving toward a netless basket, he fakes an imaginary defender, dribbles hard so the ball bounces into his hands as he rises toward a backboard so cold his skin would stick if he touched it, pauses . . . in mid-air . . . turns away from a grove of blocking arms . . . hangs suspended as he pumps the ball twice to his stomach before slamming it two-handed down the throat of the world. He is not practicing to gain the recognition of his peers or to impress girls or to get a college scholarship; at that moment he is on a trip, and for as long as he is on it, he is everything he wants to be. It should not be surprising that so many playground aces are junkies with dope, too.

Hawkins smoked grass and sniffed coke once or twice, but cheap wine was the main high of his day. Watching him play then I sometimes wondered if he was lazy or loafing along as a gesture of style or so incredibly efficient in movement that he made everything look easy. It did not occur to me that he might be high, which he wasn't. He was carefully pacing himself because years of inadequate diet and recent spurts of growth had left him with less stamina than he needed for an entire game at full tilt.

More than 200 colleges were actively recruiting Connie, including several fronting for pro teams who wanted to get him into their draft territories. The Boston Celtics, according to Wolf, were willing to pay Hawkins an under-the-table salary to attend Providence, so they could claim him in four years. Colleges offered him the standard car-apartment-sinecure. Colorado reportedly promised Connie a job clearing seaweed from the football stadium, which Wolf pointed out was more than a thousand miles from the nearest ocean. Connie took it, and went out to Boulder for summer remedial courses in reading and math. Connie took a brother along and his brother took a gun. All three were back in Brooklyn shortly.

Eventually, he decided to attend the University of Iowa. The Iowa recruiters were low-key, and they offered the next-best deal; among other perks, a weekly paycheck without a job and round-trip transportation for a neighborhood girl whenever the stud needed one. Later, when the deal was made public, Iowa received a year's probation. By then, Connie was long gone, in ruins.

The counselors at Boys and the admissions officers at Iowa were aware that Hawkins could never make it through college. One Boys teacher, working daily with Connie, raised his IQ score from 65 to 113 in a few months, and his reading level from seventh grade to eleventh. But there was no way to overcome all the years of malignant neglect during which he had drifted through school without learning how to study or organize information or take a test; all the years in which he began to think he was indeed a moron. Wolf speculates that a year in a prep school or junior college might have brought him up to a level at which he could have coped academically with Iowa. Had Iowa wanted to give him time to grow another inch, or fill out, or perfect a different type of play, he doubtless would have been farmed out for a year. But Iowa was in a hurry. Unlike any other major sport, basketball requires only one superstar to carry a whole team, to pack the fieldhouse, to plug a college into the national Good News Network.

"Connie's classes—which the recruiters had told him he could handle—were more overwhelming and humiliating than his worst experiences at Boys High," wrote Wolf in *Foul!* "Unfamiliar words buzzed about his ears like angry mosquitoes, and reading assignments for a month totaled more pages than he had read in his life. People were not unfriendly; they smiled and said how happy they were he had come to Iowa. But Hawkins soon found life on

173

the college campus dull, lonely, and sexually frustrating."

In a few years, colleges would become very sophisticated at this sort of thing, recruiting their athletes under special admission programs for minorities. There would be federally funded tutoring and relaxed grade standards for varsity eligibility. They would enlist the nearest black community to make the athletes feel at ease; they would institute black studies programs and scholarships for black girl cheerleaders to create an instant ghetto on campus. But in 1960, the problems of the high-priced black athlete in an otherwise white northern school were a private matter between the boy and his coach.

By the time Connie got to Iowa, however, he was probably past help. While his freshman basketball season was a sensation, his freshman academic year was a total wipe-out.

He was also carrying a time-bomb that would blow him off campus long before he would ever be flunked out.

The summer before he went west he had met Jack Molinas, a former Columbia all-American who had been thrown out of the NBA in the middle of a fine rookie season for betting on games. It has always been maintained that Molinas only bet on his own team to win, but by the time he met Hawkins he was mastermind of a nationwade gambling ring paying dozens of players to fix games. Connie, who had been 12 when Molinas was banned, thought the 28-year-old lawyer was just a basketball freak who bought him some meals, drove him to games, and offered him walking around money. Hawkins borrowed $200 from Molinas, which was returned by one of his brothers. There was never any evidence that Connie shaved points, gambled on games in which he played, or tried to recruit fixers. Apparently, Molinas was just softening up Connie for the future. Molinas was jailed in 1963, for five years. He was murdered in 1975.

When the 1961 college basketball scandals broke, Hawkins was one of many players hauled off campuses, locked up in New York hotel rooms with detectives, and brought before a grand jury. He was never prosecuted. But when he returned to Iowa a few weeks later, he was dismissed from school.

There was a cynical logic to this: While Iowa was perfectly willing to make an unethical arrangement with a potential all-America, it could hardly be expected to break rules for a freshman with failing grades and a tainted name. Financially, it was minimizing its losses. Had Hawkins not become involved in the investigation, Iowa probably would have found a way to keep him eligible; and had Hawkins been passing his courses, Iowa probably would have welcomed him back to school, as did other colleges whose players were mentioned in the same investigation. Iowa's action seems to have been critical to the National Basketball Association's later decision to blacklist Hawkins; other players who returned to college after a grand jury appearance were allowed to play in the NBA.

It took eight years, a painstaking investigation by lawyers and by Wolf, and the threat of a $6 million treble damage suit against the NBA for conspiring to keep Hawkins out of the league before he finally moved into the company of Wilt Chamberlain and Oscar Robertson, where he clearly belonged. By the time he got to the Phoenix Sons in 1969, Hawkins was 27, married, a father, an articulate and confident man. He was also a recent millionaire thanks to the league's sudden desire to settle the case out of court. And he had clearly been cheated, a Sports World victim lucky enough to find champions before his skills were gone. . . .

# JOHN MCPHEE

# A Sense of Where You Are

*In 1964 John McPhee interviewed the then Princeton College basketball player Bill Bradley, looking into Bradley's knowledgeable approach to the game, his use of other great players' proven techniques to perfect each of his shots. Bradley went on to play professionally for the New York Knickerbockers for ten years. Not just a fine ball player, Bradley later became a distinguished United States Senator from New Jersey, even urged by some to run for president.*

*McPhee's detailed description of how Bradley used to warm up before a game—his concentration, his thoroughness, his level of effort—makes clear the discipline and intelligence Bradley brought to honing his game. But McPhee knows it's something more than merely effort, pointing out that many basketball players could stay in a gym for five years and never make the series of left-handed hook shots Bradley could routinely make.*

Bradley is one of the few basketball players who have ever been appreciatively cheered by a disinterested away-from-home crowd while warming up. This curious event occurred last March, just before Princeton eliminated the Virginia Military institute, the year's Southern Conference champion, from the N.C.A.A. championships. The game was played in Philadelphia and was the last of a tripleheader. The people there were worn out because most of them were emotionally committed to either Villanova or Temple—two local teams that had just been involved in enervating battles with Providence and Connecticut, respectively, scrambling for a chance at the rest of the country. A group of Princeton boys shooting basketballs miscellaneously in preparation for still another game hardly promised to be a high point of the evening, but Bradley, whose routine in the warmup time is a gradual crescendo of activity, is more interesting to watch before a game than most players are in play. In Philadelphia that night, what he did was, for him, anything but unusual. As he does before all games, he began by shooting set shots close to the basket, gradually moving back until he was shooting long sets from twenty feet out, and nearly all of them dropped into the net with an almost mechanical rhythm of accuracy. Then he began a series of expandingly difficult jump shots, and one jumper after another went cleanly through the basket with so few exceptions that the crowd began to murmur. Then he started to perform whirling reverse moves before another cadence of almost steadily accurate jump shots, and the murmur increased. Then he began to sweep hook shots into the air. He moved in a semicircle around the court. First with his right hand, then with his left, he tried seven of these long, graceful shots—the most difficult ones in the orthodoxy of basketball—and ambidextrously made them all. The game had not even begun, but the presumably unimpressible Philadelphians were applauding like an audience at an opera.

Bradley has a few unorthodox shots, too. He dislikes flamboyance, and, unlike some of basketball's greatest stars, has apparently never made a move merely to attract attention. While some players are eccentric in their shooting, his shots, with only occasional exceptions, are straightforward and unexaggerated. Nonetheless, he does make someting of a spectacle of himself when he moves in rapidly parallel to the baseline, glides through the air with his back to the basket, looks for a teammate he can pass to, and, finding none, tosses the ball into the basket over one shoulder, like a pinch of salt. Only when the ball is actually dropping through the net does he look around to see what has happened, on the chance that something might have gone wrong, in which case he would have to go for the rebound. That shot has the essential characteristics of a wild accident, which is what many people stubbornly think they have witnessed until they see him do it for the third time in a row. All shots in basketball are supposed to have names—the set, the hook, the lay-up, the jump shot, and so on—and one weekend last July, while Bradley was in Princeton working on his senior thesis and putting in some time in the Princeton gymnasium to keep himself in form for the Olympics, I asked him what he called his over-the-shoulder shot. He said that he had never heard a name for it, but that he had seen Oscar Robertson, of the Cincinnati Royals, and Jerry West, of the Los Angeles Lakers, do it, and had worked it out for himself. He went on to say that it is a much simpler shot than it appears to be, and, to illustrate, he tossed a ball over his shoulder and into the basket while he was talking and looking me in the eye. I retrieved the ball and handed it back to him. "When you have played basketball for a while, you don't need to look at the basket when you are in close like this," he said, throwing it over his shoulder again and right through the hoop. "You develop a sense of where you are."

Bradley is not an innovator. Actually, basketball has had only a few innovators in its history—players like Hank Luisetti, of Stanford, whose introduction in 1936 of the running one-hander did as much to open up the game for scoring as the forward pass did for football; and Joe Fulks, of the old Philadelphia Warriors, whose twisting two-handed heaves, made while he was leaping like a salmon, were the beginnings of the jump shot, which seems to be basketball's ultimate weapon. Most basketball players appropriate fragments of other players' styles, and thus develop their own. This is what Bradley has done, but one of the things that set him apart from nearly everyone else is that the process has been conscious rather than osmotic. His jump shot, for example, has had two principal influences. One is Jerry West, who has one of the best jumpers in basketball. At a summer basketball camp in Missouri some years ago. West told Bradley that he always gives an extra hard bound to the last dribble before a jump shot, since this seems to catapult him to added height. Bradley has been doing that ever since. Terry Dischinger, of the Detroit Pistons, has told Bradley that he always slams his foot to the floor on the last step before a jump shot, because this stops his momentum and thus prevents drift. Drifting while aloft is the mark of a sloppy jump shot.

Bradley's graceful hook shot is a masterpiece of eclecticism. It consists of the high-lifted knee of the Los Angeles Lakers' Darrall Imhoff, the arms of Bill Russell, of the Boston Celtics, who extends his idle hand far under his shooting arm and thus magically stabilizes the shot, and the general corporeal form of Kentucky's Cotton Nash, a rookie this year with the Lakers. Bradley carries his analyses of shots further than merely identifying them with pieces of other people. "There are five parts to the hook shot," he explains to anyone who asks. As he continues, he picks up a ball and stands about eighteen feet from a basket. "Crouch," he says, crouching, and goes on to demonstrate the other moves. "Turn your head to look for the basket, step, kick, follow through with your arms." Once, as he was explaining this to me, the ball curled around the rim and failed to go in.

"What happened then?" I asked him.

"I didn't kick high enough," he said.

"Do you always know exactly why you've missed a shot?"

"Yes," he said, missing another one.

"What happened that time?"

"I was talking to you. I didn't concentrate. The secret of shooting is concentration."

His set shot is borrowed from Ed Macauley, who was a St. Louis University All-American in the late forties and was later a star member of the Boston Celtics and the St. Louis Hawks. Macauley runs the basketball camp Bradley first went to when he was fifteen. In describing the set shot, Bradley is probably quoting a Macauley lecture. "Crouch like Groucho Marx," he says. "Go off your feet a few inches. You shoot with your legs. Your arms merely guide the ball." Bradley says that he has more confidence in his set shot than in any other. However, he seldom uses it, because he seldom has to. A set shot is a long shot, usually a twenty-footer, and Bradley, with his speed and footwork, can almost always take some other kind of shot, closer to the basket. He will take set shots when they are given to him, though. Two seasons ago, Davidson lost to Princeton, using a compact zone defense that ignored the remoter areas of the court. In one brief sequence, Bradley sent up seven set shots, missing only one. The missed one happened to rebound in

Bradley's direction, and he leaped up, caught it with one hand, and scored.

Even his lay-up shot has an ancestral form: he is full of admiration for "the way Cliff Hagan pops up anywhere within six feet of the basket," and he tries to do the same. Hagan is a former Kentucky star who now plays for the St. Louis Hawks. Because opposing teams always do everything they can to stop Bradley, he gets an unusual number of foul shots. When he was in high school, he used to imitate Bob Pettit, of the St. Louis Hawks, and Bill Sharman, of the Boston Celtics, but now his free throw is more or less his own. With his left foot back about eighteen inches—"wherever it feels comfortable," he says—he shoots with a deep-bending rhythm of knees and arms, one-handed, his left hand acting as a kind of gantry for the ball until the moment of release. What is most interesting, though, is that he concentrates his attention on one of the tiny steel eyelets that are welded under the rim of the basket to hold the net to the hoop—on the center eyelet, of course—before he lets fly. One night, he scored over twenty points on free throws alone: Cornell hacked at him so heavily that he was given twenty-one free throws, and he made all twenty-one, finishing the game with a total of thirty-seven points.

When Bradley, working out alone, practices his set shots, hook shots, and jump shots, he moves systematically fom one place to another around the basket, his distance from it being appropriate to the shot, and he does not permit himself to move on until he has made at least ten shots out of thirteen from each location. He applies this standard to every kind of shot, with either hand, from any distance. Many basketball players, including reasonably good ones could spend five years in a gym and not make ten out of thirteen left-handed hook shots, but that is part of Bradley's daily routine. He talks to himself while he is shooting, usually reminding himself to concentrate but sometimes talking to himself the way every high school j.v. basketball player has done since the dim twenties—more or less imitating a radio announcer, and saying, as he gathers himself up for a shot. "It's pandemonium in Dillion Gymnasium. The clock is running out. He's up with a jumper. Swish!"

Last summer, the floor of the Princeton gym was being resurfaced, so Bradley had to put in several practice sessions at the Lawrenceville School. His first afternoon at Lawrenceville, he began by shooting fourteen-foot jump shots from the right side. He got off to a bad start, and he kept missing them. Six in a row hit the back rim of the basket and bounced out. He stopped, looking discomfited, and seemed to be making an adjustment in his mind. Then he went up for another jump shot from the same spot and hit it cleanly. Four more shots went in without a miss, and then he paused and said, "You want to know something? That basket is about an inch and a half low." Some weeks later, I went back to Lawrenceville with a steel tape, borrowed a stepladder, and measured the height of the basket. It was nine feet ten and seven-eights inches above the floor, or one and one-eight inches too low.

Being a deadly shot with either hand and knowing how to make the moves and fakes that clear away the defense are the primary skills of a basketball player, and any player who can do these things half as well as Bradley can has all the equipment he needs to make a college team. Many high-scoring basketball players, being able to make so obvious and glamorous a contribution to their team in the form of point totals, don't bother to develop the other skills of the game, and leave subordinate matters like defense and playmaking largely to their teammates. Hence, it is usually quite easy to parse a basketball team. Bringing the ball up the floor are playmaking backcourt men—selfless fellows who can usually dribble so adeptly that they can just about freeze the ball by themselves, and who can also throw passes through the eye of a needle and can always be counted on to feed the ball to a star at the right moment. A star is often a point-hungry gunner, whose first instinct when he gets the ball is to fire away, and whose playing creed might be condensed to "When in doubt, shoot." Another, with legs like automobile springs, is part of the group because of an unusual ability to go high for rebounds. Still another may not be especially brilliant on offense but has defensive equipment that could not be better if he were carrying a trident and a net.

The point-hungry gunner aside, Bradley is all these. He is a truly complete basketball player. He can play in any terrain; in the heavy infighting near the basket, he is master of all the gestures of the big men, and toward the edge of play he shows that he has all the fast-moving skills of the little men, too. With remarkable speed for six feet five, he can steal the ball and break into the clear with it on his own; as a dribbler, he can control the ball better with his left hand than most players can with their right; he can go down court in the middle of a fast break and fire passes to left and right, closing in on the basket, the timing of his passes too quick for the spectator's eye. He plays any position—up front, in the post, in the back-court. And his playmaking is a basic characteristic of his style. His high-scoring totals are the result of his high percentage of accuracy, not of an impulse to shoot every time he gets the ball.

He passes as generously and as deftly as any player in the game. When he is dribbling, he can pass accurately without first catching the ball. He can also manage almost any pass without appearing to cock his arm, or even bring his hand back. He just seems to flick his fingers and the ball is gone. Other Princeton players aren't always quite expecting Bradley's passes when they arrive, for Bradley is usually thinking a little bit ahead of everyone else on the floor. When he was a freshman, he was forever hitting his teammates on the mouth, the temple, or the back of the head with passes as accurate as they were surprising. His teammates have since sharpened their own faculties, and these accidents seldom happen now. "It's rewarding to play with him," one of them says. "If you get open, you'll get the ball." And, with all the defenders in between, it sometimes seems as if the ball has passed like a ray through several walls.

Bradley's play has just one somewhat unsound aspect, and it is the result of his mania for throwing the ball to his teammates. He can't seem to resist throwing a certain number of passes that are based on nothing but theory and hope; in fact, they are referred to by the Princeton coaching staff as Bradley's hope passes. They happen, usually, when something has gone just a bit wrong. Bradley is recovering a loose ball, say, with his back turned to the other Princeton players. Before he turned it, he happened to notice a screen, or pick-off, being set by two of his teammates, its purpose being to cause one defensive man to collide with another player and thus free an offensive man to receive a pass and score. Computations whir in Bradley's head. He hasn't time to look, but the screen, as he saw it developing, seemed to be working, so a Princeton man should now be in the clear, running toward the basket with one arm up. He whips the ball over his shoulder to the spot where the man ought to be. Sometimes a hope pass goes flying into the crowd, but most of the time they hit the receiver right in the hand, and a gasp comes from several thousand people. Bradley is sensitive about such dazzling passes, because they look flashy, and an edge comes into his voice as he defends them. "When I was halfway down the court, I saw a man out of the corner of my eye who had on the same color shirt I did," he said recently, explaining how he happened to fire a scoring pass while he was falling out of bounds. "A little later, when I threw the pass, I threw it to the spot where that man should have been if he had kept going and done his job. He was there. Two points."

Since it appears that by nature Bradley is a passer first and a scorer second, he would probably have scored less at a school where he was surrounded by other outstanding players. When he went to Princeton, many coaches mourned his loss not just to themselves but to basketball, but as things have worked out, much of his national prominence has been precipitated by his playing for Princeton, where he has had to come through with points in order to keep his team from losing. He starts slowly, as a rule. During much of the game, if he has a clear shot, fourteen feet from the basket, say, and he sees a teammate with an equally clear shot ten feet from the basket, he sends the ball to the teammate. Bradley apparently does not stop to consider that even though the other fellow is closer to the basket he may be far more likely to miss the shot. This habit exasperates his coaches until they clutch their heads in despair. But Bradley is doing what few people ever have done—he is playing basketball according to the foundation pattern of the game. Therefore, the shot goes to the closer man. Nothing on earth can make him change until Princeton starts to lose. Then he will concentrate a little more on the basket.

Something like this happened in Tokyo last October, when the United States Olympic basketball team came close to being beaten by Yugoslavia. The Yugoslavian team was resonably good—better than the Soviet team, which lost to the United States in the final—and it heated up during the second half. With two minutes to go, Yugoslavia cut the United States' lead to two points. Bradley was on the bench at the time, and Henry Iba, the Oklahoma State coach, who was coach of the Olympic team, sent him in. During much of the game, he had been threading passes to others, but at that point, he says, he felt that he had to try to do something about the score. Bang, bang, bang—he hit a running one-hander, a seventeen-foot jumper, and a lay-up on a fast break, and the United States won by eight points.

Actually, the United States basketball squad encountered no real competition at the Olympics, despite all sorts of rumbling cumulus beforehand to the effect that some of the other teams, notably Russia's, were made up of men who had been playing together for years and were now possibly good enough to defeat an American Olympic basketball team for the first time. But if the teams that the Americans faced were weaker than advertised, there were nonetheless individual performers of good calibre, and it is a further index to Bradley's completeness as a basketball player that Henry Iba, a defensive specialist as a coach, regularly assigned him to guard the stars of the other nations. "He didn't show too much tact at defense when he started, but he's a coach's basketball player, and he came along." Iba said after he had returned to Oklahoma. "And I gave him the toughest man in every game."

Yugoslavia's best man was a big forward who liked to play in the low post, under the basket. Bradley went into the middle with him, crashing shoulders under the basket, and held him to thirteen points while scoring eighteen himself. Russia's best man was Yuri Korneyev, whose specialty was driving: that is, he liked to get the ball somewhere out on the edge of the action and start for the basket with it like a fullback, blasting everything out of the way until he got close enough to ram in a point-blank shot. With six feet five inches and two hundred and forty pounds to drive, Korneyev was what Iba called "a real good driver." Bradley had lost ten pounds because of all the Olympics excitement, and Korneyev outweighed him by forty-five pounds. Korneyev kicked, pushed, shoved, bit, and scratched Bradley. "He was tough to stop," Bradley says. "After all, he was playing for his life." Korneyev got eight points.

Bradley was one of three players who had been picked unanimously for the twelve-man Olympic team. He was the youngest member of the squad and the only undergraduate. Since his trip to

Tokyo kept him away from Princeton for the first six weeks of the fall term, he had to spend part of his time reading, and the course he worked on most was Russian History 323. Perhaps because of the perspective this gave him, his attitude toward the Russian basketball team was not what he had expected it to be. With the help of three Australian players who spoke Russian, Bradley got to know several members of the Russian team fairly well, and soon he was feeling terribly sorry for them. They had a leaden attitude almost from the beginning. "All we do is play basketball," one of them told him forlornly. "After we go home, we play in the Soviet championships. Then we play in the Satellite championships. Then we play in the European championships. I would give anything for five days off." Bradley says that the Russian players also told him they were paid eighty-five dollars a month, plus housing. Given the depressed approach of the Russians, Bradley recalls, it was hard to get excited before the Russian-American final. "It was tough to get chills," he says. "I had to imagine we were about to play Yale." The Russians lost, 73–59.

Bradley calls practically all men "Mister" whose age exceeds his own by more than a couple of years. This includes N.B.A. players he happens to meet, Princeton trainers, and Mr. Willem Hendrik van Breda Kolff, his coach. Van Breda Kolff was a Princeton basketball star himself, some twenty years ago, and went on to play for

191

the New York Knickerbockers. Before returning to Princeton in 1962, he coached at Lafayette and Hofstra. His teams at the three colleges have won two hundred and fifty-one games and lost ninety-six. Naturally, it was a virtually unparalleled stroke of good fortune for van Breda Kolff to walk into his current coaching job in the very year that Bradley became eligible to play for the varsity team, but if the coach was lucky to have the player, the player was also lucky to have the coach. Van Breda Kolff, a cheerful and uncomplicated man, has a sportman's appreciation of the nuances of the game, and appears to feel that mere winning is far less important whan winning with style. He is an Abstract Expressionist of basketball. Other coaches have difficulty scouting his teams, because he does not believe in a set offense. He likes his offense free-form.

Van Breda Kolff simply tells his boys to spread out and keep the ball moving. "Just go fast, stay out of one another's way, pass, move, come off guys, look for one-on-ones, two-on-ones, two-on-twos, three-on-threes. That's about the extent," he says. That is, in fact, about the substance of basketball, which is almost never played as a five-man game anymore but is, rather, a constant search, conducted semi-independently by five players, for smaller combinations that will produce a score. One-on-one is the basic situation of the game—one man, with the ball, trying to score against one defensive player, who is trying to stop him, with nobody else involved. Van Breda

Kolff does not think that Bradley is a great one-on-one player. "A one-on-one player is a hungry player," he explains. "Bill is not hungry. At least ninety percent of the time, when he gets the ball, he is looking for a pass." Van Breda Kolff has often tried to force Bradley into being more of a one-on-one player, through gentle persuasion in practice, through restrained pleas during timeouts, and even through open clamor. During one game last year, when Princeton was losing and Bradley was still flicking passes, van Breda Kolff stood up and shouted, *"Will . . . you . . . shoot . . . that . . . ball?"* Bradley, obeying at once, drew his man into the vortex of a reverse pivot, and left him standing six feet behind as he made a soft, short jumper from about ten feet out.

If Bradley were more interested in his own statistics, he could score sixth or seventy-five points, or maybe even a hundred, in some of his games. But this would merely be personal aggrandizement, done at the expense of the relative balance of his own team and causing unnessary embarrassment to the opposition, for it would only happen against an opponent that was heavily outmatched anyway. Bradley's highest point totals are almost always made when the other team is strong and the situation demands his scoring ability. He has, in fact, all the mechanical faculties a great one-on-one player needs. As van Breda Kolff will point out, for example, Bradley has "a great reverse pivot," and this is an essential characteristic of a one-on-one specialist. A way of getting rid of a defensive man who is playing close, it is a spin of the body, vaguely similar to what a football halfback does when he spins away from a would-be tackler, and almost exactly what a lacrosse player does when he "turns his man." Say that Bradley is dribbling hard toward the basket and the defensive man is all over him. Bradley turns, in order to put his body between his opponent and the ball; he continues his dribbling but shifts the ball from one hand to the other: if his man is still crowding in on him, he keeps on turning until he has made one full revolution and is once more headed toward the basket. This is a reverse pivot. Bradley can execute one in less than a second. The odds are that when he has completed the spin the defensive player will be behind him, for it is the nature of basketball that the odds favor the man with the ball—if he knows how to play them.

Bradley doesn't need to complete the full revolution every time. If his man steps away from him in anticipation of a reverse pivot. Bradley can stop dead and make a jump shot. If the man stays close to him but not close enough to be turned, Bradley can send up a hook shot. If the man moves over so that he will be directly in Bradley's path when Bradley comes out of the turn, Bradley can scrap the reverse pivot before he begins it, merely suggesting it with his shoulders and then continuing his original dribble to the basket, making his man look like a pedestrian who has leaped to get out of the way of a speeding car.

The Metaphor of basketball is to be found in these compounding alternatives. Every time a basketball player takes a stop, an entire new geometry of action is created around him. In ten seconds, with or without the ball, a good player may see perhaps a hundred altenatives and, from them, make half a dozen choices as he goes along. A great player will see even more alternatives and will make more choices, and this multiradial way of looking at things can carry over into his life. At least, it carries over into Bradley's life. The very word "alternatives" bobs in and out of his speech with noticeable frequency. Before his Rhodes Scholarship came along and eased things, he appeared to be worrying about dozens of alternatives for next year. And he still fills his days with alternatives. He apparently always needs to have eight ways to jump, not because he is excessively prudent but because that is what makes the game interesting.

The reverse pivot, of course, is just one of numerous one-on-one moves that produce a complexity of possibilities. A rocker stop, for example, in which a player puts one foot forward and rocks his shoulders forward and backward, can yield a set shot if the defensive man steps back, a successful drive to the basket if the defensive man comes in too close, a jump shot if he tries to compromise. A simple cross-over—shifting a dribble from one hand to the other and changing direction—can force the defensive man to overcommit himself, as anyone knows who has ever watched

Oscar Robertson use it to break free and score. Van Breda Kolff says that Bradley is "a great mover," and points out that the basis of all these maneuvers is footwork. Bradley has spent hundreds of hours merely rehearsing the choreography of the game—shifting his feet in the same patterns again and again, until they have worn into his motor subconscious. "The average basketball player only likes to play basketball," van Breda Kolff says. "When he's left to himself, all he wants to do is get a two-on-two or a three-on-three going. Bradley practices techniques, making himself learn and improve instead of merely having fun."

Because of Bradley's super-serious approach to basketball, his relationship to van Breda Kolff is in some respects a reversal of the usual relationship between a player and a coach. Writing to van Breda Kolff from Tokyo in his capacity as captain-elect, Bradley advised his coach that they should prepare themselves for "the stern challenge ahead." Van Breda Kolff doesn't vibrate to that sort of tune. "Basketball is a game," he says. "It is not an ordeal. I think Bradley's happiest whenever he can deny himself pleasure." Van Breda Kolff's handling of Bradley has been, in a way, a remarkable feat of coaching. One man cannot beat five men—at least not consistently—and Princeton loses basketball games. Until this season, moreover, the other material that van Breda Kolff has had at his disposal has been for the most part below even the usual Princeton standard, so the fact that his teams have won two consecutive championships is about as much to his credit as to his star's.

Van Breda Kolff says, "I try to play it just as if he were a normal player. I don't want to overlook him, but I don't want to overlook for him, either, if you see what I'm trying to say." Bradley's teammates sometimes depend on him too much, the coach explains, or, in a kind of psychological upheaval, get self-conscious about being on the court with a superstar and, perhaps to prove their independence, bring the ball up the court five or six times without passing it to him. When this happens, van Breda Kolff calls time out. "Hey, boys," he says. "What have we got an All-American for?" He refers to Bradley's stardom only when he has to, however. In the main, he takes Bradley with a calculated grain of salt. He is interested in Bradley's relative weaknesses rather than in his storied feats, and has helped him gain poise on the court, learn patience, improve his rebounding, and be more aggressive. He refuses on principle to say that Bradley is the best basketball player he has ever coached, and he is also careful not to echo the general feeling that Bradley is the most exemplary youth since Lochinvar, but he will go out of his way to tell about the reaction of referees to Bradley. "The refs watch Bradley like a hawk, but, because he never complains, they feel terrible if they make an error against him," he says. "They just love him because he is such a gentleman. They get upset if they call a bad one on him." I asked van Breda Kolff what he thought Bradley would be doing when he was forty. "I don't know," he said. "I guess he'll be the governor of Missouri."

Many coaches, on the reasonable supposition that Bradley cannot beat their teams alone, concentrate on choking off the four other Princeton players, but Bradley is good enough to rise to such occasions, as he did when he scored forty-six against Texas, making every known shot, including an eighteen-foot running hook. Some coaches, trying a standard method of restricting a star, set up four of their players in either a box-shaped or a diamond-shaped zone defensive formation and put their fifth player on Bradley, man-to-man. Wherever Bradley goes under these circumstances, he has at least two men guarding him, the man-to-man player and the fellow whose zone he happens to be passing through. This is a dangerous defense, however, because it concedes an imbalance of forces, and also because Bradley is so experienced at being guarded by two men at once that he can generally fake them both out with a single move; also, such overguarding often provides Bradley with enough free throws to give his team the margin of victory.

Most coaches have played Princeton straight, assigning their best defensive man to Bradley and letting it go at that. This is what St. Joseph's College did in the opening round of the N.C.A.A. Tournament in 1963. St. Joseph's had a strong, well-balanced team, which had lost only four games of a twenty-five-game schedule and was heavily favored to rout Princeton. The St. Joseph's player who was to guard Bradley promised his teammates that he would hold Bradley below twenty points. Bradley made twenty points in the first half.

He made another twenty points in the first sixteen minutes of the second half. In the group battles for rebounds, he won time after time. He made nearly sixty per cent of his shots, and he made sixteen out of sixteen from the front line. The experienced St. Joseph's man could not handle him, and the whole team began to go after him in frenzied clusters. He would dribble through them, disappearing in the ruck and emerging a moment later, still dribbling, to float up toward the basket and score. If St. Joseph's forced him over toward the sideline, he would crouch, turn his head to look for the distant basket, stop, kick his leg, and follow through with his arms, sending a long, high hook shot—all five parts intact—into the net. When he went up for a jump shot, St Joseph's players would knock him off balance, but he would make the shot anyway, crash to the floor, get up, and sink the dividend foul shot, scoring three points instead of two on the play.

On defense, he guarded St. Joseph's highest-scoring player, Tom Wynne, and held him to nine points. The defense was expensive though. An aggressive defensive player has to take the risk of committing five personal fouls, after which a player is obliged by the rules to leave the game. With just under four minutes to go, and Princeton comfortably ahead by five points, Bradley committed his fifth foul and left the court. For several minutes, the game was interrupted as the crowd stood and applauded him; the game was being played in Philadelphia, where hostility toward Princeton is ordinarily great but where the people know a folk hero when they see one. After the cheering ended, the blood drained slowly out of Princeton, whose other players could not hold the lead. Princeton lost by one point. Dr. Jack Ramsay, the St. Joseph's coach, says that Bradley's effort that night was the best game of basketball he has ever seen a college boy play.

Some people, hearing all the stories of Bradley's great moments, go to see him play and are disappointed when he does not do something memorable at least once a minute. Actually, basketball is hunting game. It lasts for forty minutes, and there are ten men on the court, so the likelihood is that any one player, even a superstar, will actually have the ball in his hands for only four of those minutes, or perhaps a little more. The rest of the time, a player on offense either is standing around recovering his breath or is on the move, foxlike, looking for openings, sizing up chances, attempting to screen off a defensive man—by "coming off guys," as van Breda Kolff puts it—and thus upset the balance of power.

The depth of Bradley's game is most discernible

when he doesn't have the ball. He goes in and swims around in the vicinity of the basket, back and forth, moving for motion's sake, making plans and abandoning them, and always watching the distant movement of the ball out of the corner of his eye. He stops and studies his man, who is full of alertness because of the sudden break in the rhythm. The man is trying to watch both Bradley and the ball. Bradley watches the man's head. If it turns too much to the right, he moves quickly to the left. If it turns too much to the left, he goes to the right. If, ignoring the ball, the man focusses his full attention on Bradley. Bradley stands still and looks at the floor. A high-lobbed pass floats in, and just before it arrives Bradley jumps high, takes the ball, turns, and scores.

If Princeton has an out-of-bounds play under the basket, Bradley takes a position just inside the baseline, almost touching the teammate who is going to throw the ball into play. The defensive man crowds in to try to stop whatever Bradley is planning. Bradley whirls around the defensive man, blocking him out with one leg, and takes a bounce pass and lays up the score. This works only against naïve opposition, but when it does work it is a marvel to watch.

To receive a pass from a backcourt man, Bradley moves away from the basket and toward one side of the court. He gets the ball, gives it up, goes into the center, and hovers there awhile. Nothing happens. He goes back to the corner. He starts toward the backcourt again to receive a pass like the first one. His man, who is eager and has been through this before, moves out toward the backcourt a step ahead of Bradley. This is a defensive error. Bradley isn't going that way; he was only faking. He heads straight for the basket, takes a bounce pass, and scores. This maneuver is known in basketball as going back door. Bradley is able to go back door successfully and often, because of his practiced footwork. Many players, once their man has made himself vulnerable, rely on surprise alone to complete a back- door play, and that isn't always enough. Bradley's fake looks for all the world like the beginning of a trip to the outside; then, when he goes for the basket, he has all the freedom he needs. When he gets the ball after breaking free, other defensive players naturally leave their own men and try to stop him. In these three-on-two or two-on-one situations, the obvious move is to pass to a teammate who has moved into a position to score. Sometimes, however, no teammate has moved, and Bradley sees neither a pass nor a shot, so he veers around and goes back and picks up his own man. "I take him on into the corner for a one-on-one," he says, imagining what he might do. "I move toward the free-throw line on a dribble. If the man is overplaying me to my right, I reverse pivot and go in for a left-handed lay-up. If the man is playing even with me, but off me a few feet, I take a jump shot. If the man is playing me good defense— honest— and he's on me tight, I keep going. I give him a head-and-shoulder fake, keep going all the time, and drive to the basket, or I give him a head-and-shoulder fake and take a jump shot. Those are all the things you need—the fundamentals."

Bradley develops a relationship with his man that is something like the relationship between a yoyoist and his yoyo. "I'm on the side of the floor," he postulates, "and I want to play and not clutter it up. I cut to the baseline. My man will follow me. I'll cut up to the high-post position. He'll follow me. I'll cut to the low-post position. He'll follow me. I'll go back out to my side position. He'll follow. I'll fake to the center of the floor and go hard to the baseline, running my man into a pick set at the low-post position. I'm not running him into a pick in order to get free for a shot—I'm doing it simply to irritate him. I come up on the other side of the basket, looking to see if a teammate feels that I'm open. They can't get the ball to me at that instant. Now my man is back with me. I go out to the side. I set a screen for the guard. He sees the situation. He comes toward me. He dribbles hard past me, running his man into my back. I feel the contact. My man switches off me, leaving the pass lane open for a split second. I go hard to the basket and take a bounce pass for a shot. Two points."

Because Bradley's inclination to analyze every gesture in basketball is fairly uncommon, other players look at him as if they think him a little off when he seeks them out after a game and asks them to show him what they did in making a move that he particularly admired. They tell him that they're not sure what he is talking about, and that even if they could remember, they couldn't possibly explain, so the best offer they can make is to go back to the court, try to set up the situation again, and see what it was that provoked his appreciation. Bradley told me about this almost apologetically, explaining that he had no choice but to be analytical in order to be in the game at all. "I don't have that much natural ability," he said, and went on to tell a doleful tale about how his legs lacked spring, how he was judged among the worst of the Olympic candidates in ability to get high off the floor, and so on, until he had nearly convinced me that he was a motor moron. In actuality, Bradley does have certain natural advantages. He has been six feet five since he was fifteen years old, so he had most of his high-school years in which to develop his coordination, and it is now exceptional for a tall man. His hand span, measuring only nine and a half inches, does not give him the wraparound control that basketball players like to have, but, despite relatively unimpressive shoulders and biceps, he is unusually strong, and he can successfully mix with almost anyone in the Greco-Roman battles under the backboards.

His most remarkable natural gift, however, is his vision. During a game, Bradley's eyes are always a glaze of panoptic attention, for a basketball player needs to look at everything, focussing on nothing, until the last moment of commitment. Beyond this, it is obviously helpful to a basketball player to be able to see a little more than the next man, and the remark is frequently made about basketball superstars that they have unusual peripheral vision. People used to say that Bob Cousy, the immortal backcourt man of the Boston Celtics, could look due east and enjoy a sunset. Ed Macauley once took a long auto trip with Cousy when they were teammates, and in the course of it Counsy happened to go to sleep sitting up. Macauley swears that Cousy's eyelids, lowered as far as they would go, failed to cover his coleopteran eyes.

Bradley's eyes close normally enough, but his astounding passes to teammates have given him, too, a reputaion for being able to see out of the back of his head. To discover whether there was anything to all the claims for basketball players' peripheral vision, I asked Bradley to go with me to the office of Dr. Henry Abrams, a Princeton ophthalmologist, who had agreed to measure Bradley's total field. Bradley rested his chin in the middle of a device called a perimeter, and Dr. Abrams began asking when he could see a small white dot as it was slowly brought around from behind him, from above, from below, and from either side. To make sure that Bradley wasn't, in effect, throwing hope passes, Dr. Abrams checked each point three times before plotting it on a chart. There was a chart for each eye, and both charts had irregular circles printed on them, representing the field of vision that a typical perfect eye could be expected to have. Dr. Abrams explained as he worked that these printed circles were logical rather than experimentally established extremes, and that in his experience the circles he had plotted to represent the actual vision fields of his patients had without exception fallen inside the circles printed on the charts. When he finished plotting Bradley's circles, the one for each eye was larger than the printed model and, in fact, ran completely outside it.

With both eyes open and looking straight ahead, Bradley sees a hundred and ninety-five degrees on the horizontal and about seventy degrees straight down, or about fifteen and five degrees more, respectively, than what is officially considered perfection. Most surprising, however, is what he can see above him. Focussed horizontally, the typical perfect eye, according to the chart, can see about forty-seven degrees upward. Bradley can see seventy degrees upward. This no doubt explains why he can stare at the floor while he is waiting for lobbed passes to arrive from above. Dr. Abrams said that he doubted whether a person who tried to expand his peripheral vision through exercises could succeed, but he was fascinated to learn that when Bradley was a young boy he tried to do just that. As he walked down the main street of Crystal City, for example, he would keep his eyes focussed straight ahead and try to identify objects in the windows of stores he was passing. For all this, however, Bradley cannot see behind himself. Much of the court and, thus, a good deal of the action are often invisible to a basketball player, so he needs more than good eyesight. He needs to know how to function in the manner of a blind man as well. When, say, four players are massed in the middle of things behind Bradley, and it is inconvenient for him to look around, his hands reach back and his fingers move rapidly from shirt to shirt or hip to hip. He can read the defense as if he were reading Braille.

Bradley's optical endowments notwithstanding, Coach van Breda Kolff agrees with him that he is "not a great physical player," and goes on to say, "Others can run faster and jump higher. The difference between Bill and other basketball players is self-discipline." The two words that Bradley repeats most often when he talks about basketball are "discipline" and "concentration," and through the exercise of both he has made himself an infectious example to younger players. "Concentrate!" he keeps shouting to himself when he is practicing on his own. His capacity for self-discipline is so large that it is almost funny. For example, he was a bit shocked when the Olympic basketball staff advised the Olympic basketball players to put in one hour of practice a day during the summer, because he was already putting in two hours a day—often in ninety-five-degree temperatures, with his feet squishing in sneakers that had become so wet that he sometimes skidded and crashed to the floor. His creed, which he picked up from Ed Macauley, is "When you are not practicing, remember, someone somewhere is practicing, and when you meet him he will win."

He also believes that the conquest of pain is essential to any seriously sustained athletic endeavor. In 1963, he dressed for a game against Harvard although he had a painful foot injury. Then, during the pregame warmup, it bothered him so much that he decided to give up, and he started for the bench. He changed his mind on the way, recalling that a doctor had told him that his foot, hurt the night before at Dartmouth, was badly bruised but was not in danger of further damage. If he sat down, he says, he would have lowered his standards, for he believes that "there has never been a great athlete who did not know what pain is." So he played the game. His heavily taped foot went numb during the first ten minutes, but his other faculties seemed to sharpen in response to the handicap. His faking quickened to make up for his reduced speed, and he scored thirty-two points, missing only five shots during the entire evening.

# RED AUERBACH

## Russell or Bird?

*Bill Russell and Larry Bird in their own times presided over an unprecedented winning streak for Boston's basketball team, the Celtics. The players' strengths, however, were quite different. As a center, Bill Russell dominated the rebounders; Larry Bird was an unmatched forward who could not only shoot with great accuracy but could also block and rebound. Red Auerbach had the privilege of coaching both players and here analyzes whom he would choose as his first choice in a draft. His choice comes down not to who was the better player—for each player in his unique way was, according to Auerbach, the best that there was— but instead to which position determines more directly whether games are won or lost.*

People are always asking me: *Who's the best player you ever saw?*

I tell them that's not a fair question. There are so many factors you have to consider: the era a man played in; the caliber of his teammates; the types of systems his coaches installed, and how well those systems were tailored to his particular skills. These are all important considerations.

A John Havlicek, for instance, would have been outstanding wherever he played. But a Bob Cousy? No way. He would not have been an outstanding player if he ended up someplace like Chicago in the kind of slowed-down game played when Dick Motta was there. Cousy would have been stifled; he needed a running game.

Quite often, the team makes the player—more often, in fact, than the player making the team, though it can work both ways. There's an old line about how the strength of the wolf is in the pack, and the strength of the pack is in the wolf; there's some truth on both sides. But though it's nice to have a guy who'll get you 35 points a game, that's not enough to win. Bernard King can score 55 points and the Knicks might still lose. It's happened. It used to happen all the time with Wilt Chamberlain. That year he averaged 50.4 with the old Philadelphia Warriors, we finished 11 games ahead of them.

But all factors being considered, if I had to pick the best of all, the answer would be easy.

Bill Russell and Larry Bird.

And I'm not picking them just because they're my guys; I'm calling them the best of all time because they are the best of all time.

Okay, you say, but there's a draft tomorrow—the hypothetical all-time draft—and I've got the first pick. Whose name do I call? That would be the hardest thing in the world for me to decide. I'll tell you why—and then I'll tell you whom I'd pick.

When Russell quit in 1969 I knew in my heart that we'd never see anything like him again, and no one's ever come along to change that opinion.

I'll be the first to admit I didn't know what we were getting when we drafted Bird. But people forget that it was the same thing when we drafted Bill. I knew we were acquiring someone who'd get us the ball. That was our big need back in '56, the one missing element that could make us a great, great team.

I'd heard about Russell when he was a sophomore at San Francisco. My old college coach, Bill Reinhart, had seen him play. He came back and told me, "Red, you've got two years. Start planning now. This kid can be outstanding." Reinhart was the first to spot it.

So, yes, getting him was premeditated. It was no accident. We wanted Russell. And we went after him, working out a deal with St. Louis in which we gave them Ed Macauley, who was our all-star center, and Cliff Hagan, who was just coming out of the Army and was certain to be a top-notch forward. In return, we got their first pick, which was the number two pick in the draft that year. Rochester had the first pick overall, but we already knew that they were taking Sihugo Green of Duquesne. We took Russell.

Did I know what I was getting? Not really. A great rebounder? Sure. But I knew nothing about his character, his smarts, his heart; things like that. You never know those things until you actually have the guy. No one in the league really thought much about it at the time. They certainly didn't know what was about to happen: 11 Boston championships in the next 13 years.

Most of your centers in those days—Mikan, Pettit, Johnston—were also your predominant scorers, and here was a guy who, word had it, couldn't hit the backboard; that wasn't really true, but that was the rap against him.

After we made the deal to get him, Walter Brown, our owner at the time, went with me to watch him perform in an exhibition game the Olympic team was playing at the University of Maryland. He was terrible. Just awful! Walter and I sat there looking at each other all night. What in the world had we done?

But later that night, after the game, Russell came over to see us. "I want to apologize," he said. "I am really embarrassed. That was the worst game I ever played."

So we talked about it, then got onto other things and it was never mentioned again. At the end of the night, after Russell left, Walter turned to me and asked, "Well, what do you think?"

"I was worried for a while," I told him. "But after looking into his eyes and hearing him talk like that, I'm not worried anymore."

Russ joined us in December 1956, after leading the Olympic team to a gold medal in Melbourne. I brought him into my office and we had a little talk.

"You're probably worried about scoring," I suggested, "because everyone says you don't shoot well enough to play ball."

"Well, yes," he smiled, "I am a little concerned about that."

"Okay," I told him. "I'll make a deal with you today, right here and now. I promise that as long as you play here, whenever we talk about contracts we will never discuss statistics."

We never did. There was only one statistic that mattered to Russell, and it was the same one that mattered to me: Wins.

"Russ," I said, "we have a pretty good organization here. No cliques; everyone gets along real well. All we want you to do is something no one's ever been able to do for this team: Get us the ball. Forget everything else. Just get the ball."

He nodded and smiled again. "I can do that," he said.

A lot of great basketball minds didn't think he would make it, and if you analyzed their thinking, you could see their point. Take a guy like Walter Dukes. He was bigger than Russell, and he could shoot better. Why, then, was Russell so great while Dukes was just another player?

It was his ability to perform in the clutch. It was his brilliant mind. It was his great defensive anticipation, which led to his great ability to intimidate. And in addition to all of his innate abilities, Russell was a student of the game. Sure, he had quickness, reaction, all the tools he needed. But most of all, he was a thinker. If you faked him a certain way and would up making a basket or grabbing a rebound, he'd file it away in his mind, and you'd never fool him the same way again.

We played the Knicks in one of his early games with us and Harry Gallatin ate him up. Harry knew his way around. He was cute. So the next time we played New York I started telling Russ: "You take so-and-so and I'll have Heinsohn take Gallatin." He didn't say anything at first, but then he pulled me aside just before the game started.

"I'd like to play Gallatin," he said. "It won't happen again."

I said okay, and as I watched him walking onto the court I knew that this was a momentous occasion. He *killed* Gallatin. See, his pride had been wounded, and that made Russell a dangerous man to deal with. It's like they say in the jungle: Don't ever wound a lion, and God help anybody who got in his way.

I remember one day when I really got angry at him in practice. Russell hated practice. Everyone knew it, but none of us made a big deal about it because we knew the guy would give us 48 tough minutes every game. So I'd shut my eyes to the false hustle he was giving. Still, practice had its purpose, even for him, especially when we were working on plays. And sometimes I'd want him to put out just so he wouldn't upset the other players' timing. Those were the only times when I'd really get on him; otherwise, I'd allow him to set his own pace, figuring I didn't want him leaving all of his energy in a workout.

But one particular morning he was loafing more than usual, and pretty soon everyone else started goofing off, too. So I blew my whistle. "Okay," I said, "are we all done resting now? Good. Let's go! Let's have a twenty-minute scrimmage, real strong, and then we can all get out of here."

So they start in, but pretty soon they're loafing again. Now I blow my whistle and I'm steamed. "Out! Everybody out. Right now. Don't let me hear another ball bounce. Just get out."

They all scrammed, wondering what I was going to do next. But I wasn't going to do anything. The feeling just wasn't there that day, that's all. It happens sometimes. You have to know when to push and when to back off.

Now comes our next practice. "Listen up," I tell them. "We will not discuss what happened before. All I want is a good, hard practice today. Let's go."

Sure enough, Russell starts in loafing again. All he's giving me is more false hustle. I stop the practice.

"Damn it, Russell," I yelled. "You destroyed practice the other day, but you're not going to destroy this one. I'm going to go up into those stands, light a cigar, and I'm going to sit there two hours, three hours, four hours—whatever it takes—until I see a good 20-minute scrimmage. I don't care if you're here all day long. I'm going to see a workout, so make up your mind to that now."

I grabbed some cigars, went into the stands and blew the whistle for them to start.

They began to play, and after five minutes I started to laugh. I couldn't help it. Russell must have blocked 9,000 shots. He'd grab a rebound, throw the outlet pass, race downcourt to stuff in a shot, then beat everybody back on defense, where he wouldn't allow anyone to get within 18 feet of the basket. I watched this incredible display and thought to myself, "If I don't stop this right now, he's going to leave his next game right here in the Cambridge Y."

I decided the only way to handle it was to make a joke of it, so I blew my whistle and walked back onto the court.

"Russell," I said, "what the hell am I going to do with you? I didn't mean for you to play *that* good. Can't you give me a happy medium!"

Bill's calling card, his speciality, was the blocked shot. I began to notice that he didn't block shots the way all the other big guys blocked them. Chamberlain and all those other guys were what I called shot-swatters—seven-foot fly-swatters—who'd knock the ball out of bounds, or else belt it into the open court where anybody could retrieve it.

Russell didn't do that. With his great timing and body control, he'd hit the bottom of the ball, forcing it to pop up into the air like a rebound, which he'd then grab. Or else he'd redirect it into the hands of one of his teammates.

Either way, we ended up with possession. He turned shot-blocking into an art, and he's the only man I've ever seen who could do that on a consistent basis. No one's ever been able to duplicate his style, although Bill Walton came the closest when he was healthy.

Russell took that one great skill and revolutionized the game by terrorizing the league. As word spread and his reputation grew, he began instilling fear into the hearts of all the great shooters. He didn't react the way other centers reacted, so these shooters never knew how to react to him. Most shot-blockers, anticipating a shot, would go into the air with the shooters. Not Russell. He was so quick, so fast, that he wouldn't make his move until after the ball had left the shooter's hand. Against other centers, they'd just go behind a screen, or fake, or maybe double pump. That didn't work with Russell. He'd just stand there, watching you, waiting for you to commit yourself. The moment you released the ball, he'd be on it like a cat.

Shooters would come racing down the court, stop, and go up for a jumper—but hesitate just long enough to ask themselves, *"Where is he?"* And that split-second was all it took for one of our other guys to catch up to them. In situations like those, which we saw all the time, Russell didn't have to move an inch to break up a play. His presence alone was so unnerving that opposing players would blow their shots just worrying about what he *might* do.

I used to lead teams of NBA stars on State Department tours all over the world. One summer our tour took us to Yugoslavia. When we offered to put on clinics, as we did wherever we went, the officials there told us they weren't interested. Apparently some AAU team had been there before us and was beaten easily by the Yugoslavian national team.

We tried to explain that there was a big difference in our country between pros and amateurs, but they didn't want to hear anything about it. All they knew was that the guys they had whipped had worn USA on their jerseys. There was nothing they wanted to learn from us, they said, and they were pretty arrogant about it.

That irritated me. I wanted to set the record straight, to show the fans over there that they hadn't seen the best America could offer, because of course that's never explained to them whenever poorly-trained pickup teams of American kids get their asses handed to them by pros behind the Iron Curtain.

Yugoslavia had this redheaded center who was the leading scorer in all of Europe. So I pulled Russell aside just before the game got under way. "Look," I told him, "don't worry abut the ball tonight. Don't worry about rebounds. Let Pettit and Heinsohn worry about that stuff. All I want you to do is guard that big kid over there. If he scores one basket, I'm going to break your neck. Understand?"

We start the game and the kid gets the ball. He

fakes right, bounces once to his left, then goes up into the air—and you can see this big smile on his face. All of a sudden, Russell uncoils his arm. Blocked shot. We take the ball to the other end of the court and score.

This happened agin. And again. And again. Russell blocked about six shots in a row, and now the kid's going bananas. He comes down the court a seventh time, takes two steps backward and throws the ball like a baseball.

"Damn it, Russell," I yell, "you let him hit the backboard!"

Russ looks at me. Now he's figuring he's got to find a way to get both the kid and me off his back. So the next time the guy takes a shot, instead of blocking it again he smacked it as hard as he could and it hit the kid in the face. He began screaming, going into a tantrum like a three-year-old, and he winds up kicking the ball into the crowd.

That was it for him. Technical foul. They threw him out of the game—the hero of the country, mind you. He had seen all he wanted to see.

That's what Russell could do when he put his mind to it.

Would we have had the success we enjoyed without Bill Russell? No way. But would he have had the same success if he played for another coach? I don't know.

I do know this. When I let it be known at the start of the 1965-66 season that I was beginning my final year of coaching, he came to me, more than once, and urged me not to quit. He called my wife and urged her not to let me quit.

Then one day late in that season, when he realized my mind was made up, he came to me and said he'd like to take over as coach when I retired. His reason was that he didn't want to play for anyone else. Suppose he didn't like the new guy? Or suppose the new guy brought in a different system after all these years?

Well, my mind started moving pretty fast. Suppose the new guy didn't understand Russell? Suppose they weren't able to develop a productive chemistry? I started thinking the same way Russell was thinking.

"I don't want to play for anybody else," he told me. "If I can't play for you, I'd rather play for myself, if you'll let me have the job."

I jumped at the idea. What better way to motivate Russell, I thought to myself, than to make him accountable for the whole team's performance? Remember, the year I left the bench we won our eighth championship in a row. Every season it became more difficult to sustain the intensity. But I knew Russell's pride, and if anybody could get the most out of Russell the player, it would be Russell the coach. Now there would be two reasons he had to win! Talk about a great self-motivating situation.

At our breakup banquet that spring, after all of the other speakers had been to the mike, Russ got up and talked about replacing me. He was leading up to a point, and when he got there he turned and looked directly at me.

"People say Red was lucky to have me," he said. "And he was. But I was lucky to have him, too. Red, you and I are going to be friends until one of us dies."

My throat got tight and my eyes filled and I had to look away. Lucky to have him? You bet I was.

I'm not much for showing my emotions in public, but I did that night.

I almost did it again when they had that big weekend for me in Boston. After all of my old players, from the '50s, '60s, '70s, right down to the present club, had assembled on the Garden court, they announced my name, and I walked out into the middle of a tremendous ovation. It was very emotional, but I was in full control as I started shaking hands with each old Celtic.

Then as I started moving toward Russell he held his arms out, and I stretched my arms, and the next thing I knew he was lifting me off the floor and holding me in a bear hug. Everyone was cheering, but all I was thinking was that I didn't want to cry because I was afraid I might not be able to stop. I almost cracked, but I got through it.

You see, what Russell and I share will always be special. My wife loves the guy. I love the guy. I understand him, just like he understands me. As he once said, we have the most essential ingredient for friendship, and that's mutual respect. He made no demands of me, and I made no demands of him. As he likes to say, we "exchanged favors."

One year, the night before training camp opened, I called him to my room. "Russ," I told him, "I'm going to yell at you all day long tomorrow. I may yell at you all week long. Don't pay any attention to it, okay? You see, if I can't yell at you, then I can't yell at anybody." He said that would be okay, so for the next couple of days I really climbed all over him, and he didn't react. I figured that was because of the little agreement we'd made. It wasn't until later that he told me I'd gotten him so mad he wanted to kill me. I was such a good actor that I guess I forgot I was acting.

Other times he'd come to me and ask if he could skip a practice, or maybe travel ahead by himself and meet the team on the road. It didn't happen often, but if I thought it really meant a lot to him I'd sometimes go along with his request. And I'd always add one condition: "You owe me one."

He'd laugh and say okay. Some night, maybe a month or two later, we'd be getting ready for a tough one and I'd go over to him.

"You owe me one, right?"

"Right."

"Well, I want it tonight."

Then he'd play his heart out.

Today, when I look back in private thoughts, I enjoy reflecting on some of the things I did which helped win games. And I'm sure Bill, in his private thoughts, enjoys the same type of reflections. Many of those thoughts—his and mine—go hand

in hand. We were a lot alike: Two strong person-
alities, both having the same goals, the same phi-
losophies, both doing anything and everything we
could to achieve the triumphs that meant so much
to both of us.

I think it's safe to say there's a bond between
us that very few men will ever be privileged to
share.

I've always wished the public could know the
Russell I know, but he's a very private man who's
hard to get to know. He just wants to be left alone.

There have been things he's said and done—like
refusing to let us formally retire his number,
which we did without him; or refusing to attend
his own enshrinement in the Hall of Fame—that
I have not agreed with, and I've told him so.

Yet throughout his playing days I didn't want
to go into his personality or eccentricities unless
I felt I had to. That was Russell. That was his
thing, so to speak. Other than giving advice where
I felt it was welcome or needed, I made no attempt
to change him. Who knows? If I had tried to
change his personality it might have affected the
way he played.

I'll always remember the time I heard him
speaking off the cuff to some students at Notre
Dame. We were there for an exhibition, as I recall,
and it was during the period of great campus upheaval: Civil rights, Vietnam, protests. It seemed
students were mad at everyone and raising hell
every chance they got.

I watched Bill sit on the edge of a stage and

rap with those kids, and all the respect I had for him doubled. He was so articulate, so down-to-earth, so open and honest—and all these kids, including the long hair types, sat with their eyes wide open, fascinated by what they were hearing. I don't know of anybody else in the country who could have held that particular audience under that kind of control. Even today, if he'd go around talking to kids the way he did back then, he'd do a better job of communicating with them than just about anybody else in the nation.

That's the Bill Russell too few people ever get to know.

Will there ever be another Russell?

I don't know. I think the next Dr. J is already here; his name is Michael Jordan. And we might be seeing the next Bob Cousy in Isiah Thomas.

But another Russell? I don't know about that. Patrick Ewing's no Russell. He's a great player and a super kid, but he's a power center; Russell was a finesse center. A guy who'd have a shot at being a Russell-like center if he wasn't so offensive-minded is Ralph Sampson; he's got the quickness, the smarts and the reactions. Akeem Olajuwon? Keep your eyes on him. He might be the one.

I'll always remember what Russell said the first year of his retirement when Kareem Abdul-Jabbar, then known as Lew Alcindor, came into the league with a great flourish. Someone asked

Russell, "How would you have done against Alcindor?"

I think that bothered Bill. He was never one to use the word "I" a lot; he never had that kind of ego. But here was this kid, this great offensive machine, creating such a stir that already people were forgetting the way Russell had dominated every center he ever faced.

"The question," he told the interviewer, "is not how I would have done against Alcindor, but rather how Alcindor would have done against me."

It was a great line, and he was absolutely right to have said it.

When you think about it, maybe that's the only way to measure the *next* Bill Russell: How would he have done against the original Bill Russell? Personally, I don't think I'll live to see the man who might have beaten him.

You're always looking, always hoping, to find the next great one, and back in 1977 we started hearing rumors about this kid out at Indiana State. No one ever said he was great at that time, but the word was that he was good, very good. So I watched him on TV a couple of times, and then, during his junior season, I went to see him in person for the first time.

Like Russell, Larry Bird showed me what I wanted to see the first time I laid eyes on him. Here was a kid who could shoot and who knew how to handle the ball. He was going to be eligible for the draft that spring, 1978, even though he was a junior, because he started his collegiate career at Indiana and then sat out a year. But he made it known he intended to play his senior season. Anybody drafting him would have to wait a year. Most teams don't want to do that, but we looked at it differently. Back in 1953 I drafted *three* Kentucky players—Frank Ramsey, Cliff Hagan and Lou Tsioropoulos—a year before they graduated. Like Bird, they were all junior-eligibles.

Why? Because you'd rather have potential *great* fresh blood than potential *good* fresh blood coming into your organization. Any good player you draft probably won't make that big a difference, but a great player can make all the difference in the world. So what's one year? It goes by very quickly, and it's well worth the wait if the player you're talking about has the potential for making a major impact upon your team.

Larry, I felt, had that potential—yet I didn't even dream of the surprises which were to come. I didn't realize how quick he was. I had no knowledge of his rebounding abilities. I knew he had a court presence on offense, but I didn't realize he had one on defense, too. And I had no sense of his leadership qualities, or his ability to motivate other people as well as motivating himself.

I had no great insight into his character, or his personality, or his willingness to play in pain. I have never had an athlete in my 39 years in the league who liked to play more than Larry does and who would make every effort to play, whether he was hurt or not. He symbolizes that old line *if he can walk, he can play* better than any athlete I've ever met.

Yet he was drafted solely on the premise that he was a damned good ballplayer who could put some points on the board and move the ball around. That's all I was expecting, just as I was only expecting Russell to get us the ball.

We had a terrible season in 1977-78 (32–50) but the one thing it gave us was the sixth pick in the first round. So we waited until the first five names were called: Mychal Thompson, Phil Ford, Rick Robey, Mike Richardson and Purvis Short. Then it was my turn to speak: *Boston takes Larry Bird of Indiana State.*

The following spring, after his senior season, I opened negotiations with his agent, Bob Woolf. They lasted three months and at times were somewhat heated, though a lot of that was just newspaper talk.

I knew Larry was going to cost us some money, and I was prepared to pay a reasonable price, but the point I kept hammering home was that no forward ever *made* a franchise in our league. And historically, I was correct. The only guys who ever had the ability to turn around an entire franchise were centers: Mikan, Russell, Chamberlain, Reed, Jabbar, Walton, Malone. All of your other players, no matter how great they were, were contributors. Look at Dr. J—as great as he is, he didn't win it all until Malone joined him. No forward could do it by himself, because forwards are at the mercy of the guards; the guards control the ball.

That's why no forward ever *made* a franchise—until Larry Bird made ours. He was the first exception, and he may go down in history as the only exception.

The day he walked into our rookie camp was the day my eyes were opened: The way he shot the ball; the way he passed it around; the way he crashed the boards; the way he raced up and down the court; the way he controlled the tempo and action; the way he seemed to make *no* mistakes. As I sat there watching, all I could think of was the day Havlicek first showed up 17 years earlier. It was the only thing I could compare it to.

John had just been cut from the Cleveland Browns camp. He flew into town, someone picked him up, and the next thing I knew he was walking onto the court. Ben Carnevale, the Navy coach, was with me at the time. We started watching John, and after about three minutes I turned to him and said, "Oh my God, what have I got here?" Ben looked at me and said, "I don't know, but I've got a hunch it's going to be something good."

That's how it was with Larry, though maybe not as dramatic—because, remember, I wasn't coaching now. My first thought was simply that this kid was worth every nickel we ended up giving him, which at that time amounted to the richest rookie contract ever signed in any sport.

Larry's very stoic, very unemotional in his expressions, so the more you watch him, the more you appreciate him. He's the consummate pro: He's got a job to do, and anything that might get in the way of doing that job is simply shrugged off, disregarded. Knock him down. He gets back up. He gives as much as he gets in that department. Very seldom does he blow up; diving onto the floor, getting hit with elbows, whatever it is, the look on his face never changes. He just keeps doing the job.

You know what he reminds me of? A street guy with class. That's the only description what keeps coming to my mind: A tough kid off the streets who exudes nothing but class.

I'll tell you something else about him: He's got more mental toughness than any player I've ever seen, including Russell. And I know that Russell has tremendous respect for Bird's ability and for Bird as a person.

There are very few players I would pay to see. I would have paid to see Calvin Murphy play at Niagara. He was spectacular. I'd have paid to see Russell, just to admire the art of his defense. But I wouldn't have paid to see Chamberlain or Jabbar; they don't excite me that way. Don't misunderstand; they're great. But I'd find them monotonous. I wouldn't have paid to see Mikan; he was like a robot. But I'd pay to watch Isiah Thomas, and I'd have paid to watch Dr. J in his prime. Years ago I'd have paid to watch an Elgin Baylor or a Bob Cousy.

As a rule, however, I very rarely jump out of

my seat to applaud a player. I guess I've seen too many over the years to react that way anymore. Yet Larry has lifted me out of my seat more than any other player ever has.

It's those moves, that variety of shots, that way he has of improvising and he goes along so that you just don't know what he's going to do, what's coming next. He keeps coming up with the damndest plays I've ever seen. It's like watching Cousy in his prime—yet we're talking about a forward who rebounds like a center!

He is—and I say this unequivocally—the greatest all-around player who ever lived.

Larry's a student of the game in a different way than Russell. Russ might have thought to himself: "If a guy's standing next to me in the pivot here, and I put my hip into him this way, then he can't make the following moves . . ."

Larry doesn't break it down like that. He just sees a shot go up and tells himself: "I'm gonna get it." Yet Bird, in my opinion, would be a better coach than Russell was. Russell hated the nitty-gritty stuff. Even though he loved to think about the game, he hated all the routines.

Bird *sees* what has to be done, *feels* what has to be done, *knows* what has to be done, and he can teach. I've heard him telling things to guys. I've even asked him, on occasion, to explain certain things to players, things I thought they should know which he might not volunteer unless he was asked. He's sensitive to the fact some people might resent it.

Yet he reminds me of something I once heard about Bobby Orr. They say no teammate ever resented a dollar or a drop of ink that came Orr's way, because he was such a team player they all realized how lucky they were to have him on their side. They appreciated his greatness and his humility, and as a result they became his biggest fans.

That's how it is with the Celtics and Bird. They love the guy. Can you blame them?

From the day Larry started playing in the fall of '79, we haven't had an empty seat in Boston Garden.

People contrast that to the 13 years in which Russell played there, when the average attendance was 8,406.

I don't think the comparison's fair. For years and years we were selling basketball to an area which was predominantly interested in hockey. It took a long time to educate people, to get them to appreciate what our game was all about. And then we started to win with such regularity that our success became a problem, too. What's the point of watching the Celtics? You *know* they're going to win easily. That became a very prevalent mood. It was as if we had become too good for our own good, as ridiculous as that might seem. We were filling houses all around the league, but in Boston no one seemed to get too excited until the playoffs rolled around, and then we played to capacity crowds.

If Bird had played *with* Russell on some of those great teams we had back then, we still wouldn't have sold out. And if Russell had come along five years later, and retired five years later than he did, he'd have been performing for sellout crowds, too. It was just a matter of timing, of educating the public.

I'll say this for Larry, however: He's sold more tickets, as an individual attraction, throughout this league than any player before him. He's become the best box office draw in the history of the NBA. Of all the stars who've made up basketball's galaxy, he shines brightest.

So draft day comes tomorrow and I've got the number one pick of all time. I can have my choice of any player who ever wore an NBA uniform. I can't pick three. I can't pick two. I can pick only one.

So who do I pick: Russell or Bird? They're both *my* guys.

The only way to go about it is coldly and logically. Let's say I take Bird. The next guy takes Russell, and after him it's Walton, Jabbar, Malone and Chamberlain. In that first round, all the top centers go, and then they start in with the greatest forwards and guards. Meanwhile, I'm left with no center, which means I've got a big problem, assuming I can't win in a league like that with Bird as my center.

See, when I build a ballclub—again, realizing Bird's an exception—my number one priority is my center. My second priority is my guard, the one who's going to be handling the ball most of the time, like a Cousy or an Isiah Thomas. Those are the guys you're going to win or lose with. Then come your forwards.

So, let's say I have Russell as my center: Since everyone else is taking centers, there are still some great forwards around when I get my second pick, though none are quite the same as Bird.

Now let's say I've got Bird as my forward, and I team him with an average center, say a Rich Kelley or a James Edwards.

Would I be better off with the first combination? Or the second? That's what you've got to ask yourself: How am I going to round out my team?

In other words, If I can pair a Russell with a Havlicek, am I going to be better off than I would be with a Bird and some other center?

The answer's got to be yes.

So when they call my name I've got to say: *Boston takes Bill Russell.*

And then I've got to start working on a trade.

# TOM CALLAHAN

## An Ominous Giant's Farewell

*Kareem Abdul-Jabbar of the Los Angeles Lakers, master of the sky hook, moves to the end of his notable career. At the age of forty-one, he has seen many of his contemporaries come and go, and has outlasted them all. He ends his career with two records that will probably be hard to break—for playing in the most games and for scoring the most points (38,028) in history. Like all athletes, he must prepare for the end of an active-playing career, but Abdul-Jabbar has staved off the inevitable for twenty-four years, far longer than most.*

If he was forbidding to start with and inaccessible for so long, consider that Kareem Abdul-Jabbar once looked for what he calls "positive role models" and found them in inanimate objects. "The Empire State Building," he says. "The redwoods." They represent an 86-in. man and his 24-year journey from New York City to California, nearly done. History's greatest basketball player is in his last season.

"At first," he says, "basketball was something I did when the lights were on in the playground just because I liked it." He was Lew Alcindor then, a bookish Harlem Catholic constructed of high-tension wires connected at right angles. He developed a hopping hook shot, calling to mind a praying mantis assembling a foldout lawn chair, out of early necessity; all his straightforward attempts were being blocked. He made a style of coming at things from a different angle.

"I saw a movie, *Go Man Go,* about the Harlem Globetrotters," he recalls. "In one scene, Marques Haynes dribbles by Abe Saperstein in a corridor. After that, I worked at handling the ball. I didn't want to be just a good big man. I wanted to be a good little man too." For Power Memorial, a high school that no longer exists, he was everything and led the team to 71 straight victories.

At UCLA, the rules were changed expressly to thwart him. Dunking, jamming the ball into the basket from above, was temporarily outlawed by the National Collegiate Athletic Association. Still, with a sullen grace and dispassionate touch, he showed UCLA to 88 wins in 90 games and three national titles. He was the NBA's first draft choice of 1969.

"Professional demands are different; they take most of the fun out of it," says Abdul-Jabbar, who embraced Islam during his second season with the Milwaukee Bucks. His new name meant "generous and powerful servant of Allah." He jilted a girlfriend and wed a woman selected by his mentor, Hamaas Abdul Khaalis. (The marriage ended after nine years and three children.) In 1973 seven members of Khaalis' family were murdered by Black Muslims in a Washington house bought by Kareem. Four years later, Khaalis participated in a siege of Government offices. He is now in a federal penitentiary.

Kareem's association with Khaalis was brief, but a vague connection to mystery and darkness lingered. Unlike Wilt Chamberlain, who slouched in layup drills and favored finger rolls over slam dunks, Kareem lacked the good taste to be chagrined by his size, to shrink himself down to tradition, to hide the shame of his incongruous talents. He was as tall as Chamberlain and yet as agile as Bill Russell. "His sky hook," says Russell, who seldom rhapsodizes, "is the most beautiful thing in sports."

Kareem was not the only ominous giant in the game. On dreary airport mornings, when soldiers and civilians customarily brush by one another, the common exchanges foul everyone's mood:

"Are you fellows basketball players?"

"No, we clean giraffes' ears."

But Kareem's scowl became the definitive one. "My inability to enjoy my successes, or at least to show my enjoyment," he says, "made it hard for people to enjoy me." But he went on. He transferred to the Los Angeles Lakers in 1975 and kept going on. And on. "Just thinking of it now is strange," he says.

Here's one way to think of it: 20 years ago, Kareem and 208 other men were playing in the

NBA. By the end of the '70s, 18 of them remained. In 1983, two. When Elvin Hayes—Kareem's particular college rival—retired from the Houston Rockets in 1984, one. Since then, just Kareem. He has amassed the most games (1,525) and points (38,028) in history, but the telling indicator is that only three scorers in the league today have been even half as prolific. Recalling players past, he says, "They've come and gone by generations. I'm still here."

Riding the great Laker wave of back-to-back NBA titles in 1987 and 1988, his fifth and sixth all told, Kareem returned this season for one last $3 million campaign at 41. But from November to January, he looked so soft and spent, the Los Angeles papers pleaded with him to stop. It seemed he was going around again just for the money (a stream of failed investments has him at public loggerheads with his agent) or maybe for the curtain calls at all the final stops (testimonials have included a motorcycle in Milwaukee and a chunk of Boston's parquet floor).

At his low point, annoyed teammates actually waved him out of the pivot. "I wasn't just window dressing," he says, "but I was headed that way. Your mind is what makes everything else work. Mine was on other years. but I think I've turned it up a notch in the past few games."

He has. The Lakers are not as overpowering as they were, but the Western division is probably still theirs, and the East continues to fear them. Trying to stay in the game, Kareem can't yet block out every thought of passage. His favorite year was 1985, "when we finally beat the Celtics." The special coach was UCLA's John Wooden, who "never let his goals separate him from his ideals." The ultimate teammates were Oscar Robertson and Magic Johnson. "Playing with Oscar in Milwaukee was a privilege. No nonsense, no frills. And being with Magic has been wonderful. His flair and joy."

The singular event, though, may have been the fire in 1983 that burned his home, his rugs, his art, his jazz records and just about every other material thing he owned. "The public sympathized with me, reached out to me," he says, "and even tried to replenish my record collection. I realized how self-absorbed I'd been and started to look at the fans differently. They started to see me too." Because other centers were elected, this week's All-Star game almost went on without him. But when Johnson was injured, Commissioner David Stern ruled that a center could replace a guard, and Kareem was called. This time, the rules were changed to include him.

# GOLF

GOLF

# PETER DOBEREINER

## How It All Began and Two Unforgettable Lies

*Many medieval games existed involving whacking a ball around the countryside, but who was the one responsible for thinking of putting a tiny ball into a hole in the ground? Looking into the obscure origins of golf, Peter Dobereiner, with a light touch, gives arguments in favor of both the Dutch and Scotch origins, and settles the issue for himself. He also reports on two other confounding rounds of golf, one played from a boat to the green, and the other from within the clubhouse.*

It would be pitching it a bit strong to say I lie awake at night pondering the origins of golf. I have better things to ponder during bouts of insomnia, but the subject is intriguing enough.

Scholars have probed long and deep to discover how and where golf began. No one with any feeling for the game's past can examine the historical evidence without wondering where the credit for inventing golf rightly belongs.

There have been two main schools of thought on the subject. Some (mainly Scottish) historians maintain stoutly that golf was invented by the

Scots. Other (mainly Dutch) historians claim with equal vigor that golf was invented in the Low Countries. The evidence is not conclusive either way.

It is quite certain, as we know from local authority records and paintings, that a golflike game was played in Holland long before the first official record of golf in Scotland.

The Dutch game of *spel metten colve* ("game played with a club") was well established in the thirteenth century, and over the years it developed into separate forms and the name evolved through *colf* to *kolf.* One version was miniaturized and played in a courtyard, or on ice, but mainstream *kolf* was a cross-country game, played in a series of separate "holes" with implements remarkably similar to early golf clubs and with wooden balls of about two inches in diameter. The ball was even teed up on a small cone of sand exactly as we venerable codgers did in our youth.

All that evidence was purely circumstantial, or totally irrelevant, according to the Scottish school. After all, club and ball cross-country games of one kind or another had been played since Roman times. The point was that all the early Flemish paintings depicting *kolf* showed the participants playing to targets such as church doors, and golf's greatest distinction was that it involved a secondary game, the totally original concept of putting-out into a hole in the ground.

The argument thus revolved around the question: "What is golf?" If it is accepted that the holing-out process makes golf unique, setting it apart from the Continental vesions, then it is possible that a Scot invented this all-important refinement. There is not a shred of evidence to this effect, but at least it leaves the question open.

Mr. S.J.H. Van Hengel, who is the foremost authority on the origins of *kolf,* has made some important discoveries. He managed to date an early beech-wood ball, which was discovered driven deep into the earth under the pile of a dockside building, by turning up the records of the building.

The excavations for the new Amsterdam underground railway system turned up remnants of clubheads that are similar to early golf clubs.

But the most significant discovery, in the context of the golf argument, was that *kolf* was eventually formalized to the extent of playing to a pole. Doors and the like had proved to be too easy as targets so the pole was introduced. These poles in their turn went through a process of evolution, becoming beautifully carved and ornamented artifacts. Indeed, they were so attractive that people started to steal them.

Now, what happens if a thief in the night walks off with a pole that has been stuck into the ground? Exactly, my dear Watson—a neat round hole is left on the exact spot where *kolf* players are accustomed to competing in each phase of their cross-country club and ball game.

What would you do in those circumstances?

"My goodness, Hans, the pole is not there. How shall we finish?"

"There's nothing for it, Jan, old boy, but for us to knock our rollers into the hole."

Thus, surely, was born the putt. And with it, golf. The evidence is presumptive but overwhelming. Here we have the missing link in the chain. It explains why later paintings of the Flemish School show *kolf* being played to a hole. (The idea that golf was re-exported from Scotland was never very convincing).

Once we take the plunge and discard the Scottish theory—and it is an emotional wrench to abandon those fanciful ideas of shepherds putting acorns into rabbit holes on the linksland of Fife— then everything else falls into place.

Quite apart from Scottish military expeditions to the Continent, there was a flourishing trade link between Edinburgh and St. Andrews and the Low Countries. It would be natural for the crews to pick up the game and bring it back to their homeland.

We already know that wooden balls were exported from Holland to Scotland, and that the Dutch switched to the *sajet ball* (uncombed wood stuffed into a leather cover) before the Scots began making their featheries.

St. Andrews has had tremendous mileage out of calling itself the home of golf, but I'd suspect strongly that the noble city is an imposter. If that is right, the real home of golf is more likely to have been the village where a challenge match was played in the year 1296 and repeated annually for the next 430 years. That was the game that evolved into golf.

Move over, St. Andrews—you are usurping the historic birthright of the village of Loenen on the Vecht.

*Come hell or high water—and plenty of both*

Chivalry forbids identifying the lady in question but the prize for the biggest bundle in a serious competition probably goes to a competitor in the qualifying round of a women's tournament at the Shawnee club. As it happened the number of entrants was exactly the same as the number of qualifying places but it was decided to hold the qualifying round anyway since prizes had been put up for it. That decision was to provide a bleak footnote in the annals of golf.

Our anonymous heroine was probably not in line for one of the special prizes when she came to a short hole with a stream running in front of the green. And she was certainly out of the running for a silver spoon to commemorate finishing as top qualifier a few minutes later when she plopped her tee shot into the water.

Do not tell me that she could have dropped another ball short of the water and pitched into the hole to save her par. This was a player brought up in the stern tradition of playing the ball as it lies, no matter what. Come hell or high water she would get a club to the ball without recourse to effete legal concessions. She and her husband climbed into a boat and rowed out to the floating ball. She stood in the prow, her club raised like a harpoon, and called navigational instructions to her spouse. 'Port your helm.' 'Stop engines,' and 'Slow astern.' When the craft was manoeuvred into position she lashed at the ball, sending up a waterspout which drenched the two of them.

Sad to relate, her efforts were shabbily rewarded. As the frantic pursuit continued she gritted her teeth and became, if truth were known, slightly obsessive. She would get that ball out of the water if she died in the attempt. Most of us lesser mortals would surely have cut our losses after about 20 or 30 attempts but here was the true frontier spirit in action.

She had to complete the course in order to qualify—and she was going to complete the course her way, come what may. Pedants may argue that technically the ball was out of bounds after the first hundred strokes, because by now the boat had progressed a mile and a quarter downstream, and then, in triumphant vindication fo the exhortation that if at first you don't succeed then you should try, try and try again, she cracked the problem of how to hit a golf ball from water. She cracked it all too well, for her mighty swipe sent the ball deep into a wood.

The mariners made landfall and continued the chase on foot. As pedestrians they got on much better and she eventually holed out on her 166th

stroke. At something in excess of 3500 yards it
had been quite a par three.

*Is the barman a loose impediment?*

There must be something about the air surrounding the 18th green at Moortown golf club,
near Leeds. Down the years this area has earned
a reputation as golf's Bermuda Triangle, the
scene of numerous events which defy logical explanation. In the 1980 European Tournament
Players' Championship, for instance, Severiano
Ballesteros had a bare 120 yards to the flag for
his approach shot. His ball lay sweetly on the
close-cropped fairway turf and a good shot would
give him the title.

By this stage of his career Ballesteros was no
longer an excitable youth with adrenalin squirting
from every pore at the prospect of winning a tournament. He was a battle-hardened champion and
he took his time, checking the yardage and as-
sessing the contours and condition of his target
landing area. He selected his nine-iron and played
a languid, three-quarters shot. The ball started
off dead on line as it soared into the calm air of
a summer's evening. It was still rising as it flew
over the flagstick. On and on it flew, over the
green, over the back fringe, over the horseshoe
of grandstands behind the green. It pitched
among the startled golfers who were improving
the shining hour by honing their strokes on the
practice putting green. Don't ask me how or why

this freak shot happened. Above all, do not ask Ballesteros for he does not take kindly to intrusion into his private grief.

You might try asking the amateur, Nigel Denham, for he too was a victim of the Moortown Phenomenon and he might have a theory. In the 1974 English Amateur Strokeplay Championship he too was astonished to see his approach shot fly the green. The ball pitched on a pathway in front of the clubhouse, bounced up the steps through the open door, hit a wall and rebounded into the bar. Moments later the perplexed Demham followed, having first been ordered to remove his golf shoes in accordance with the rules of the club. He found his ball sitting on the carpet and surrounded by members in whom alcoholic refreshment had released unsuspected talents for ribald remarks.

Denham consulted the local rules and confirmed that the clubhouse was not out of bounds. It followed that his ball lay within an obstruction from which no relief was available. He could move a chair or a table but, having done so, there was no interference with his stance or the intended area of his swing. Therefore, he reasoned, he must play the ball as it lay. He had 20 yards to the green and, to facilitate the shot, he opened the window. He played a crisp shot through the open window and the ball finished 12 feet from the hole, to a resounding ovation from the drinkers.

In the fullness of time the details of this daring stroke were conveyed to the Rules of Golf Committee at St Andrews for adjudication. The committee ruled that Denham should have been penalized two strokes for opening the window. Chairs, tables, beer mats and sundry impediments could be cleared aside with impunity as movable obstrucions but the window, as an integral part of the immovable obstruction of a clubhouse, should not have been moved.

Meanwhile the committee of Moortown pondered the incident and declared the clubhouse out of bounds.

# PAUL GALLICO

## Bob Jones

*The tenor of the brilliant, nine-year career of the amateur Bob Jones contrasts sharply with the win-at-all-costs careers of the professional athletes of today. Relaxed and confident, in 1930 Jones played—and won—his way through golf's grand slam—the British Amateur, the British Open, the U.S. National Open, and the U.S. Amateur. In his affectionate tribute to this sportsman and gentleman, Paul Gallico explains why Jones inspired the adulation that he did. As he observes, "if we couldn't all be Dempseys, Tildens, Weismullers, or Red Granges, we could—at least occasionally —vicariously experience the glory that was Jones." Most impressively, Jones's accomplishment— as an amateur—is one sports record that may never be broken.*

There is a picture that remains embedded in the recesses of memory, of a locker room of a country club in Minneapolis, late on a steamy, hundred-degree, humid afternoon of July 1930 and a gang, some with towels about their middles, sitting around relaxing after the day's play.

The occasion was rather a serious one. The club

was Interlachen, the play had been for the U. S. National Open championship, and it had been won by Bobby Jones who, previously that year, had captured the British Amateur and the British Open.

Somebody asked the chunky little man nursing the Georgia Corn-and-branch, "What are you going to do when you retire, Bob?"

There was a moist and mischievous gleam in the champion's eye from the soothing effects of his first drink during the four grueling days of the tournament and, grinning, he turned to another who was likewise celebrating with sour mash and said, "You'd better tell them, O.B.—you know."

O. B. Keeler, golf writer for the Atlanta *Journal*, lifelong, intimate friend and Boswell to Jones, fastened his towel securely around his loins and arising, sonorously declaimed from memory the lines of Helaire Belloc:

If I ever become a rich man,
Or if ever I grow to be old,
I will build a house with a deep thatch
To shelter me from the cold,
I will hold my house in the high woods
Within a walk of the sea,
And the men that were boys when I was a boy
Shall sit and drink with me.

And when he had thus recited, the new champion got up and joined him; the two men put their arms about one another's shoulders and chorused

251

the last two lines in unison, swept an exaggerated bow, hoisted their glasses once more, and serious drinking was resumed.

Later on, when the locker room had almost emptied, Jones, his father "the Colonel," O. B. Keeler, the late Grantland Rice and a few others, lingered on for some quartet singing, heads together in deep harmony and from behind the rows of steel lockers one heard the strains of:

> Honey, honey bless yo' h'aht,
> Mah honey that Ah loves so well,

missing out on none of the lovely, barber shop swipes.

In this vignette is much that was best, memorable, and likable about Robert Tyre Jones, Jr., who, on that particular day, was three legs up on his incredible journey to his Grand Slam effort of winning the British Open, the British Amateur, the U. S. Open, and the U. S. Amateur all in one year. He was the finest golfer and competitor ever produced in the United States, or anywhere else, the King himself of the Golden People.

We have seen two of our heroes of yesteryear, Ruth and Cobb, calling their shots at some portion of a single ball game and then delivering the goods. Jones called his on the Grand Slam, except that only two people knew it—his father and Keeler. Yet, Jones started the year 1930 with both the hope and expectation of winning the four major championships. His modesty shines through his reason for not making his intentions public: "I felt reluctant to admit that I considered myself capable of such an accomplishment."

And if by now you are not fed to the teeth with superlatives, stay with me, I beg of you, for this closing session of the Old Codgers' or Beard-Mumblers' Club. I would like to tell you a little something about the man who, of all those I met and knew during my fourteen years as a sportswriter, spanning 1922 through 1936, impressed me as being the best sportsman, the greatest gentleman, and the champion of champions.

When I knew him and tagged at his heels as a reporter, he was a stockily built young fellow of medium height, with sandy-brown hair and a pleasant, open face. Again, he stripped not like an athlete, but an ordinary man in good trim with no visible musculature. He had a warm, all-embracing grin and a fine, derisory expression about his eyes and mouth when telling one against himself. He had the gift of laughter and self-ridicule. He enjoyed a drink, a funny story, and companionship, and had an enviable and fluent repertoire with which to correct the line of a ball in flight.

He was that rare person, a genuine amateur, in a time when the whole concept of amateurism in the United States was being shattered. He loved golf for the fun of it, the fellowship of the foursome, the jokes, the lies at handicapping time, the scrapping and struggling to win a dollar Nassau. And there was more truth than childish ignorance to the anecdote that when he was a boy and going around the Eastlake course with his father, he asked, "Dad, what do people do who don't play golf on Sunday?"

A part of Jones was that warm and amusing relationship he had with his parent. Bob preferred to play with the old gentleman more than with anyone else because, as he said, "Dad used to get so mad." "The Colonel," of course, was taking perpetual golf lessons from his famous son. Jones, Sr. always appeared in the galleries of Jones, Jr.

I remember that final day at the Merion Country Club at Ardmore, Pennsylvania where Jones completed the Slam by winning the U.S. Amateur championship. A group of us, Colonel Jones, O. B. Keeler, Chick Ridley, and a mess of writers, were standing on a hillside with field glasses, like generals in an old print, watching Jones and his opponent Gene Homans coming up to the green of the long fourth, the afternoon of the 36-hole finals.

The distant, tiny figure of Jones stepped up to the ball and seemed merely to wave his arms. It climbed into the sky and sailed to the pin.

"My word, Colonel," said Grantland Rice, "your boy almost strained himself to death hitting that one!"

"I wasn't looking at him hitting it," said father Jones, "I was looking at that sign that boy is carrying. It says, 'JONES NINE UP.' Man, that's the finest-looking sign I ever saw."

The game, for the duffer who competes in no

more than an occasional club handicap, is probably the least strenuous physically, and visually the least dramatic sport of any, and is recommended by the medical profession to old gaffers with too much suet collecting around their middles. But to my generation Jones was the be-all and end-all of this royal and ancient pastime, the Grand Panjandrum, the mighty wizard, warlock, shaman, high priest, the Great God Golf himself. Thousands of people followed him when he played in the hope as well as quite possibly belief, that if they only watched him play or were near him, some of his magic would rub off onto them.

Like every other sport, golf enjoyed an explosive boom in the 1920s. Five years before that date it was estimated that there were no more than a quarter of a million addicts in the country, half a million by 1920, and ten years later at least five million trying to control that pesky little white ball.

The explanation for this was: more leisure time, more money, more golf courses, and—Jones.

The popularity and publicity attained by this modest young Southerner, born in Atlanta, Georgia on St. Patrick's Day 1902, set an entire nation golf-crazy. Membership in a country club became practically obligatory for status. The ritual of the Sunday morning foursome was almost more rigid than church attendance. And as the final accolade of arrival, the low handicap golfer could get himself a cushy job as a customer's man with any brokerage house or Wall Street concern, with duties no more onerous than playing a round or two with a visiting moneybag and murmuring, "Oh, good shot, sir!" when same connected with a ball which landed anywhere within bounds.

These elements and the worship of Jones tied in with the fact that golf was a game that everyone of every age could play. It had been blessed by the doctors and was healthful. One did not have to be endowed with muscles or more than ordinary coordination. In the playing of it one was not hit, stabbed, bruised, or knocked down and, best of all, the ball was not thrown. It remained immobile, giving one a chance to get set to take a swipe at it. Everywhere municipalities were constructing public links, and anyone who could afford the price of a set of mallets could join in the fun.

True, there were some complications in that the golf swing was not a natural one and the ball showed irritating tendencies to fly off at tangents and come to rest in unwholesome parts of the landscape. But there were professionals galore to initiate beginners into the hang of the thing, and after a few lessons away they would go, happily hacking and blasting.

And Jones, the amateur, was our boy—the shining star in the sky that beckoned us on. If we couldn't all be Dempseys, Tildens, Weissmullers, or Red Grangers, we could—at least occasionally—vicariously experience the glory that was Jones when, by sheer accident, we managed to put together three good shots in a row and rack up a bird on a par 4 hole.

We were Jones and Jones was us, because all through his career he was the only one who really behaved like the ordinary, everyday golfer who attended to his job and played at weekends. His business then was to grow up and acquire an education. During some of his greatest tournament years he was at Georgia Tech and later Harvard Law School, and in 1928 was admitted to the Bar. He could do all this and still go up to an Open championship and wipe the eyes of professionals of the caliber of Walter Hagen, Gene Sarazen, Tommy Armour, Bob Cruickshank, the Smiths, Horton and MacDonald, Leo Diegel, Johnny Farrell, and others of that class.

This filled us with all of the naughty boy's glee experienced when teacher falls on his face in front of the class, and everybody felt a share in these triumphs.

The tremendous satisfaction it afforded us, our gratitude and the affection we felt for him exploded upon his return from abroad, after he had won the British Amateur and the British Open consecutively and reached the halfway mark on his journey to the Grand Slam. We did not even know at the time that he was after it, but no American ever before had won the two big British titles in the same year and so we gave him "the treatment"; the ticker-tape ride up Broadway just as we had to Ederle, Lindbergh, and others.

Aboard the city tug *Macom,* Grover Whalen

snatched Jones off his liner at Quarantine, ferried him to The Battery, plunked him into a cavalcade of cars, and drove him up Broadway through the blizzard of torn-up paper to be received by Mayor Walker. Today, I doubt whether a similar feat by an American on the golf course, that is to say the winning of the two British championships, would manage to break out of the sports pages up onto page one, much less instigate a traffic-stopping delirium. But that's what we were like then and what Jones meant to us.

Bob Jones was a born golfer. Everything about the game suited his body, his character, and his competitive spirit. Chromosomes must have been collecting in ancestors down through the ages to produce this curious young man who, at the age of seven, when other kids were running about playing baseball, was swinging a lone golf club for hours in imitation of a Scottish professional by the name of Stuart Maiden, whom he watched giving lessons at the Eastlake club in Atlanta. This same boy at the age of twelve posted a card on the club bulletin board, "Out in 36, back in 34," tying the amateur record for the course.

Maiden took him in hand, taught and developed him, but his swing, timing, and pivot were gifts from the gods, the most perfect combined action the game has ever known. Where every other man and woman has had to struggle against the illogicality of a right-handed person having to hit the ball a backhanded stroke with the *left hand,* with Jones it was wholly natural and comfortable from the very beginning. He whistled that club-head through the ball and dropped the missile on target two hundred yards away.

But the gods, though lavish, first had to have their little joke. Thus, in addition, they bestowed upon him the ambition of a perfectionist and the temper of a mandrill. He passed through seven hellish teenage years losing tournament after tournament from sheer petulance, throwing clubs and even once quitting under fire, until in the end he beat those fun-loving but always jealous Olympians at their own game by developing an enchanting sense of humor and learning to master himself.

From that time on, which was the year 1922, when he tied for second after Gene Sarazen in the Open at Skokie, he was never out of the spotlight, never without some major title through 1930. After his Grand Slam, which he felt he could never hope to duplicate, he retired quietly into the wings and brought our fabulous era to a close.

Jones was probably the only championship competitor who ever came near to being loved out of winning many of the titles which studded his brilliant career.

Even his opponents universally liked and admired him, and the reason for this lay in the nature of the game itself, which inspires all those who indulge in it with affection. Jones played so beautifully, he was such a joy to watch in action—the quiet elegance and smooth rhythm of his stroke, the arc and pattern of the flight of his ball, that he reached the hearts of even the sourest or most misanthropic old pros. And, too, as a sportsman and strict interpreter of the rules, he was a credit to their game. He called strokes upon himself which cost him important tournaments, when the ball had moved no more than the width of an eyelash while addressing it, and no one but himself had seen it.

But to return to this love business, Jones had millions of worshipers—amateur duffers whose flag he was carrying into every tournament and who were rooting for him to win.

And then there were his personal friends from Atlanta of which there were so many, and friends of his father and family, and friends of friends who doted on him and turned up at his tournaments to follow him in the gallery through every hole, exuding worry, pride, and affection. The looks they cast upon him were moist, benign, and misty with adoration, their voices bated and caressing, their attitudes maddeningly adulating to a man who was trying to keep sharp his competitive edge.

They put upon him such a burden of love that he fairly staggered under it and turned sick with nerves and the pressure of trying to win, not for himself but for them, and not to let down the side. This over and above the yahoos he did not even know, who came galumphing after him between tee and green to shout, "I've got a big bet on you,

Bobby boy!"—or more likely, "Bobby lad." And how Jones hated to be called "Bobby" and "lad." He was "Bob" to his intimates.

Anyone who has played any kind of a game knows that there is nothing that so stimulates the winning spirit as a little bit of underdogism or hatred, to get a competitor's back up to the point where he produces that extra championship something to turn the trick. Consider yourself, now, in Jones' plight, suffocating in treacly waves of affection and well-wishing, carrying the load of everyone's goodwill and prayers and back-patting and this in a game which, while not physically grueling, is in other ways the most nerve-racking and finicky in the world.

In medal play Jones could not even work up a grudge against an opponent. His sole enemies were himself and the landscape; friendly, smiling nature, lush grass, beautiful, spreading trees, silvery babbling brooks. Even the rude, irresponsible gallery was a paradox, for while its bad manners, insensitivity, and monstrous lack of consideration were a constant and harrying handicap, it was nonetheless composed of adoring people who were just like overgrown, uncontrollable, lolloping, and slobbering puppy dogs.

This was one of the problems that Jones had to overcome and did, along with the other hazards of the game.

Jones' winning of the four major championships of Great Britain and America, the Grand Slam, has probably had more words written about it than any other sporting event, for the odds against such a feat were astronomical.

And one of the most interesting features of these odds was that they were not entirely restricted to golf and his chances of surviving four of the most difficult and testing competitions in the world. For the operative word here is "surviving." Who would have dreamed that twice between July and September of the year of the Grand Slam, that is to say between his winning the U. S. Open and competing in the U. S. Amateur, Jones would escape death by a fraction of a second and the proverbial eyelash.

A more superstitious era would have sworn that the gods were angry at the temerity of this man in challenging them by setting out to accomplish this feat. During a round of golf at Eastlake that summer, they fired two lightning bolts at him and each time scored near-misses. The first one hit where the Jones foursome ought to have been had they continued on, instead of hesitating about what to do under the circumstances of the sudden thunderstorm.

Then as Jones passed by the clubhouse on his way to the locker room, "they" had one more shot and bull's-eyed the clubhouse chimney. Jones' umbrella was smashed, his shirt ripped down to his waist, and there was a six-inch scratch on his shoulder, but he was otherwise unharmed. After the storm he found the spot where he had been littered with masses of brick and mortar, any one of which would have killed him had it struck him on the head.

Next, the Jealous Ones tried a different method. They sent a runaway automobile after him as he was walking toward the Atlanta Athletic Club, where he had a luncheon engagement. Occupied with his thoughts, he did not hear the juggernaut approaching until a voice behind him called, "Look out, mister!"

Jones turned, saw, and reacted with a jump which he himself said would have done Jesse Owens credit. The car passed exactly over the spot from which he had leaped, and crashed into the wall of the clubhouse. But for the lone pedestrian's warning, he would have been crushed to death. After that the gods gave up and he had only to contend with the amateur golfers of the United States and Canada.

Jones alone would be capable of revealing the nerve strain he endured through those four tournaments; tensions ever increasing and multiplying, to the last test—the American Amateur at Merion—in which he took his final thirty-six-hole match from his opponent, Gene Homans, by the overwhelming score of 8 and 7. He does so, in fact, in his splendid book, *Golf Is My Game,* published in 1960, and it is not at all certain that a severe illness suffered in later life was not attributable as the price paid for these strains.

There have been those inclined to laugh at us in that era for the purple prose we often injected into our accounts of Jones' accomplishments.

After all, what was there to this game of walking leisurely through manicured country on a sunny, summer's afternoon, pausing occasionally to strike at a ball that wasn't even moving compared to the eye needed to knock a baseball pitch out of a park, the courage to crash a football line, the speed of reaction and agility to return a fireball tennis service, or the endurance to survive a pounding in the ring and come on to win?

The fact remains that of all sports, golf in one sense is the most taxing in that it calls for absolute self-control. Those adrenalins which in the boxer, ballplayer, or footballer can whip him to a fighting frenzy and produce a sometimes seemingly miraculous, winning performance are of no use whatsoever to the championship golfer. If anything they are a handicap. He wants no part of this kind of chemistry to upset the precarious balance of nerve and muscle. As I wrote once in a column in the long, long ago, golf is a backwards game; a descent from *crescendo fortissimo* to *pianissimo*. Instead of working up to a climactic effort, the booming drive comes first and at each hold for the finale, with every taut nerve screaming and twanging, the player most impart the most delicate impetus to the ball to cause it to roll over an often rough and uneven lawn and pop down a very small mole hole.

In a golf championship, whether he is playing the seventy-two holes of an Open, or the week's competition of the Amateur, the contender must go on doing exactly the same thing at the end that he has done at the beginning—play against the course and hit the ball in a calm, cool, and relaxed manner. Yet, as he nears the final flag, the tensions are entirely different from what they were at the start. In addition to the other competitors breathing down his neck, he is carrying the burden of wrongly played holes and lost strokes.

And, it must be remembered as well, that he is playing the same layout over and over again. Each hole acquires an identifiable personality and a history of triumph or trouble, so that as the player approached it, he cannot help but be thinking of the mess he made of it the last round. And this mounting strain Jones endured not once, but four times as he battled on toward the completion of the Grand Slam. Let no one underestimate his suffering during that year of near-miraculous accomplishment, or what it took out of him. I do not hesitate to call this the supreme athletic effort of the decade.

But the four major titles in one season was only the climax to a nine-year career which has not been equaled since.

In nine consecutive attempts at the U. S. Open and, remember, always playing against professionals who were hot and edged from continued winter and spring competition, Jones finished first four times and second four times. Two of the latter he lost in playoffs, indicating that he hit the leading score on six occasions, the last four of them in a row. He won three out of four British Open championships in which he competed, and had a fifty-fifty split in his two tries at the British Amateur.

With practically every record set up then wiped off the books by the more skilled and efficient athletes of the present, the question naturally arises whether anyone will ever equal or surpass the accomplishment of Jones.

Like every other game or sport, golf has become improved and refined to the point where it is far more demanding than ever before. Jones won most of his Open championships with scores ranging between 290 and 296, which today will get you a yard or so of crying towel in the locker room and little more. To have a look in at a modern tournament, you must be at least ten strokes under that total, a reflection of the steel-shafted clubs, beefed-up ball and above all, the fierce and continuing cut-throat battle among the professionals for the big money prizes.

I am convinced that the duplication of Jones' feat is slipping farther and farther away due to the primary condition to be fulfilled by one who wants to match it. For to begin with he must be an amateur.

And he must win that first one, the British Amateur, where he will encounter not only the best players in the British Isles, but wind and weather, and rain sometimes fired by the bucketfull in his face as he stands trying to address the ball. Jones' problem was made even more difficult by the fact that in those days, after the qualifying rounds, they played eighteen-hole elimination matches morning and afternoon, before the thirty-six-hole final. Eighteen holes in championship golf is equivalent to sudden death. If you found yourself one or two down on the back nine, your opponent could halve you out of the tournament in no time. Twice in this tournament Jones was carried to the eighteenth green to win, and once by Cyril Tolley to an extra hole, the nineteenth, so that his narrow escapes and the tensions they set up can be imagined.

Well, if such a player-for-fun comes along and does win the British Amateur, he must thereafter take over the world's best professionals—British, American, Canadian, French, Argentine, or whatever is going, in two tournaments of the most difficult and nerve-racking medal play conceivable.

Since the days of Jones there has been only one non-professional who has captured an Open championship. This was our own Johnny Goodman, who took the U.S. title in 1933, but won nothing else that year. The world itself has changed so greatly, socially and physically, within the last forty years that it is doubtful whether such an amateur as Jones could mature, even though he were to duplicate all Bob's endowed mental and physical genius.

The late Grantland Rice, the most graceful of all sportswriters, put it this way in an article written in 1940: "There is no more chance that golf will give the world another Jones than there is that literature will produce another Shakespeare, sculpture another Phidias, music another Chopin. There is no more probability that the next five hundred years will produce another Bob than there is that two human beings will be born with identical fingerprints."

And so we old ones proudly nominate Jones as the best of the best and the best of all.

We yield that nobody in our day jumped over a bar set at 7 feet 2 1/2 inches, ran a mile in under four minutes, broke the 60-yard sprint barrier or swam, hurdled, or skied as fast as they do today. But the picture of Robert Tyre Jones, Jr. still hangs over the bar of the Old Codgers' and Beard-Mumblers' Club, unassailed and unassailable. None of us who knew him then or, for that matter, even the present or the next generation of sportswriters, will be around to see him shot down.

# DUNCAN CHRISTY
## Playing Through

*The eighties ushered in a new era in sport, characterized by refinements in sports medicine and advances in physical and mental training techniques. As a result, athletes began to extend their careers. Now past fifty years of age, Jack Nicklaus, who has spent more than thirty years as a professional golfer and won every major tournament, joins other determined athletes— such as pitcher Nolan Ryan and Olympic track star Edwin Moses—who have performed superbly past what used to be considered their prime. Although Nicklaus himself admits that the power in his game has diminished, the mystique of this consummate golfer lives on. Plagued by back problems, Nicklaus scorns the less stressful senior tour and participates in the regular tournaments. Why does he persist? Writer Duncan Christy suggests that the reason may be the allure of the public's adulation.*

Jack Nicklaus is in agony. Just minutes ago he was telling a press conference at a tournament in Florida that his back—which has nagged him recurrently through most of the 1980s and cost him the patina on his peerless game—was "excellent.

269

I've been playing golf without medicine, and I'm delighted about how I've been hitting and feeling." But no sooner had the crowd dispersed than a sudden spasm knocked his breath away, and left his hands groping at his immobilized hips.

Now the PGA's Player of the Century is flat on his back on the carpet of the conference center, his knees tilted up over a chair, his face reddening. His aides are horrified as he gently attempts to stretch the afflicted muscles and discs, but he waves them away: "No, I don't want a pillow, thanks, I'm going to keep my head down."

Why can't Jack Nicklaus just stop playing golf? Part of him certainly wants to, after 30 years on the tour and a record of victories that will never be equalled. And in the months since his 50th birthday in January—the date that made him eligible for the senior tour—he's projected a very public ambivalence about matching his skills against the young lions of the regular tour and the middle-aged lions of the senior one.

He doesn't need the money: the scope of his business enterprises has no peer among sportmen. So why does he continue to play, when he can count all the victories he's had in the last decade on one gloved hand?

"I'm in a quandary over what I want to do," says the Golden Bear frankly. "I need to get my own head screwed on properly." Precious few athletes know when to hang up the shoes, that precise moment when their awesome skills are in retrograde even as they stand at the pennacle. Nicklaus himself passed on the greatest opportunity any sportsman has ever had to go out on top, his Masters victory four years ago. "That was my greatest triumph," he remembers. "Nobody expected me to win, including me." But on that Sunday afternoon, 46-year-old Jack Nicklaus devoured the competition, as he had so many times before, and slipped the winner's green blazer over his shoulders for an unprecedented sixth time.

In a lesser man this persistence would simply be a case of rampant ego blinding the possessor to his inevitable decline. The ego is there, in Nicklaus, although outward glimpses of it are as rare as holes-in-one. His skills have eroded. He admits this. "Twenty to 30 yards on my long game," he says, "and the power to hit the ball high out of the deep rough."

But ego is too pat an explanation when it comes to Nicklaus. To challenge himself, he recently set the goal of becoming the first player to win on both the regular and the senior tours and promptly won his first senior tournament. With any other 50-year-old golfer—with the possible exception of Lee Trevino—the reaction would be total skepticism; "he's kidding himself." But the Nicklaus mystique persists, the professional golfing world's long-time nightmare of being chased down the fairway by the Golden Bear with a tournament on the line.

Golfer Payne Stewart thinks that Nicklaus' chances are slim on the regular tour. "He doesn't play that much anymore," says last year's PGA champion. "And he doesn't have the feel that he had when he was 30." But paradoxically, says Stewart, "the tournaments I can see him winning would be majors"—the hallowed Masters, the U.S. and British Opens, and the PGA—"because he can get himself into a zone for majors better than anybody."

In fact, there are powerful incentives for Nicklaus not to play golf. One of them is the global scope of his business interests, a $350 million-a-year machine that builds golf courses all over the world, promotes and handles his many endorsements, and keeps the public continually provided with Jack Nicklaus golf equipment, accoutrements and sportswear. "I've got a darn good business," he says, "which I feel may be more important than playing golf. I want to grow that for my five kids."

A second is the memory of his father, who died of cancer at the age of 56. "Here he was a vital part of our lives," Nicklaus remembers, "and all of a sudden he was gone. I want to see my kids"—who range in age from 28-year-old Jack II to 16-year-old Michael—"grow up, and not spend my whole life on a golf course or a plane. I want to play, but I don't want it to dominate my life the way it has for 30 years."

A third is the unique situation Nicklaus faces as an aging champion making his debut on the senior tour. "He's got everything to lose and nothing to gain," says golfer Chi Chi Rodriguez. "He's the first guy to hit the senior tour like that. Jack has more pressure than anybody: if he wins, everybody says that he should, and if he loses, his reputation suffers."

The senior tour appears to offer Nicklaus all the pleasures of the famous definition of a tie game—"like kissing your sister." And try as he might to be gracious about it, he continues to land in a conversational bunker. "Senior golf doesn't give me any goal," he was quoted as saying in a recent interview. "To be honest, playing pro-ams on short courses with no rough"—senior tournaments are three-day events over shorter, more forgiving course layouts—"doesn't motivate me." As for the competition, Lee Trevino's string of victories notwithstanding, "most of the guys who are playing well, with a few exceptions, are the guys who were marginal players when they played on tour." Namely, those who lagged far behind Nicklaus in the fine print of the sports reports.

Strong words from a man normally regarded as a diplomat for the sport. And despite the storm of reaction—particularly from the "round bellies" on the senior tour—Nicklaus keeps on hacking. "I'm having a hard time being 50," he says. "I'm having a hard time being a senior. Does being 50 mean that I'm supposed to run to the senior tour?"

So the question remains—Why does he continue to play?

Nicklaus says that he feels he "owes it to the public to be visible. The public has been very good to me." This begs the question. More likely it is an adulation which has barely dwindled even as he finishes further and further from the top. When he recently played near the top of the Doral Open, he was the guy mobbed at press conferences. "Could Big Jack win again?" the scribes wanted to know, paying only perfunctory heed to the real leaders.

So instead of resolutely turning to business, he's consulting with a new teacher to recover the fundamentals of his swing. Instead of accepting the identity of the "ceremonial golfer"—the figurative ride in the golf cart—he practices an aggressive program of aerobics to strengthen his back.

"My days of being the best competitor, the best golfer in the world are over—I know that," he says. "But no one likes to give that up; you don't want to give up where you think you are in your life."

# HERBERT WARREN WIND

## Trevino

*In the previous essay in this volume the reader learns of the later years of one of golf's legends—Jack Nicklaus. In this essay are the beginnings of the winning career of Lee Trevino, who began caddying and playing golf at the age of eight. Trevino's difficult ascent to becoming one of golf's great players took him through a partnership in a pitch-and-putt course to a stint in the Marines to working as a club professional in El Paso, Texas. During one period of his life Trevino had a golf club in his hands for almost fifteen hours a day. In Wind's estimation, Trevino's doggedness yielded one of golf's most superb shot-making techniques. Trevino's story is a reminder that the road to the top usually demands years of dedication.*

Three facets of Trevino's career and personality seem to me unusually fascinating and well worth further examination: his background, his singular technique, and some of the key moments of his major victories. His life has a strong Dickensian quality, partly because of the hard times he endured as a boy and a young man, and partly because of the improbable turns of fate that marked his road to the top. He left school when he was fourteen and in the eighth grade, and found a job helping out at a driving range in Dallas that was owned and operated by a professional named Hardy Greenwood. Trevino had already been around golf for several years. While his grandfather's shack had many limitations, it also had a few advantages. There was a lake behind it, along with some big willow trees and a beautiful cottonwood that he remembers wistfully. More to the point, the shack was situated a hundred yards from the Glen Lakes Country Club. Trevino had started caddying at Glen Lakes when he was eight. He also started playing at that age, for he got to know the greenkeeper's son, and they would go out together and hack around the course during the hours when it was empty. It didn't take Trevino long to become a pretty fair little golfer and also to become thoroughly enamored of the game. That is why he gravitated to the driving range in 1954 when he left school and went looking for a job. The following winter, he helped Greenwood build a nine-hole par-3 course on twelve acres adjacent to the driving range. They did all the work themselves: they designed the holes, installed the pipes for the watering system, mixed the sand and loam and peat moss for the fairways and greens, seeded the course, and, when the grass came through, mowed it and spruced up the green areas. The longest hole at Hardy's pitch-and-putt course was 120 yards, and the shortest was 65 yards. The course was lit at night, and it was a highly profitable operation. Trevino was happy with this life for a while, but late in 1956 he grew restless and signed up for a four-year tour of duty in the Marine Corps. He spent a good deal of it on Okinawa and got in a lot of golf on a course called Awase Meadows. At this time, Trevino was, in his own estimation, "just a good 4-handicap golfer," although he turned in some low rounds in interservice matches. (One of the golfers he played against was Orville Moody, then in the Army and stationed in Japan, who subsequently won the 1969 U.S. Open.) "My main trouble in those days was that I was a right-to-left player," Trevino recalled during our talk. "On some rounds, I would hit the most awful-looking hooks you ever saw, and I paid the price for them. I had to do something about my method of hitting the ball, I realized, or I would never become a really sound golfer."

Upon getting out of the Marines, Trevino went back to Dallas and to his old job at the driving range and the par-3 course. One day shortly after his return, he was invited to play at Shady Oaks, in Fort Worth, Ben Hogan's home club. As usual, Hogan was hitting out practice balls. Trevino stopped and watched him from a distance. He was impressed by two things: every shot that Hogan hit was cut slightly—that is, it curved a shade from left to right—and on shot after shot the caddie never had to move; the ball hopped up into his hand on the first bounce, as if it were on a string. Hogan, like Trevino, had struggled for years with a hook when he was a young man, and he didn't become a champion until, completely altering his approach to the game, he started hitting the ball not from right to left but from left to right and patiently mastered a controlled fade that made him the most accurate golfer since Harry Vardon. Trevino, like all golfers, had heard about this, but it was watching Hogan in action that drove the point home. In a word, when a right-to-left player hits the ball badly and hooks it, the spin on it carries it sharply and fast to the left, and it frequently ends up in heavy rough or even out of bounds, but when a left-to-right player hits the ball badly, it spins in a comparatively soft and slow arc to the right, often stops in the fairway, and rarely causes him much grief.

Back at the driving range, Trevino got down to the job of learning to cut the ball. He took a very open stance, aiming well to the left of his target, and, after some experimentaion, he developed an individual way of achieving the results he was after. He used an exceptionally strong grip on the club, and he took it back with the club face closed. Then, as he came into the ball, he tried to open the club face just before impact. He worked on developing a firm left side on the downswing, knowing that if he didn't he'd spray the ball all over the place. He also worked on keeping his body down low in the hitting area; the longer a player stays down at impact, the less he can pronate his arms and hands, and too much pronation causes hooking. As he hit through the ball, he extended his club as far forward as possible. This exaggerated extension was not at all a natural move for him. One gimmick he found invaluable in training himself to do this was to pretend that there were four balls lined up in a row and on his downswing try to hit through all four of them, and not just the first one.

It took Trevino about a year of daily practice before he felt confident that he could fade the ball more or less as he wanted to. He began to play very well, so he continued with the method he had devised. Off the tee, he would aim for the left-hand rough and slide his low, buzzing drives ten or fifteen yards to the right and comfortably onto the fairway. On his irons, if the pin was positioned on the left side of the green he aimed for the left edge and slid his approach into the pin. It should be noted that in the mid-nineteen-seventies, after his back trouble, he had to modify his technique slightly. He couldn't stay down as low in the hitting area and also had to come up a little more quickly, and this meant he couldn't keep the club face on the ball as long. In addition, the right hand got into the shot more. Consequently, after setting up in his open stance he did not try to cut across the ball from the outside in on the downswing to give the ball the outer spin that made it fade; instead, he swung straight through the ball almost on the direct line to the target. This is the technique he employs today. On his full shots with his woods and most of his irons, the ball falls in a shade from the left. On some of his short irons, he actually draws the ball a fraction from right to left. Unlike most athletes with an unorthodox style, who are interesting mainly because they nevertheless manage to get results, Trevino is an aesthetic delight. On his best days, there is no visible exertion at all as he moves into his shots; his magnificent hand action and timing quietly do the work. He strikes the ball much more purely than most of the paragons of copybook style, and it flies toward the flag with perfect rotation and on just the right parabola. The fact is that he is not only one of the finest strikers of the ball in modern times but one of the best shotmakers in history.

One of the most important stretches of Trevino's life is the period we know least about—the years between his return home from the service at the end of 1960 and his sudden explosion on the national golf scene in 1967. Soon after getting back to Dallas and reestablishing his ties with Hardy Greenwood's driving range and par-3 course, he turned professional and joined the Professional Golfers Association. He quickly fell into a daily regimen. He would rise before daybreak and arrive at Tenison Park, a public golf course, at around five. Tenison Park received a lot of play, but at that early hour it was empty, and Trevino, if he wished, could whirl around the eighteen holes in no time at all. Other mornings, if he had a match lined up—and he often did, since Tenison Park was a harbor for hustlers—he would play a few holes before the match to get warmed up for his morning's work. He nearly always wore Bermuda shorts, and as often as not he played barefoot. When his practice round or his match was over, he would move to the practice tee and hit dozens and dozens of balls. After that, he would take a shower, put on his work clothes (slacks and a golf shirt), and drive to Hardy's. He began work there at two in the afternoon and closed the place down between eleven and midnight. He alternated between its two facilities: one day he would run the driving range and the next day the par-3. During slow afternoons, he hit out more balls. Trevino estimates that during those years he had a golf club in his hands an average of fifteen hours a day. It is unlikely that any other golfer in the country in the nineteen-sixties practiced as hard or as long. By 1965, when he won the state open championship, he was probably a good enough golfer to have made it on the P.G.A. tour, but personal problems prevented him from taking that step. In any event, he was very much at home at Tenison Park and was prospering to some degree from his matches there. He was also able to augment his salary from Hardy's by playing matches on the par-3 course. His chief difficulty was that he had become so expert at pitching and putting on that familiar terrain that it wasn't easy to get people to play him. Finally, after running out of even those customers who were willing to take him on provided he played right-handed with left-handed clubs, he hit upon a gimmick that, once he was firmly ensconced in the big time, received reams of publicity. His new specialty involved the use of a twenty-six-ounce Dr Pepper bottle—made of very heavy glass—which he wrapped with adhesive tape, so that it would not shatter when he hit a golf ball with it. Wearing a glove on his right hand, he held the bottle at the neck, tossed the ball in the air, and batted the ball with the big end of the bottle. He practiced with the bottle almost as much as he did with his regular clubs. After a while, he could flight the ball in the proper arc for a golf shot, and he could also hit it 120 yards—the length of the longest hole on the par-3 course. He putted billiards style, with the neck. Trevino's average score for nine holes with the bottle was 29 or 30—two or three strokes above par. He was able to persuade his opponents to give him half a stroke a hole, which meant that if he tied them on a hole they lost it. The stakes generally were fifty cents or a dollar a hole. He accepted all challenges for over three years and never lost a match with the bottle.

In the winter of 1966, the course of Trevino's life changed abruptly. Shortly before, he had quit his job at the par-3 and the driving range, and for a while his only income came from his matches at Tenison Park. One night that January, he received a phone call from El Paso. A man he had never met was calling him. "He was connected with the Horizon Hills Country Club, and he wanted me to come out and play a golf match for him," Trevino explained to me. "You see, quite a few people were getting beat pretty badly at Horizon Hills in matches with a certain guy. One young fellow who had lost his shirt had been asked, 'Do you know someone who can play—someone nobody knows?' This kid told them, 'Yeah. I know a Mexican boy in Dallas who can really play, and no one's ever heard of him.' Well, this man at the other end of the phone said he'd send me a plane ticket and give me three hundred dollars if I'd come out to El Paso and play for him for two days. I told him I'd have to ask my wife about it. She was working then as a file clerk at Blue Cross-Blue Shield for fifty-five dollars a week, and that's what we were basically living on. We were having a hell of a time making ends meet. So I told Claudia—that's my wife—about the proposition this guy had offered. When she heard the numbers, she said, 'O.K. You can go.' I flew out to El Paso, went to Horizon Hills, and played two rounds—one each day—against a very good golfer, a well-known pro on the tour. I beat him soundly both rounds. About a month later, this man from El Paso phoned me again. There was an amateur who wanted to play me, he said. I said I was interested. 'You got a job yet?' he asked me. I told him no, and after a moment he said, 'Why don't you come out to El Paso to stay?' I had a 1958 Oldsmobile, and I rented a small U-Haul trailer and threw everything into it. When we arrived in El Paso, that's all we had, along with fifty dollars in cash."

Trevino easily defeated the amateur challenger. He then went to work for Horizon Hills as the club professional. He received only thirty dollars a week for his services as the pro, but he gave some lessons and had ample time to play matches with the members, so his take-home pay amounted to a respectable sum. By spring, he was well started on a new life. He qualified for the 1966 U.S. Open, held that year at the Olympic Club, in San Francisco, and he made the thirty-six-hole cut, but he finished with two unimpressive 78s, mainly because of his inability to cope with the bunkers. There hadn't been a single bunker at Tenison Park. The next year, he didn't feel much like trying to qualify for the Open, but his wife set aside the necessary twenty dollars and sent in his entry. He did very well in the local and sectional qualifying tests. Two of the key men in the operation of Horizon Hills, Jesse Whittenton (who had played cornerback for the Green Bay Packers) and his brother Don, lent him four hundred dollars to help him meet the cost of the long trip East. At Baltusrol, he had the good fortune early in the week to meet a club member—Chuck Smith, now deceased—who found him delightful company. At the close of each day's play, they spent part of the evening together, Smith working on his gin-and-tonics, Trevino on a succession of beers. There is no question in Trevino's mind that Smith's friendship had a good deal to do with his feeling almost as much at home at Baltusrol as he had at Tenison Park, and that that put him in the proper frame of mind to play his best golf. After his fifth-place finish in the Baltusrol Open, he was on his way.

# JOHN UPDIKE

# Thirteen Ways of Looking at the Masters

*Using Wallace Stevens's "Thirteen Ways of Looking at a Blackbird" as a point of departure, John Updike takes various sharp looks at the most prestigious golf match in America—the Masters. From his analysis of the golfing styles of Snead and Palmer to his descriptions of the ham sandwiches served and his characterizations of three generations of female spectators, Updike captures the flavor of the occasion. Each of Updike's sections, without fail, brings its own reward, as, for instance, his thought about the young golfers on the course, burdened with the hopes of parents, teachers, backers, "and with the difference between success and failure so feather-fine."*

### 1. As an Event in Augusta, Georgia

In the middle of downtown Broad Street a tall white monument—like an immensely heightened wedding cake save that in place of the bride and groom stands a dignified Confederate officer—proffers the thought that

No nation rose so white and fair;
  None fell so pure of crime.

Within a few steps of the monument, a movie theater, during Masters Week in 1979, was showing *Hair,* full of cheerful miscegenation and anti-military song and dance.

This is the Deep/Old/New South, with its sure-enough levees, railroad tracks, unpainted dwellings out of illustrations to Joel Chandler Harris, and stately homes ornamented by grillework and verandas. As far up the Savannah River as boats could go, Augusta has been a trading post since 1717 and was named in 1735 by James Oglethorpe for the mother of George III. It changed hands several times during the Revolutionary War, thrived on tobacco and cotton, imported textile machinery from Philadelphia in 1828, and during the Civil War housed the South's largest powder works. Sherman passed through here, and didn't leave much in the way of historical sites.

The Augusta National Golf Club is away from the business end of town, in a region of big brick houses embowered in magnolia and dogwood. A lot of people retire to Augusta, and one of the reasons that Bobby Jones wanted to build a golf course here instead of near his native Atlanta, was the distinctly milder climate. The course, built in 1931-32 on the site of the Fruitlands Nursery property, after designs by Dr. Alister Mackenzie (architect of Cypress Point) and Jones himself, has the venerable Augusta Country Club at its back, and at its front, across Route 28, an extensive shopping-center outlay. At this point the New South becomes indistinguishable from New Jersey.

## 2. As an Event Not in Augusta, Georgia

How many Augusta citizens are members of the Augusta National Golf Club? The question, clearly in bad taste, brought raised eyebrows and a muttered "Very few" or, more spaciously, "Thirty-eight or forty." The initial membership fee is rumored to be $50,000, there is a waiting list five years' long, and most of the members seem to be national Beautiful People, Golfing Subspecies, who jet in for an occasional round during the six months the course is open. When Ike, whose cottage was near the clubhouse, used to show up and play a twosome with Arnold Palmer, the course would be cleared by the Secret Service. Cliff Roberts, chairman of the tournament from its inception in 1934 until his death in 1977, was a Wall Street investment banker; his chosen successor, William H. Lane, is a business executive from faraway Houston.

A lot of Augusta's citizens get out of town during Masters Week, renting their houses. The lady in the drugstore near the house my wife and I were staying in told me she had once gone walking on the course. *Once:* the experience seemed unrepeatable. The course had looked deserted to her, but then a voice shouted "Fore" and a ball struck near her. The ghost of Lloyd Mangrum, perhaps. The only Augustans conspicuous during the tournament are the black caddies, who know the greens so well they can call a putt's break to the inch while standing on the fringe.

### 3. As a Study in Green

Green grass, green grandstands, green concession stalls, green paper cups, green folding chairs and visors for sale, green-and-white ropes, green-topped Georgia pines, a prevalence of green in the slacks and jerseys of the gallery, like the prevalence of red in the crowd in Moscow on May Day. The caddies' bright green caps and Sam Snead's bright green trousers. If justice were poetic, Hubert Green would win it every year.

### 4. As a Rite of Spring

"It's become a rite of spring," a man told me with a growl, "like the Derby." Like Fort Lauderdale. Like Opening Day at a dozen ballparks. Spring it was, especially for us Northerners who had left our gray skies, brown lawns, salt-strewn highways, and plucky little croci for this efflorescence of azaleas and barefoot *jeunes filles en fleurs.* Most of the gallery, like most of the golfers, had Southern accents. This Yankee felt a little as if he were coming in late on a round of equinoctial parties that had stretched from Virginia to Florida. A lot of young men were lying on the grass

289

betranced by the memories of last night's libations, and a lot of matronly voices continued discussing Aunt Earlene's unfortunate second marriage, while the golf balls floated overhead. For many in attendance, the Masters is a ritual observance; some of the old-timers wore sun hats festooned with over twenty years' worth of admission badges.

Will success as a festival spoil the Masters as a sporting event? It hasn't yet, but the strain on the tournament's famous and exemplary organization can be felt. Ticket sales are limited, but the throng at the main scoreboard is hard to squeeze by. The acreage devoted to parking would make a golf course in itself. An army of over two thousand policemen, marshals, walkway guards, salespersons, trash-gleaners, and other attendants is needed to maintain order and facilitate the pursuit of happiness. To secure a place by any green it is necessary to arrive at least an hour before there is anything to watch.

When, on the last two days, the television equipment arrives, the crowd itself is watched. Dutifully, it takes its part as a mammoth unpaid extra in a national television spectacular. As part of it, patting out courteous applause at a good shot or groaning in chorus at a missed putt, one felt, slightly, *canned.*

### 5. *As a Fashion Show*

Female fashions, my wife pointed out, came in

three strata. First, young women decked out as if going to a garden party—makeup, flowing dresses, sandals. Next, the trim, leathery generation of the mothers, dressed as if they themselves were playing golf—short skirts, sun visors, cleated two-tone shoes. Last, the generation of the grandmothers, in immaculately blued hair and amply filled pants suits in shades we might call electric pastel or Day-Glo azalea.

### 6. *As a Display Case for Sam Snead and Arnold Palmer*

Though they no longer are likely to win, you wouldn't know it from their charismas. Snead, with his rakishly tilted panama and slightly pushed-in face—a face that has known both battle and merriment—swaggers around the practice tee like the Sheriff of Golf Country, testing a locked door here, hanging a parking ticket there. On the course, he remains a golfer one has to call beautiful, from the cushioned roll of his shoulders as he strokes the ball to the padding, panther-like tread with which he follows it down the center of the fairway, his chin tucked down while he thinks apparently rueful thoughts. He is one of the great inward golfers, those who wrap the dazzling difficulty of the game in a impassive, effortless flow of movement. When, on the green, he stands beside his ball, faces the hole, and performs the curious obeisance of his "side-winder" putting stroke, no one laughs.

291

And Palmer, he of the unsound swing, a hurried slash that ends as though he is snatching back something hot from a fire, remains the monumental outward golfer, who invites us into the game to share with him its heady turmoil, its call for constant courage. Every inch an agonist, Palmer still hitches his pants as he mounts the green, still strides between the wings of his army like Hector on his way to yet more problematical heroism. Age has thickened him, made him look almost musclebound, and has grizzled his thin, untidy hair; but his deportment more than ever expresses vitality, a love of life and of the game that rebounds to him, from the multitudes, as fervent gratitude. Like us golfing commoners, he risks looking bad for the sake of some fun.

Of the younger players, only Lanny Wadkins communicates Palmer's reckless determination, and only Fuzzy Zoeller has the captivating blitheness of a Jimmy Demaret or a Lee Trevino. The Masters, with its clubby lifetime qualification for previous winners, serves as an annual exhibit of Old Masters, wherein one can see the difference between the reigning, college-bred pros, with their even teeth, on-camera poise, and abstemious air, and the older crowd, who came up from caddie sheds, drove themselves in cars along the dusty miles of the Tour, and hustled bets with the rich to make ends meet. Golf expresses the man, as every weekend foursome knows; amid the mannerly lads who dominate the money list, Palmer and Snead loom as men.

## 7. As an Exercise in Spectatorship

In no other sport must the spectator move. The builders and improvers of Augusta National built mounds and bleachers for the crowds to gain vantage from, and a gracefully written pamphlet by the founder, Robert Jones, is handed out as instruction in the art of "letting the Tournament come to us instead of chasing after it." Nevertheless, as the field narrows and the interest of the hordes focuses, the best way to see anything is to hang back in the woods and use binoculars. Seen from within the galleries, the players become tiny walking dolls, glimpsable, like stars on a night of scudding clouds, in the gaps between heads.

Examples of Southern courtesy in the galleries: (1) When my wife stood to watch an approach to the green, the man behind her mildly observed, "Ma'am, it was awful nice when you were sittin' down." (2) A gentleman standing next to me, not liking the smell of a cigar I was smoking, offered to buy it from me for a dollar.

Extraordinary event in the galleries: on the fourth hole a ball set in flight by Dow Finsterwald solidly struck the head of a young man sitting beside the green. The sound of a golf ball on a skull is remarkably like that of two blocks of wood knocked together. *Glock*. Flesh hurts; bone makes music.

Single instance of successful spectatorship by this reporter: I happened to be in the pines left of the seventh fairway on the first day of play, wondering whether to go for another of the refreshment committee's standardized but economical ham sandwiches, when Art Wall, Jr., hooked a ball near where I was standing. Only a dozen or so gathered to watch his recovery; for a moment, then, we could breathe with a player and experience with him—as he waggled, peered at obtruding branches, switched clubs, and peered at the branches again—that quintessential golfing sensation, the loneliness of the bad-ball hitter.

Sad truth, never before revealed: by sticking to a spot in the stands or next to the green, one can view the field coming through, hitting variants of the same shots and putts, and by listening to the massed cheers and grunts from the other greens, one can guess at dramas unseen; but the unified field, as Einstein discovered in a more general connection, is unapprehendable, and the best way to witness a golf tournament is at the receiving end of a television signal. Many a fine golf reporter, it was whispered to me, never leaves the set in the press tent.

The other sad truth about golf spectatorship is that for today's pros it all comes down to the putting, and that the difference between a putt that drops and one that rims the cup, though teleologically enormous, is intellectually negligible.

### 8. As a Study in Turf-Building

A suburban lawn-owner can hardly look up

from admiring the weedless immensity of the Augusta National turf. One's impression, when first admitted to this natural Oz, is that a giant putting surface has been dropped over acres of rolling terrain, with a few apertures for ponds and trees to poke through. A philosophy of golf is expressed in Jones's pamphlet: "The Augusta National has much more fairway and green area than the average course. There is little punishing rough and very few bunkers. The course is not intended so much to punish severely the wayward shot as to reward adequately the stroke played with skill—and judgment."

It is an intentional paradox, then, that this championship course is rather kind to duffers. The ball sits up on Augusta's emerald carpet looking big as a baseball. It was not always such; in 1972, an invasion of *Poa annua,* a white-spiked vagabond grass, rendered conditions notoriously bumpy; in remedy a fescue called Pennlawn and a rye called Pennfine were implanted on the fairways and greens respectively and have flourished. Experimentation continues; to make the greens even harder and slicker, they are thinking of rebuilding them on a sand base—and have already done so on the adjacent par-three course.

From May to October, when the course is closed to play, everything goes to seed and becomes a hayfield, and entire fairways are plowed up: a harrowing thought. The caddies, I was solemnly assured, never replace a divot; they just sprinkle grass seed from a pouch they carry. Well, this is a myth, for I repeatedly saw caddies replace divots in the course of the tournament, with the care of tile-setters.

## 9. As Demography

One doesn't have to want to give the country back to the Indians to feel a nostalgic pang while looking at old photos of the pre-World War II tournaments, with their hatted, necktied galleries strolling up the fairways in the wake of the baggy-trousered players, and lining the tees and greens only one man deep.

The scores have grown crowded, too. The best then would be among the best now—Lloyd Mangrum's single-round 64 in 1940 has not been bettered, though for the last two years it has been equalled. But the population of the second-best has increased, producing virtually a new winner each week of the Tour, and stifling the emergence of stable constellations of superstars like Nelson-Hogan-Snead and Palmer-Player-Nicklaus. In the 1936 and 1938 Masters, only seven players made the thirty-six-hole score of 145 that cut the 1979 field to forty-five players. Not until 1939 did the winner break 280 and not again until 1948. The last total over 280 to win it came in 1973. In 1936, Craig Wood had a first-day round of 88 and finished in the top two dozen. In 1952, Sam Snead won the Masters in spite of a third-round 77. That margin for intermittent error has been squeezed from tournament golf. Johnny Miller chops down a few trees, develops the wrong muscles, and drops like a stone on the lists. Arnold Palmer, relatively young and still strong and keen, can no longer ram the putts in from twenty feet, and becomes a father figure. A cruel world, top-flight golf, that eats its young.

## 10. As Race Relations

A Martian skimming overhead in his saucer would have to conclude that white Earthlings hit the ball and black Earthlings fetch it, that white men swing the sticks and black men carry them. The black caddies of Augusta, in their white coveralls, are a tradition that needs a symbolic breaking, the converse of Lee Elder's playing in the tournament.

To be fair, these caddies are specialists of a high order, who take a cheerful pride in their expertise and who are, especially during Masters Week, well paid for it. Gary Player's caddie for his spectacular come-from-nowhere victory of 1978 was tipped $10,000—a sum that, this caddie assured an impudent interrogator, was still safe in the bank. In the New South, blacks work side by side with whites in the concession stands and at the fairway ropes, though I didn't see any in a green marshal's coat. I was unofficially informed that, at the very time when civil rightists were agitating for a black player to be invited to play even if one did not earn qualification—as Elder did in 1975—blacks were not being admitted to the tournament *as spectators.* I wonder about this. On pages 26–27 of the green souvenir album with a text by Cliff Roberts, one can see a photograph of Henry Picard hitting out of a bunker; behind him in the scattering of spectators are a number of ebony gentlemen not dressed as caddies. At any rate, though golf remains a white man's game, it presents in the Masters player and caddie an active white-black partnership in which the white man is taking the advice and doing the manual work. Caddies think of the partnership as "we," as in "We hit a drive down the center and a four-iron stiff to the pin, but then he missed the putt."

## 11. As Class Relations

Though the Augusta National aspires to be the American St. Andrews, there is a significant economic diffence between a Scottish golf links thriftily pinked out on a wasteland—the sandy seaside hills that are "links"—and the American courses elaborately, expensively carved from farmland and woods. Though golf has plebeian Scottish roots, in this country its province is patrician. A course requires capital and flaunts that ancient aristocratic prerogative, land. In much of the world, this humbling game is an automatic symbol of capitalist-imperialist oppression; a progressive African novelist, to establish a character as a villain, has only to show him coming off a golf course. And in our own nation, for all the roadside driving ranges and four o'clock factory leagues, golf remains for millions something that happens at the end of a long driveway, beyond the MEMBERS ONLY sign.

Yet competitive golf in the United States came of age when, at The Country Club, in Brookline, Massachusetts, a twenty-year-old ex-caddie and workingman's son, Francis Ouimet, beat the British legends Vardon and Ray in a playoff for the U.S. Open. And ever since, the great competitors have tended to come from the blue-collar level of golf, the caddies and the offspring of club pros. Rare is the Bobby Jones who emerges from the gentry with the perfectionistic drive and killer instinct that make a champion in this game which permits no let-up or loss of concentration, yet which penalizes tightness also. Hagen acted like a swell and was called Sir Walter, but he came up from a caddie's roost in Rochester. The lords of golf have been by and large gentlemen made and not born, while the clubs and the management of the Tour remain in the hands of the country-club crowd. When genteel Ed Sneed and Tom Watson fell into a three-way playoff for the 1979 Masters title, you knew in your bones it was going to be the third player, a barbarian called Fuzzy with a loopy all-out swing, who would stroll through the gates and carry off the loot.

### 12. As a Parade of Lovely Golfers, No Two Alike

Charles Coody, big-beaked bird. Billy Casper,

once the king of touch, now sporting the bushy white sideburns of a turn-on-the-century railroad conductor, still able to pop them up from a sandtrap and sink the putt. Trevino, so broad across he looks like a reflection in a funhouse mirror, a model of delicacy around the greens and a model of affable temperament everywhere. Player, varying his normal black outfit with white slacks, his bearing so full of fight and muscle he seems to be restraining himself from breaking into a run. Nicklaus, Athlete of the Decade, still golden but almost gaunt and faintly grim, as he feels a crown evaporating from his head. Gay Brewer, heavy in the face and above the belt, nevertheless uncorking a string-straight mid-iron to within nine inches of the long seventh hole in the par-three tournament. Miller Barber, Truman Capote's double, punching and putting his way to last year's best round, a storm-split 64 in two installments. Bobby Clampett, looking too young and thin to be out there. Andy Bean, looking too big to be out there, and with his perennially puzzled expression seeming to be searching for a game more his size. Hubert Green, with a hunched flicky swing that would make a high-school golf coach scream. Tom Weiskopf, the handsome embodiment of pained near-perfection. Hale Irwin, the picture-book golfer with the face of a Ph.D. candidate. Johnny Miller, looking heavier than we remember him, patiently knocking them out on the practice tee, wondering where the lightning went. Ben

Crenshaw, the smiling Huck Finn, and Tom Watson, the more pensive Tom Sawyer, who, while the other boys were whitewashing fences, has become, politely but firmly, the best golfer in the world.

And many other redoubtable young men. Seeing them up close, in the dining room or on the clubhouse veranda, one is stuck by how young and in many cases how slight they seem, with their pert and telegenic little wives—boys, really, anxious to be polite and to please even the bores and boors that collect in the interstices of all well-publicized events. Only when one sees them at a distance, as they walk alone or chatting in twos down the great green emptiness of the fairway, does one sense that each youth is the pinnacle of a buried pyramid of effort and investment, of prior competition from pre-teen level up, of immense and it must be at times burdensome accumulated hopes of parents, teachers, backers. And with none of the group hypnosis and exhilaration of team play to relieve them. And with the difference between success and failure so feather-fine.

### 13. As a Religious Experience

The four days of 1979's Masters fell on Maundy Thursday, Good Friday, Holy Saturday, and Easter Sunday. On Good Friday, fittingly, the skies darkened, tornadoes were predicted, and thousands of sinners ran for cover. My good wife, who had gone to divine services, was prevented from returning to the course by the flood of departing cars, and the clear moral is one propounded from many a pulpit: golf and churchgoing do not mix. Easter Sunday also happened to be the anniversary of the assassination of Abraham Lincoln and the sinking of the *Titanic,* and it wasn't such a good day for Ed Sneed either.

About ninety-nine percent of the gallery, my poll of local vibes indicated, was rooting for Sneed to hold off disaster and finish what he had begun. He had played splendidly for three days, and it didn't seem likely he'd come this close soon again. When he birdied the fifteenth and enlarged his once huge cushion back to three strokes, it seemed he would do it. But then, through no flagrant fault of his own, he began "leaking." We all knew how it felt, the slippery struggle to nurse a good round back to the clubhouse. On the seventeenth green, where I was standing, his approach looked no worse than his playing partner's; it just hit a foot too long, skipped onto the sloping back part of the green, and slithered into the fringe. His putt back caught the cup but twirled away. And his putt to save par, which looked to me like a gimme, lipped out, the same way my two-footers do when I lift my head to watch them drop, my sigh of relief all prepared. Zoeller, ten minutes before, had gently rolled in a birdie from much farther away. Sneed's fate seemed sealed then: the eighteenth hole, a famous bogey-maker, waited for him as ineluctably as Romeo's missed appointment with Juliet.

He hadn't hit bad shots, and he hadn't panicked; he just was screwed a half-turn too tight to get a par. The gallery of forty thousand felt for him, right to the pits of our golf-weary stomachs, when his last hope of winning it clean hung on the lip of the seventy-second hole. It so easily might have been otherwise. But then that's life, and that's golf.

# HORSE RACING

# BILL BARICH

## Bloodlines and Speed

*How breeders over the years have attempted to develop faster horses, and some of the more or less correct systems of breeding they applied. In the past, breeders trusted in their own mystic formulas for success: some believed that a pregnant mare received infusions of blood from the male that affected not just the one pregnancy but even her successive foals sired by other stallions; other breeders studied the stud book for past winners over many generations and searched for patterns of bloodlines; yet others emphasized the quality of the female line in their research. But if you want to learn how breeders attempted to "stamp the get," and how the lame Crooked One gave birth to an outstanding succession of females, read on.*

All horses are descended from the so-called dawn horse, whose fossil remains were discovered in 1838 near Suffolk, England, and subsequently dated to the Lower Eocene epoch some seventy million years ago. Because the skeleton was small, measuring less than twenty inches high at the shoulder, scientists grouped it mistakenly among the ratlike huraxes and named it *Hyracotherium*.

By the time similar finds were made in northern Europe and the upper Mississippi Valley, Darwinian theory had gained a purchase in scientific circles, and the fossils in question were reclassified as relatives of the present-day horse. Charles Marsh of Yale contributed a new taxonomic label, *Eohippus*. Out of this little fox-sized animal the modern thoroughbred evolved.

The evolutionary path was convoluted, though, winding intricately through several species before arriving at the modern horse's true progenitor, *Equus caballus*. There was *Mesohippus*, the first horse adapted to grazing; *Parahippus*, about three inches taller and bearing stripes on its coat; *Merychippus*, whose humped withers and dentition provided another advance; and *Pliohippus*, taller still, with more delicate legs and toeless feet. *Equus caballus* flourished during the Pleistocene age; the animal was about fifty-two inches high at the withers, strongly built, and of a hardy constitution. The great Pleistocene floods wiped out the species in the Americas, but it survived throughout Europe and Asia. One herd disappeared into the Mongolian wilderness and was not discovered until the last century, when the Russian explorer who found the herd lent it his name: *Equus przewalskii*.

By 4000 B.C. the first horses had been domesticated and were used for pulling carts. In Greece, circa 1700 B.C., the carts metamorphosed into the famous two-horse chariots of *Ben Hur*. Though these chariots were primarily instruments of war,

Greeks did race them on occasion and bred special horses in the Peloponnesus to pull them. Columbus reintroduced horses to North America on his second voyage in 1493, leaving behind some representative Andalusian stock in the West Indies. Horses soon became part of the cargo on almost every ship bound for the New World, and Amerindian tribes in Texas and New Mexico were quick to latch on to as many of them as they could. Apaches and Comanches raided Spanish encampments and traded stolen horses to more northerly tribes, as did French and Spanish traders (though less flamboyantly), and by 1730 even the Yakima in Washington owned stock.

The lightest, fastest, and in many ways finest descendants of *Eohippus* were by then to be found in North Africa. Two closely related types, the Arab and the Barb (for Barbary Coast, now Libya), had been inbred meticulously over centuries to maintain their purity and prepotency, that all-important ability to transmit signal characteristics to an offspring (called, in breeding terminology, *stamping the get*). In Africa the cult of noble blood was born. Never be hard on a fine horse, the Arabs said, for his nature will cause him to rebel. At night, out on the desert sands, the Arabs brought prized mounts into their tents and treated them like members of the family. Then there is the Saharan legend of the original horse breeder, Ishmael. A mare of Ishmael's gave birth to a filly who was too weak to keep up with the caravan, but rather than destroy the foal—her blood was noble—Ishmael ordered his men to wrap her in goatskin and carry her along. This saved her life but crippled her legs. She became known as the Crooked One, but in spite of her deformity she achieved high honor as the taproot, or base, mare for an excellent line of females, the *Benat el-A'waj,* Daughters of the Crooked One, who in turn became the *Kehila.* In Arabic Kehila means *purely* or *thoroughly* bred.

By the early sixteenth century horses were in short supply in England because so much stock had been lost during the War of the Roses. Henry VIII, a sportsman dependent on horses for hunting and tournaments, took measures to improve the situation. Primarily, he relied on neighboring countries for imports, which complemented an edict of his predecessor, Henry VII, who in 1496 had banned the export of stock from Britain. The accent was on speed and lightness, and away from the qualities embodied by a prior favorite, the great horse, a big strong animal bred for combat and capable of transporting a man-at-arms and sixty pounds of armor into a fray. Francesco Gonzaga, Marchese di Mantova, sent Henry broodmares and Barb stallions. Ferdinand of Aragon contributed two Spanish horses worth a thousand ducats; the gesture was so grand it caused speculation about Ferdinand's sanity. Over the years more and more Arabs and Barbs found their way into the king's stables at Greenwich. The Master of the Horse interbred them, and the offspring were raced in gentlemanly contests against horses from the stables of Henry's friends and acquaintances. Gradually this racing fever spread to the populace. When municipal race-courses like those at Chester, Newmarket, and Croyden opened, the demand for animals bred exclusively to race increased.

The problem of breeding such a horse fell to the wealthy and their studmasters. No real break-through occurred until by luck three exceptionally prepotent stallions arrived in Britain within a forty-year period. In 1688 Captain Byerley cap-tured at the siege of Vienna a handsome "Turk"—actually an Arab courser who'd been bought or stolen by the Turkish officer riding him—and brought him home; in 1704 Richard Darley pur-chased from Syrian friends in Aleppo a four-year-old Arabian and sent him to his brother in Yorkshire; and in 1730 the second earl of Go-dolphin acquired from Edward Coke of Derby-shire an Arabian who'd been foaled in Yemen and had once purportedly belonged to the King of France. From the get of these stallions, the three great thoroughbred bloodlines were created. Characteristics of the Godolphin Arabian were disseminated by Matchem (foaled in 1748) and those of the Byerley Tork by Herad (foaled in 1758). But the most important line proceeds from the Darley Arabian's relative Eclipse, born in 1764, the year of the great eclipse of the sun. Eclipse was a champion who won all his races without ever being whipped, spurred, or headed, and when he went to stud in 1771 he rode to the stables in a cart, so precious had he become. The moment was a triumphant one for *E. caballus*, reversing as it did the earliest images of domestication. The horse was in ascendance, fully pedigreed, the subject of oil paintings that hung above mantelpieces in the parlors of princes and magnates, captivating them just as its ancestors had captivated the cave dwellers at Lascaux.

This, then, was the thoroughbred, an offshoot of human longing, a particle of nature molded to fit within a construct, derived from Arabian stock tainted only slightly in couplings with royal mares and a few mares of mysterious and perhaps humble origins. But the progress from concept to flesh was not so orderly as some track historians make it sound. Breeding went on all over Britain, without much supervision or control, and the genealogical records of sires and broodmares were often confused or faked and sometimes unavailable. Names of horses were changed frequently, almost always when ownership changed, and were abbreviated or misspelled or otherwise fudged—Matchem was actually Match 'Em, and Herod more rightly *King* Herod. Occasionally the same name was bestowed on two or three animals in succession, father and son, mother and daughter. The terms Barb, Arab, and Turk were used interchangeably, and not every mare billed as "royal" came in fact from the king's stables. John Cheney, editor of *An Historical List of all Horse-Matches Run, And of all Plates and Prizes Run for in England in 1727*, the first known attempt at a stud book (a record of stallions' bloodlines and performances on the track), couldn't vouch for the accuracy of the pedigrees he included. A later competitor named Heber confessed in the preface to his *Calendar* that mistakes were unavoidable when cataloging genealogical data. Despite these complications the thoroughbred, simply by having been brought into existence, posed a new problem, that of refinement. How could breeders improve a horse's speed and stamina? They started with blood.

The blood of thoroughbreds is thick and hot, with more hemoglobin and red cells and a higher cell density than are found in ordinary horses, but it isn't the medium in which characteristics like speed and stamina are suspended or by which they're transmitted to offspring. Breeders in the days before Mendel thought it was. For them blood held the resonances of generations, all the secrets, and they were engaged in a perpetual search for a master formula to guide them in their tinkering. Their approach was alchemical. How do you extract the gold of a perfect racehorse from the base substances of sire and dam? What are the correct proportions? How much sprinter in the mix, how much router, and from which family? Darley Arabian's? Byerley Turk's?

Some breeders believed in telegony. In telegonic theory, a pregnant mare received infusions of the stallion's blood from her developing fetus, through "channels as yet unknown to Science,"

313

and retained even after foaling a few of the sire's precious traits. She could pass them along to subsequent foals even if they were the get of a different stallion. Her blood became twice-prized, hermaphroditic, offering breeders a double hit of male potency, a second set of masculine characteristecs for the price of one. Colonel Vuillers's dosage system was somewhat more sophisticated, but equally useless. Vuillers attempted to concoct a recipe for mixing blood in perfect ratio. He traced the history of each horse listed in the stud book of his day back through twelve generations, recording its four thousand ancestors. Patterns began to emerge, certain horses showing up time and again in the lineage of champions. Counting each ancestor as a unit of blood, Vuillers could then specify the right mix for, say, a speedy filly: combine 288 parts Birdcatch, 351 parts Touchstone, 186 parts Voltaire . . .

Mendelian genetics brought to a close the era of corpuscular mysticism, but breeders continued to look for a definitive way to predict the outcome of pairings. Though broodmares were known to be more effective than stallions at passing along their characteristics, most systems concentrated on studs and their ability to stamp their get. An exception was the Bruce Lowe system, which still has currency today. Lowe, an Englishmen, examined the pedigrees of the winners of three major English classics, the Derby, Oaks, and St. Leger, and traced them back in *female* line to their earliest known ancestors, as recorded in volume one of the stud book. The descendants of Tregonwell's Natural Barb Mare had won most often, so Lowe ranked this family first in importance. The descendants of Burton's Barb Mare were second-best at producing winners and became Bruce Lowe Family Number Two. In all Lowe ranked forty-three families. While his work was useful, pointing out the strengths and weaknesses of several lines, it was attacked immediately in the States. Americans protested the inherrent bias against United States-born or -bred mares (their foals seldom competed in European classics even if they were outstanding racehorses), and other breeders with mares who'd been slighted criticized Lowe for devising a system bound to perpetuate itself. His "prophecy" was self-fulfilling. Top-ranked mares would be bred to top-ranked stallions and naturally produce superior foals. Later on, experts poked holes in Lowe's research, but Lowe still has defenders in breeding circles, perhaps because he chose to focus on feminine principles in a world skewed radically toward the masculine.

Other breeding techniques have gone in and out of vogue as their results have been demonstrated on the track. Inbreeding, the practice of mating two closely related horses, maintains genetic purity and intensifies familial characteristics, both positive and negative, to varying degrees. A sire and a dam who share great speed and a nasty disposition may well yield a comet-like colt, but the colt might also be too troublesome to handle. Sometimes two families show an affinity for one another, called a nick, and breeding between family members produces excellent foals. But nicks are not infallible. The energy around them always dissipates, often in a single generation, and inferior specimens begin to issue. In the end there are no shortcuts, no formulas that have infallibly proven their worth over an extended period. When you talk to breeders they speak of simple commonsense principles. Use quality stock, they say. Learn your bloodlines. Watch for peculiarities. Does a stallion transmit more of his characteristics to his fillies than to his colts? Then he's a broodmare-sire. Cover your mares with stallions who'll complement them, supplying talents they lack, or try breeding speed to speed or stamina to stamina in hopes that the desired characteristic will be emboldened. There's not much else you can do, they mutter, moving dirt around with a boot tip, feeling handicapped because another force is a work and they can't quite get to it, something beyond eugenics, the crackling around the bodies of lovers bent on conceiving, heat lightning, what the mystic says in saying nothing: a hole in the smoke. Every now and then a breeder makes contact with this energy, harnessing it briefly.

# CAROL FLAKE

# The Hopeful

*The world of horse racing usually is depicted as tough, fast talking, and ruthless. However, as Carol Flake reminds us, beneath the brashness are hints of why the horse—and particularly the noble thoroughbred—holds a special place in mythology. Freedom, courage, "worldly longing," and a bond with the natural world are just a few of the qualities that horses represent. In this affecting piece Flake explains why she decided to leave the "clutter" of urban culture and become a part of the racing world. Her quest was to follow the development during one year of a two-year-old who might end up a contender for the Triple Crown—the Derby, the Preakness, and the Belmont. Racing's dark side is also here—the toll on the people and horses, what Flake calls the "pain/payoff quotient"—in the tragic death of the filly Ruffian.*

In the spring of 1984, I stopped worrying about culture and politics, about bombs and computers, and I began looking for a horse: not a horse to buy or even to ride, but a horse who would give me a quick getaway nonetheless. I was looking for a champion: a beast with a destiny, a horse who had been born in a year of biotech businesses and trivial pursuit, of space shuttles and designer jeans, who would somehow charge through all the clutter and emerge a hero.

The horse I was looking for was not an animal who could pull a plow or a carriage, who could prance in a show ring, who could cut cows from a herd. By birth and training, he would be able to do only one thing. He would be able, however, to do it better than any other kind of animal; he would be able to do it better than any other breed of horse; and better still than 99.9 percent of his own breed. He would be able to run very fast, carrying a human on his back.

Like nearly everybody involved with the business and sport of horse racing, I was looking for a thoroughbred who could win the Kentucky Derby.

This quest, however, had as much to do with Walter Farley, Robin Leach and Boethius as with Secretariat. It had something to do with the deep, mythic bond between human and horse; it had to do with America's morbid fascination with wealth and fame; and it also had to do with a dark, ironic element of fate that seems to set the world of horse racing apart from other endeavors.

Horse racing may have begun as the sport of kings and gentlemen, but it remains a humbling experience for most of those involved in it. Racing is a ride on the wheel of fortune, where money counts, but where neither wealth, hard work, nor social standing is any guarantee of success.

My quest for a Derby horse was a return, with a twist, to the dreams of my youth.

As a kid, I had never owned a real horse of my own, only an improvised hobby horse, a broomstick and stuffed sock, with a leather belt for reins and shreds of yarn sewed on for a mane. But that broomstick was my Bucephalus, on which I conquered the neighborhood; I was a centaur, both horse and rider, both beast and master. Sometimes I would run away with myself.

When I learned to read, I devoured anything that had to do with horses—my father's old collection of Will James books about the West, biographies of great racehorses like Exterminator and Black Gold, and of course Walter Farley's Black Stallion series. Farley's rogue stallion, an animal too fierce to be ridden by anyone except his young friend Alec, had little to do with the cute and cuddly creatures of the animal kingdom usually portrayed in children's books; he was something out of myth, more heroic than any human protagonist. And, it must be admitted, he was sexy: "His mane was like a crest, mounting, then falling low. His neck was long and slender, and arched to the small, savagely beautiful head. The head was that of the wildest of all wild creatures—a stallion born wild—and it was beautiful, savage, splendid." What's more, the Black could put his wildness to good use; he could win races.

All that wild splendor seemed too grand for the quiet little town where I grew up; it belonged to another world somewhere, another world I might find someday. A fast horse, I thought, could really take you places.

In the meantime I tried to get it all down on paper. Over and over, I tried to draw the ineffably regal and spirited creatures I dreamed about. Like the cave paintings at Lascaux, they were ritual beasts—magic animals that held the key to power and success.

Sometimes, when I was bored or lonely, I would conjure up an image of the perfect horse, the creature I could never get right on paper. When we would set out on long trips to my grandmother's farm in East Texas in the family station wagon, I would imagine myself riding alongside the car on my wild steed; sometimes I would become the horse rather than the rider, trying to imagine what it would be like to run that fast, so fast that the wind would bring tears to my eyes.

My grandmother had long since sold all her horses, so my only riding experiences had been on pony rides at various carnivals and fairs. The reins were always tied down, and the ponies were trained to plod calmly around a circle, so there wasn't much challenge involved. But a couple of times I managed to undo the restraints, and I had the ponies trotting snappily, their fat little bellies bouncing, before the irate managers could catch me.

One day, when I was nine years old or so, a horse

magically appeared in my grandmother's cow pasture: a big, shaggy colt with a piece of rope tied around his neck. I suggested to my friend Andrea, who had come along for her first visit to a farm, that we hop on the horse and go for a ride. We searched in vain for a bridle in the cobwebbed tack room in the abandoned barn where my grandparents had once stabled their draft horses. That was enough to discourage Andrea, who was always a sensible sort. But I felt certain that the horse had somehow materialized on the farm as an answer to my nightly prayers, and I was destined to ride him. I convinced Andrea that I was a terrific rider, an Indian-style veteran who had no need of saddle, bridle, or bit. Lugging an old milk-stool up beside the horse, who was grazing peacefully, I clambered aboard. Andrea climbed up behind me, and with a whoop we were off.

The horse moved directly into a gallop without benefit of a walk or trot, and we headed directly toward the barbed wire fence at the far end of the pasture. I clung to his mane, and Andrea clung to my waist. The horse was running flat out, like a racehorse, and the going was remarkably smooth, despite clumps of tall grass and weeds that loomed up along the way. When we seemed certain to crash into the fence, I yanked the horse's mane to the left, and he spun around neatly, executing a hairpin about-face. I hung on, but Andrea let go of my waist and went flying into the fence.

The strange horse and I galloped around and

around the pasture, until he wearied of the game and slowed to a walk. Andrea had extricated herself from the fence and gone for help. When my grandmother arrived, after daubing Andrea liberally with Mercurochrome, she told me that the horse I had commandeered was her neighbor's champion cutting horse, an extremely valuable quarter horse trained to herd cattle by running very fast and making very sharp turns.

And so it was that my dream horse proved to be as real as my friend's wounds. Unknowingly, I had encountered my first blood-and-money horse—a well-bred horse whose speed meant risk, whose ability meant gain. A horse who gave you the edge.

What was it that horses represented to me? Part of it undoubtedly was the kind of sublimated sexuality that makes men smile knowingly when you talk about girls and horses. A lot of young girls do "grow out" of their horse fever when they get interested in boys—hence the stereotyped notion, as poet Maxine Kumin has described it, that "girl children long to sit astride the muscular power and rhythmic motion of a horse out of deep sexual urges," a longing that eventually is redirected "toward its natural object of fulfillment, the adolescent boy." Horses, in a sense, suggest to a young girl the kind of sensual intimacy that might exist between living beings, a relationship based on body language—on touch and trust.

Horses, however, also represented another impulse as primal as sex—a desire to be linked to the natural world. To be linked with an element of wildness, and yet to retain a measure of control.

Farley's proud horses, forever wild, suggested the kind of primal power D. H. Lawrence had been so obsessed by: "Horses, always horses . . . You were a lord if you had a horse. Far back, far back in our dark soul the horse prances. He is a dominant symbol: he gives us lordship . . . And as a symbol he roams the dark underworld meadows of the soul." Without the horse, Lawrence felt, man had lost touch with something vital and became diminished: "Within the last fifty years man has lost the horse. Now man is lost. Man is lost to life and power—an underling and a wastrel."

I think horses meant the same thing to me that "horsepower" did to many boys and men—they meant freedom. Like the spotted horses that ran amok in Faulkner's *The Hamlet,* the horses that roamed my imagination challenged the boundaries between the "wild" and the "domestic."

Prancing and snorting on the edges of our consciousness, like vestiges of a myth, certain horses seem to suggest a means of venturing out into the world and conquering it. And racehorses, with their inordinate will to win, represent the ultimate symbol of worldly longing. With racehorses, whether you own them, watch them, or bet on them, you seem to be reverting to some older, darker way of looking at the world, a way of testing your fate, of finding your place in the scheme of things.

Horses can be great equalizers. Put a short man on a horse, and you have a king, a conqueror, or a jockey; Louis XIV, Napoleon, or Willie Shoemaker. According to a medieval bestiary dating from the twelfth century, *equus,* the Latin word for horse, is derived from a word meaning "level" or equal. But as the bestiary's anonymous monk goes on to explain, horses, like their masters, want to win: "The spiritedness of horses is great. They exult in battlefields, they sniff the combat; they are excited to fight by the sound of the trumpet . . . They are miserable when conquered and delighted when they have won." Consequently horses have also been a means and a symbol of lordship.

As Diana Vreeland put it in an explanatory note to her 1985 "Man and the Horse" exhibit at New York's Metropolitan Museum, "A man mounted on his horse is twice the man he is on the ground." Virtually the entire exhibit was given over to the engraved armor, the tricorne hats, the whips, the crops, the crested livery and the racing silks that have made the horse a mount of the ruling class.

The Arabian horse had given Muslims the means to conquer North Africa and to invade southern Europe, while the invention of the stirrup gave Charles Martel and his Franks a means to defeat them at the beginning of the age of chivalry—an age inspired by the horse. And eventually the fast, long-winded horses that the British bred by crossing their big, sturdy mares to the light, swift Arabians became the most aristocratic of all horses—the thoroughbred.

A good thoroughbred can still make a commoner a kind of king. Racing in America, which grew out of county fairs, tobacco-field challenges, and wild duels through colonial streets, continued to pay homage to the English stud book—the family Bible of the thoroughbred, in which the pedigree of every thoroughbred in England had been inscribed since 1793. Americans themselves might betray a mongrel pedigree, but their race-horses could trace their ancestry back to the same three foundation sires as their English counterparts. And America named its most famous race after an English peer—Lord Derby, for whom the English Derby had been named in 1771.

Nevertheless, winning the Triple Crown of racing—the Derby, the Preakness, and the Belmont—has become a very American sort of quest, a quest begun by sporting tycoons, the would-be lords of the American turf, and continued in recent years by men and women with new money and new ways of approaching the game. Long before the Super Bowl, the World Series, and the Indianapolis 500, winning the Derby meant reaching the pennacle of the sports world. And yet, except for the Derby, racing has never attracted the kind of broad public interest that such all-American sports as baseball and football have amassed. Racing, which, after all, involves a form of gambling, has been considered a game of kings and touts, with very little social ground in between. There have always been more Puritans than cavaliers in America.

Racing, too, has had few stars of any longevity to attract a following the way baseball and football do. Every year, racing may have its prodigies—its Dwight Goodens and its Darryl Strawberrys—but its Reggie Jacksons have long since been retired. Except for the great geldings like Kelso, Forego, and John Henry, the best horses are rushed off the track to the breeding shed at age three or four, to "improve the breed," before they can progress from star to legend. Frequently, because they begin running at such a tender age, they retire with the ankles and the knees of disabled veterans.

There was a long, dry spell for equine horses between Native Dancer, the gray ghost, in 1953, and Secretariat, the chestnut cover boy of three different news magazines when he won the Triple Crown in 1973. And there has been another dry spell since 1980, when the mighty Spectacular Bid went undefeated in his fourth year and the stalwart Genuine Risk became the first filly since Regret, in 1915, to win the Derby.

My own interest in racing, which survived puberty and survived college, had not, however, survived a terrible accident that occurred on the track in 1975. Like millions of other Americans, I had tuned in on a bright July afternoon to watch a match race between Derby winner Foolish Pleasure and Ruffian, the undefeated filly champion. Ruffian, who had won the New York Racing

Association's Triple Crown for fillies by a combined total of 25 lengths, was perhaps the greatest filly in the history of American racing. The fillies of her generation had never been able to challenge her, and so it seemed a natural step for her to take on the fastest colt of her generation.

Ruffian had come along at the height of the feminist movement, and she had become a symbol of achievement to many women. And oddly enough, she aroused the kind of resentment among certain men on the track as feminists had in the business community. One trainer was heard to say, "No filly can run that fast; she must be a dyke." And so, in that match race, there were those who were rooting against her, just on principle.

And so, when Ruffian, who was leading the race by half a length near the half-mile pole, snapped her right front ankle in two but kept running, her body propelled, stumbling, in fear and pain, the late Moody Jolley, known on the backstretch as the meanest man in racing, was heard to say, "You throw a fast half-mile at the bitch, and she comes unbuckled." And so, at a subsequent press conference, Moody's son Leroy, the trainer of Foolish Pleasure, did not express his regrets, but said that racing was not for those who wear "short pants."

At the time, Ruffian seemed to symbolize, in the most tragic fashion, what might happen to talented females who tried to keep up with the boys. But in retrospect, I think her death had less to say about feminism than it had to say about racing: about human hubris, which had created a breed of horse so fast, so beautiful, and yet so fragile.

Eventually I learned that men, too, had been affected by Ruffian's death—sportswriters, in particular, who had come to think of her as some kind of super-horse, a vision of strength and grace. Jack Mann, who wrote Ruffian's obituary for the *Horseman's Journal,* and who had stayed up all night after the accident while the vets tried to save her, said that "she was as special as Willie Mays. There was an extra dimension to her." When she had gone out to the track before the race, he said, "she was like a young girl, so strong and fresh. And when they brought her back, she looked like an old lady." He prefaced her obituary with lines from Coleridge's "Epitaph on an Infant":

> Ere Sin could blight or Sorrow fade,
> Death came with friendly care.

Before Ruffian's death, I had ignored the dark side of racing—the toll it takes on horses, on those who love them, on those who depend on them for a living. I had finally learned what race-trackers learn from day one: the pain/payoff quotient. For every winner there are scores of losers; for every victory there is a heavy cost.

With Ruffian, the cost, I think, had been the momentum of the sport. Two years earlier, Secretariat's remarkable achievements had gotten people interested in racing again. But her death had told the public that racing wasn't for people in "short pants." It wasn't, in other words, for those who loved animals; it was for cool-headed gamblers, for professionals who could look at horses as numbers or chances in a lottery. Racing, always precariously balanced between sport and game of chance, seemed to belong now more completely to the world of casinos than to the world of ballparks and playing fields.

Sportswriters who had allowed themselves to get attached to certain horses found themselves backing away. One sportswriter told me that after Ruffian he never again allowed himself to care for a horse. Suddenly a huge audience had learned the hardest lessons racing can teach about the cruelty of fortune, the overreaching nature of man, the fleeting nature of success. It was not a lesson that mainstream America was interested in learning in such a fashion.

I didn't get interested in horse racing again until the summer after I had lost a job in New York. I had been fired by an elderly bon vivant who scribbled his criticism of my work in purple Magic Marker memos and who would call for his assistant every day before lunch to bring in his raspberry yogurt and to tie a purple bib around his neck. This man and I had different priorities, beginning with our choice of favorite colors. At the time, I was interested in the farm crisis, country music, the political peccadillos of television preachers, while my mauve-mad boss was hot for the latest scandal behind the baffles at the New York City Ballet.

I had climbed my way up from my sleepy Texas hometown into a high-profile New York publishing job, only to find that my real roots and my priorities lay elsewhere.

I had grown uneasy in the trendy cafes and style emporiums of New York, and I dreaded the apotheosis of the upscale, gourmet-kitchen consumers who would later that year be labeled as Yuppies. I dreaded the possiblity that I had become part of a poached-peaches-and-Gucci tide. I found myself longing for a world where men with purple Magic Markers had no power, where almond croissants had no cachet.

If I had been younger, and if I had lived in a different time, I might even have thought about running away to the circus. But this was an era when daredevils were dwarfed by their Super Dome arenas, and lion tamers made silly television commercials for American Express.

I had forgotten about the places where grownups could still run away, where men and women rode untamed animals, where fortunes could be made in a day.

And so it was that, twenty years after the magic cutting horse had made my fantasies come true, horses came to my rescue again. While recuperating from urban malaise in my rented shack in the Berkshires, I used to drive past a sign proclaiming that horse racing would be taking place for two weeks at the Great Barrington Fair. The setting was wonderful—a small bullring of a track, a rickety grandstand, and a mountain backdrop.

Out of curiosity, my boyfriend and I showed up for the races one afternoon. We didn't buy a *Racing Form*, figuring that the horses were so old and decrepit that knowledge of previous performances would be of little help. Gradually, though, we got hooked on the strange menagerie of animals that filled the backstretch of Great Barrington's fairgrounds, and we found ourselves returning every afternoon.

Some of the horses boasted excellent bloodlines, with sires even I could recognize. There was the gorgeous Zation, a strutting chestnut who looked as though he should be running at Saratoga instead of the fair circuit, but who lacked the lungs and the courage to win even a cheap claiming race; ancient Trumpeter Swan, of royal breeding, who had won some big races and more than a quarter of a million dollars earlier in his career, but who was now grinding it out week by week; the reliable Prince Jac O, who could never have won at a respectable track but who won five in a row at Great Barrington.

This bizarre collection of backyard pets, winded losers and aging veterans astonished me with their courage and willingness. They tore around the track as though their lives depended on it—which, in many cases, it did, since the fairs were the last stop before the glue factory or meat-packing plant for many worn-out horses. The previous year, I learned, a Connecticut plant had cleaned out the

331

fairs to fill a huge demand for canned horsemeat in France.

Thoroughbreds, it seemed to me, had experienced, more than any other creature, the heights and depths of human stewardship. They had played the role of king, king-bearer, or sacrificial lamb, depending on the needs of those who owned them. The world they belonged to seemed an older, more primitive world than the one where I had made my way—a world of quests and exploitation, of great victories and unexpected tragedies. It was a feudal world of lords and serfs, of wealthy owners and track-bound grooms, where one's destiny was determined less by hard work or money than by bloodlines and the whims of fate.

Every day owners and horseplayers alike were trying to beat the odds, trying to make the payoff before the pain or the losses became too great. For every Secretariat, there were a million Zations, and there were a million long shots who never came in.

Some horseplayers, however, claimed to have found the clue to all mysteries, the edge that would finally beat the game. And there were newcomers to the sport who were trying to minimize the fateful element of racing, to make it conform to rules of supply and demand, to the cost/benefit models they had learned in business school or in making their fortunes in ship-building, oil exploration, computer design. Others were applying the most practical strategy of all—using OPM,

Other People's Money, to invest in horses. The sport of kings and tycoons was becoming a business of multiple partnerships and syndicates.

Eventually the horses that had drawn me away from Madison Avenue, to Kentucky and Saratoga, let me back to Wall Street and Seventh Avenue. The marketing of thoroughbreds, like the marketing of art, was a speculative business that depended on brokers who could sell their product to high rollers and investment-seekers on the basis of promise rather than substance. The thoroughbred breeding business depended on the buyer's willingness to gamble, balanced against his desire for a good investment or his desire for prestige.

And yet there was still one great quest, one great dream, that set racing apart from all other pursuits, that kept everything going, from grooms who scraped by on $225 a week to breeders who paid half a million dollars for one mating of a mare to the stallion Northern Dancer. It was the hope for a classic horse—for a fast, precocious two-year-old who would be able at age three to extend his speed for the grueling mile-and-a-quarter of the Derby, the mile-and-three-sixteenths speed trap of the Preakness, and the mile-and-a-half marathon of the Belmont.

I decided that I wanted to be part of such a quest, to hitch a vacarious ride on the wheel of fortune. And so, in the spring of 1984, I began looking for a young thoroughbred with the "look of eagles"; a contender.

My plan was to follow this "chosen" colt for

the most crucial year in his life, from his debut as a two-year-old through his campaign for the Triple Crown. The odds of finding such a colt, I knew, were very high. Out of the 38,483 registered thoroughbreds born in 1982, only a dozen or so would make it to the Derby in 1985.

Even choosing a colt that became two-year-old champion would be no guarantee of success. After Spectacular Bid, the only top two-year-old to make it as far as the starting gate of the Derby had been a plucky gelding named Rockhill Native, who never managed to win a big race longer than a mile. And even as I was beginning my search, Devil's Bag, the most promising young horse in recent years, was showing signs of imminent failure; he never made it to the Derby.

I began calling my hypothetical colt the Hopeful, after the big race for two-year-olds at Saratoga that had been won by so many promising young horses who had gone on to prove themselves: Man o' War, Native Dancer, Nashua, Secretariat, Affirmed.

I knew I was going to have to do a great deal of hoping once I chose my horse. I was going to have to hope that he would stay sound, that he would stay healthy, and that he would stay a contender—three wishes that seldom came true for the owners and trainers of young horses. The stressful, high-stakes road to the Derby tested horses and their handlers alike, and few proved equal to the test.

I was hoping, too, that my chosen horse could

help me outdistance the deadening ambitions of the overly networked, overly analyzed, and overly jazzercised world from which I had grown so alienated, a world that had lost its connectedness not only to the earth but to the spirit. The Hopeful was to become my getaway horse, a flesh-and-blood hero who would lead me in a quest through the strange, self-enclosed world of the track, a quest for the sense of wildness and wonder I had lost so long ago.

# RED SMITH

# The Belmont Starts with George

*A behind-the-scenes study of the man responsible for pressing the button to start one of the most celebrated racing events in America, the Belmont Stakes. The starter must intuit the exact second when all horses and riders are ready to go. A clean start is what George Cassidy was after, and it appears he had a special gift for taking in the whole confusing scene in one all-encompassing look, and knowing when the time was right. Cassidy had followed in his father's footsteps, the well-known starter Mars Cassidy, pushed into his first race when he substituted for Mars at age twenty-two. Although George had simply shut his eyes and let the horses go, the stewards were amazed at the skillful start—and this marked the beginning of a notable career.*

George Bennett Cassidy, ruddy, smiling and faultlessly tailored, climbs a short flight of stairs beside the inner rail at Belmont Park and stands watching while assistants lead the horses into the starting gate. The moment the doors are closed, four or five urgent voices rise: "No, boss, not yet!" "No chance, boss!" "Not ready!" Almost immediately, Cassidy's thumb presses the button at the end of an insulated cord. A strident bell rings, doors fly open with a metallic clang, the jockeys whoop like Comanches. They're off in the Belmont Stakes.

"In gate at 5:35," the chart in Sunday morning's paper will report. "Off at 5:35, Eastern dayight time. Start good." With only minor variations, charts have been saying this about every Belmont since June 7, 1930, when Cassidy sent a field of four away and saw Gallant Fox come home in possession of the Triple Crown.

George Cassidy has let horses go from walkup starts, from a belt of webbing stretched across the track, from the Australian barrier—six strands of rope designed to trip horses and strangle jockeys —and from the infernal machines that were the immediate precursors of today's electric gate. Five times while Belmont Park was closed for reconstruction he started the stakes on Aqueduct's stretch turn, where a race of a mile and a half had to begin on a track measuring a mile and an eighth.

"Start good," forty-two of the charts reported. "Start good for all but Determined Man," read the single exception in 1964 when Bill Boland's mount reared just as Cassidy hit the switch.

In Cassidy's time the Belmont has had as few as three starters—in 1931 when only Sun Meadow and Jamestown chased Twenty Grand—and as many as 13—in 1954 and 1971. If Secretariat can add this race to his Kentucky Derby-Preakness double he will become the first Triple Crown winner in 25 years, so Cassidy will take special pains to get a clean start.

He does not anticipate trouble, even though Secretariat is habitually nonchalant leaving the gate. "I can't remember any Belmont that was trouble," he said yesterday, "since the early days before we had the gate. There's just a little more tension than the ordinary race. I guess the year Canonero was here [1971] was our biggest field, plus the fact that there were so many of those South Americans hopping around.

"Canonero was supposed to be a bad actor in the gate. They had to blindfold him and load him last, but in New York we load 'em by post position, from the inside out. We blindfolded Canonero but loaded him seventh, when his turn came. Once he was standing, we took the blindfold off and he never made a move."

It doesn't worry Cassidy that $6-million or more may be riding on the races he starts Saturday. He is a blithe spirit, as patient as he is good-humored, and responsibility rests lightly on those exquisitely groomed shoulders.

Experiance has polished a gift that Eddie Arcaro likens to the split vision of a quarterback surveying all his receivers in one glance. "He seems to sense the instant when a bad horse is going to stand," the former jockey says. "Sometimes, sitting on a skittish 2-year-old in the old Widener Chute, I'd marvel at how he could get 28 of us off together."

Maybe this is because Cassidy, like Secretariat, was bred for his job. In 1890 his father, Mars, who owned and trained thoroughbreds and trotters, was pressed into service as starter at Iron Hill, a Maryland track now lost from memory. In 1903 Mars was invited to New York, and he worked the big wheel until his death in 1929.

Mars was distinguished by a high bowler hat, handlebar mustaches, a temper that boiled at 98.6 degrees and a vocabulary that would bring blushes to the foredeck of a Portuguese freighter. All three of his sons worked as his assistants but only George stayed with it. Marshall became a steward and Jockey Club official highly influential on the national scene. A variety of adventures at the post convinced Wendell that his future lay in the oil fields.

Once, as occasionally happens with a horse notoriously reluctant to start, Wendell was assigned to stand behind a sluggard and encourage him with a bullwhip. He slipped his wrist through the thong at the butt of the whip and, on signal, fetched the steed a manly swat. The lash took a half-hitch round the horse's tail.

"Wendell went the first eighth in a little better than 12," George says, "before the whip pulled free."

When George was 22 and schooled in esoteric wiles like biting a rogue's ear to make him stand, the stewards at Saratoga sent word for him to start the first race in the absence of his father, who had been unavoidably detained. In those days, a talent for beating the start was esteemed as the loftiest refinement of the equestrian art. Riding in the first race were Pony McAtee, Laverne Fator, Earl Sande, Mack Garner and Jim Burke, all capable of removing a starter's coat and vest without getting caught.

They walked up to the tape, George shut his eyes and let them go. The stewards couldn't believe their binoculars. It was the best start of the meeting. The stewards didn't know that on the way to the post the desperadoes had made a compact: "Good kid, young Cassidy. Give him a break." After that beginning it was inevitable that George would succeed his father.

Soon after he did, an owner named Reilly demanded that his horse be removed from the schooling list of bad actors forbidden to start until their manners at the post improved. "We had Prohibition then," Cassidy says, "with rumrunners and hijackers, and this Reilly belonged to the armpit artillery. He said he'd make it tough for me. His horse stayed on the list but I had Reilly insomnia for a few weeks."

As far as the jocks were concerned, all friendship ceased when the Cassidy kid officially became The Man. The first to test him was Earl Sande. He tried to beat the barrier and Cassidy gave him a five-day suspension. He tried again and got five days more. This cost him a stakes assignment on Gallant Fox.

"I stopped in a butcher shop," Cassidy says, "and here was this guy with a white apron and red arms, a horseplayer, whacking up a side of beef with a cleaver and saying how he'd like to get his hands on the louse that took Sande off Gallant Fox. I took my business elsewhere."

# WILLIAM NACK

## Secretariat: The Making of a Champion

*The stunning physical beauty of the regal Secretariat and his extraordinary track record—winning over one million dollars during his two-year career —earned him the title of "horse of the century." Capturing the imagination of the general public as few race horses have, Secretariat became a client of the William Morris advertising agency and one of the most photographed horses in history. Unlike other big winners on the track Secretariat's speed and will to win were not at first obvious when he began his training as a plump two-year-old. Speed is bred into a thoroughbred's bloodline but learning to relax amidst the noise and crowding of the field of horses, taking the bit, falling into a rhythm of running, and "leveling out" and reaching for the ground are all qualities that must be taught to the budding race horse through daily sessions with jockeys. Here William Nack gives us a sampling of this "aesthetic marvel's" schooling and a description of why the accolades were deserved.*

The van door opened in Florida on that January

day of 1972, and Secretariat first stepped foot on the racetrack at Hialeah Park.

Like Bold Ruler, Secretariat emerged into a new kind of world, insular, superstitous, and perpetually on the make, a world forever in bivouac— whole armies of grooms and hot walkers, exercise boys and trainers and jockeys' agents, feed men peddling alfalfa and medicine men with horse aspirins weighing sixty grains, clockers and jockeys —ready on a moment to move on to other tracks, north to Maryland, New York, New Jersey, California, or Chicago.

Flies on all the windowsills, rows of stalls in rows of barns, hooves clicking on cement, metal gates clanging, springs whining, liniments and alcohol for rubbing, a pint of whiskey holstered like a wallet in the pocket, tips hot at six o'clock in the morning, lukewarm at three, cold at dinner over ham hocks or enchiladas.

As a young two-year-old—plump as he was off the farm—Secretariat had begun to grow into an aesthetic marvel of anatomical slopes and bulges, curves and planes that were stressed and set off by the color of his coat, a reddish gold that ran almost to copper. His shoulders were deep, his bone of good length, and there was no lightness of bone under the knee, as Miss Ham once suggested there might be. He had a sloping rump, the imprimatur of the Nearco tribe, and the slightly dished face of an Arabian. The quality of his head and face set him apart at once from many other Bold Rulers, including Bold Ruler himself.

His sire was coarse about the head, with the jug-headedness common to trotters, and transmitted this trait to not a few of his offspring.

Secretariat didn't inherit Bold Ruler's lengthiness; he was shorter of back, more barrel chested and muscular in his physical development. But he had what Bull Hancock regarded as a mark of quality in all the Bold Rulers that could run. "You can pick the Bold Rulers out on their conformation," Bull once said. "I see the same musculature as Nasrullah. They all had an extra layer of muscle beside their tail running down to their hocks. It is a good sign when you see it in a Bold Ruler. It means strength and speed."

All he had was physique in the beginning, the look of an athlete. Lucien Laurin was wary of appearances. In his years spent on the racetrack, he had seen too many equine glamor boys come and go. To Laurin, Secretariat was just another untried thoroughbred.

To jockey Ron Turcotte, he was a potential mount, no more than that. The day after Secretariat arrived from the farm, Turcotte was at the barn at Hialeah, where he worked mornings exercising horses for Laurin. He walked up the shed to see Riva Ridge and glancing down the barn, two stalls away from his Kentucky Derby favorite, he saw the white star, the ears pricked forward, and the neck a mass of red. Secretariat was glancing back at him

Turcotte went to the stall, took a closer look, and called up the shed to Henny Hoeffner, the assistant trainer. It was the first time Turcotte ever saw Secretariat, whom he described as "a pretty boy."

Penny Tweedy, when she first saw him said, simply, "Wow!"

But the game is a horse race, not a horse show, and the axiom among horsemen is: "Pretty is as pretty does." Secretariat, in the opening weeks, did not do much.

He didn't awe the clockers with the bursts of speed that Bold Ruler loosed at Hialeah as a youngster. There were no quarter-mile workouts in 0:22, no leveling off into a flat run, all business, from the quarter pole at the top of the stretch to the wire. He was still the overgrown kid.

Ron Turcotte was with Lucian Laurin one morning at Hialeah when four two-year-olds were let from the barn and began circling them, grooms holding the bridles.

Turcotte jumped aboard Secretariat that morning for the first time, guiding him out to the racetrack with the others in Indian file, reaching the dirt track and turning right, counterclockwise. Laurin told them to let the youngsters gallop easily, side by side, in a schooling exercise designed to accustom them to having other horses running next to them. The drill was the same as Secretariat had done two months earlier, under Bailes, at the farm. The four colts took off at a slow gallop around the mile-and-an-eighth oval, galloping abreast. The riders stood high in the saddle, going easily, Secretariat almost lackadaisically. The red horse plopped along in casual indifference, his head down, a big, awkward, and clumsy colt, Turcotte thought. Galloping past the palm trees and the infield lake, jockey Miles Neff, riding Twice Bold, reached his stick over and slapped Turcotte on the rump. Turcotte yelled. There was laughter on the backstretch. With Charlie Davis riding inside him on All or None, Turcotte leaned over and jammed Davis in the butt with his stick. Davis almost went over All or None, screaming. This was not all intended for fun. Exercise boys often do this to get young horses accustomed to quick movement, to shouts, to noise, to horse racing.

The colt next to Secretariat drifted out and banged against him and the red horse countered with a grunt.

He didn't alter course, drifting back and taking up the same path he had before the bumping. "He was just a big likeable fellow," Turcotte said. "His attitude was 'Stay out of my way.' " But they didn't. The colt beside him came out again, side-swiping him a second time.

Turcotte remembered the same drill a year before on Riva Ridge. The rangy bay was timid, shy, and leery of all contact. If Riva Ridge had been sideswiped like that when he was a young two-year-old, he would have leaped the fence to get away. Not this one.

Ron Turcotte liked him instantly because he was "a big clown," likable and unruffled among crowds, a handsome colt who relaxed while on the racetrack, who behaved himself, going as kindly as if out in the morning for a playful romp in the Florida sun.

Secretariat became the most popular of the baby two-year-olds to gallop, and one after another the exercise boys and jockeys who worked for Laurin climbed on him. There was Cecil Paul, a thirty-year-old jockey from Trinidad, who jumped aboard one morning and remembered hearing Lucien tell him, "He's a nice colt, Mr. Paul, and he's just a baby. You take care of him."

Mr. Paul galloped Secretariat frequently on those balmy mornings. On his back went Miles Neff, too, the jockey who was about to retire after thirteen years of knocking about on racetracks, and off went he and the colt into an easy gallop.

Neff especially liked the way he moved, feeling something a rider feels after straddling many horses over many years. Part of it had to do with size and strength, but some of it was just a feeling, a sense. "This is your best two-year-old, Mr. Laurin," Neff said one morning, as he slid off Secretariat.

As the days chased one another like colts in a pasture, Secretariat's bearing, his ease and kindliness, increased his popularity among the exercise boys until they were actually competing for his stirrups. Gold Bag, a youngster owned by Lucien Laurin, was quicker on his feet but he was headstrong—rank and speed crazy—often trying to run away with riders in the morning. Twice Bold pulled so hard on the reins that riders used to dismount rubbing the soreness in their arms. All or None, the filly, would buck, jump, kick, spin, and wheel; no one wanted to ride her. "Everyone wanted to gallop Secretariat," Turcotte said. "All you had to do was sit there." As the days passed, Cecil Paul felt him begin to take hold of the bit.

That was pivotal. Turcotte also felt the colt lean against the bit, fall into it, grab it in his mouth, and run against it in a communion transmitted from mouth to hands through the lines stretched taut between them.

"You want to make him think he's doing something, so you sit against him, take a hold of him, and make him think he's doing everything on his own. You have to build his ego. You have to give him confidence," Turcotte said.

Not even confidence came easily for the red horse. In late February Laurin boosted Turcotte on Secretariat for a quarter-mile workout, not an easy gallop but a speed drill, in company with Gold Bag, Twice Bold, and a colt named Young Hitter. It was time to teach them how to run, how to level out and reach for ground, something all horses have to learn.

"No race riding, boys!" Lucien called out to the four as they walked their horses to the racetrack that morning, through Sunny Fitzsimmons Lane and out the quarter-mile bend under the spanking brightness of the morning. The four riders reached the racetrack and moved into a gallop around the turn. They headed for the three-eighths pole at the top of the stretch, then pulled to a stop, lining up abreast and walking several yards. Then they clucked to their horses and went into a jog, picking up speed slowly.

Nearing the quarter pole, the four riders chirped again and the horses started leveling and reaching out, bodies lower to the ground. Twice Bold, Gold Bag, and Young Hitter accelerated rapidly, gathering speed from a gallop to a run as they raced past the quarter pole at the top of the straight.

Turcotte picked up Secretariat's reins and chirped to him, trying to give the colt a feel for the game, not yelling, but urging quietly. He sensed bewilderment in the colt, so he gathered Secretariat together and gave him time to steady himself and get his legs under him, synchronized and meshing. The three others blew away from him. Far up the racetrack, as Secretariat battled along by himself down the stretch, Turcotte saw the three more precocious horses far down the lane as Secretariat started to find himself and gather momentum.

They all dusted Secretariat easily that morning, beating him by about fifteen lengths and racing the quarter mile in 0:23. Secretariat finished in about 0:26.

Periodically, as Secretariat worked out in Florida, Penny Tweedy would ask Laurin about the red horse, and he hardly reflected buoyant hope.

"He hasn't shown me much," Lucien would say. Or, "He's not ready. I have to get the fat off him first." Or, "I have to teach him to run. He's big, awkward, and doesn't know what to do with himself."

Secretariat was beaten more than once in workouts that winter at Hialeah. Gold Bag beat him again. So did Twice Bold and All or None, the filly. So did a colt named Angle Light, a two-year-old bay owned by Edwin Whittaker, a Toronto electronics executive. He wasn't beaten by fifteen lengths again, but the crowd of young horses did beat him by five lengths another time.

Riva Ridge remained the luminary of the Meadow barn. The champion worked sharply for the seven-furlong Hibiscus Stakes March 22, and when he won it briskly coming off the pace, Laurin honed him for the Everglades Stakes—the same race won by Citation twenty-four years earlier—on April 1. That was the day Turcotte sensed a change in Secretariat during a workout. The track was muddy that morning when Laurin put Turcotte on the red horse, Neff on Angle Light, and Charlie Davis on All or None. The filly had thrown Turcotte earlier, so Laurin put Davis, a strong and experienced exercise boy, on her.

He told them he wanted them to work an easy three-eighths of a mile.

It was about eight o'clock. It had been raining heavily earlier in the day, but it had lightened to a drizzle by the time the set of horses headed down the backstretch to the three-eights pole, midway through the turn for home. About seventy yards from the pole, in unison, the riders took hold of the reins and eased their horses toward the rail, keeping them about five feet out. Turcotte could feel Secretariat fall against the bit, heavy-headedly, and he could see a horse on each side of him. He eased down in the saddle. The tempo picked up as the horses raced past the three-eighths pole and banked into the stretch. Suddenly the horse on the inside of Secretariat drifted out, glancing off his side.

Turcotte steadied Secretariat. Recovering from the bump, the red horse started slowing down, easing himself back. Turcotte reached forward with his whip and waved it in front of the colt's right eye and he picked it up again, slipping back into the breach. He stayed there through the run down the lane, striding hard against the bit to the wire, finishing head and head with the others in 0:36, breathing easily, a sharp move for young two-year-olds in the mud at Hialeah. They had run at a perfect "twelve-clip." It was a fast workout. Secretariat was learning how to run.

Running times vary considerably from track to track, from condition to condition, and according to the sex and age of the horses, so what is fast is relative. But most horsemen agree that horses are stretching out on a fast track when they run a furlong—a distance of 220 yards or one-eighth of a mile—in 0:12. When horses string a few 0:12 furlongs back to back, they are moving at what horsemen call a "twelve-clip."

A twelve-clip is the rate of speed horses must

average or maintain to win major stakes races at American middle and classic distances, distances from a mile to a mile and a quarter.

Most horses, even young two-year-olds like Secretariat, Angle Light, and All or None, should be able to run at a twelve-clip for a few furlongs—at least four.

That means they would be running one-eighth of a mile in 0:12, one-quarter in 0:24, three-eighths in 0:36, a half mile in 0:48.

At that rate of speed, a horse would run six furlongs, or three-quarters of a mile, in 1:12, which would win races on some tracks. If a horse strung two more furlongs together at a twelve-clip, he would be running a mile in 1:36, a time that equals or betters the clocking for six of the dozen runnings of the $50,000-Added Jerome Handicap at Belmont Park between 1961 and 1972. The degree of difficulty in sustaining a twelve-clip beyond a mile, unlike sustaining it from four furlongs in 0:48 to five furlongs in one minute, increases in quantum jumps. The degree of difficulty increases vastly beyond a mile.

For another furlong in 0:12 would send a horse a mile and an eighth, or nine furlongs, in 1:48, a clocking that would have won every running of the $100,000 Wood Memorial since it was run at that distance in 1952. And another 0:12-second furlong would send a horse a mile and a quarter in 2:00 flat, which was the Kentucky Derby record set by Northern Dancer in 1964; and a mile and three-eighths in 2:12, two and one-fifth seconds faster than Man o' War's American record; and a mile and a half in 2:24.

That workout was the first time Turcotte could sense that the big clown had any ability at all, any speed. He fell against the bit and ran with two fast youngsters, handling the mud well, handling it better than Riva Ridge did that afternoon in the Everglades Stakes.

Hemmed in on the rail with no place to go, bumping the rail in the stretch, and never getting near the lead, Riva Ridge finished fourth in the race, the first time he had been beaten since the summer of '71. Laurin said he was grateful to get the horse back in one piece. Turcotte was sharply criticized for his ride in the race, and Penny and Lucien talked about firing him and finding another rider. But the big races were coming up, so they decided to keep him on the colt.

It would not be the last time that Turcotte nearly lost a Meadow Stable mount.

It was nearing the time of the spring classics, and Riva Ridge was shipped north to Lexington, Kentucky, for the Blue Grass Stakes on April 27, his final prep race for the May 6 Kentucky Derby. Secretariat and several stablemates were vanned north to Long Island and to Barn 5 at Belmont Park, an indoor shed with a row of stalls that abutted the fence of the clubhouse parking lot. Barn 5 lay just 200 yards from the main track, the biggest oval in America—at one and one half miles in circumference—and there the humdrum of routine began.

In their first workout in New York that year, Angle Light and Gold Bag beat Secretariat badly on a sloppy racetrack, running a half mile in 0:49. Secretariat ran in 0:50 1/5 with urging, not a sharp move. A fifth of a second is equal to a length, so Gold Bag and Angle Light beat him by six.

In mid-April, on a gray wet morning when the track was a mire, apprentice jockey Paul Feliciano, who worked under contract for Lucien, hopped aboard Secretariat for a routine gallop on the training track about a quarter mile away.

Feliciano had his feet out of the stirrups, dangling them at Secretariat's side, when Laurin spotted him and raised his voice in warning.

"Put your feet in the irons!" he yelled. "Be careful with that horse! Don't take no chances. He plays and he'll drop you, I swear to God."

Feliciano's feet rose into the stirrups, which he was wearing too short, and someone dimly recalled Laurin's calling to Feliciano, "Drop your irons." What Laurin wanted Feliciano to do was lengthen his stirrups for surer balance.

The horses moved toward the training track, and Laurin turned to Dave Hoeffner, Henny's son, and said, "Hey, you want to take a ride to the training track with me?" They slipped into Lucien's station wagon.

Laurin, muttering and still peeved at Feliciano, told Hoeffner in the car, "I bet that horse throws this kid. He's frisky and I bet he throws him. The kid's not listening to what I'm saying."

Secretariat, and the other horses in the set,

strode through the stable area to the gap leading to the training track. They walked onto the muddy surface and began, one by one, to take off at a slow gallop. Feliciano, his reins loose, guided Secretariat near the outside rail and stood up in the saddle as the colt cantered through the long stretch toward the clocker's shed, passed the shed, and began heading into the first bend. He heard a horse working to his left, on the rail, his hooves slapping and splashing at the mud as he drilled past on the rails.

"I heard the noise. It was a split-second thing. He stopped, propped and wheeled, and turned left and I knew what was going to happen. I think he knew I was going off, too, already slipping, because he turned around from under me. I landed on my face."

Secretariat, riderless, his head and tail up and his reins flapping across his neck, took off clockwise around the racetrack, the wrong way, racing back toward the gap. Laurin saw him and, in an instant, was speeding out of the training track infield.

The car zipped through the tunnel and reentered the fence at the stable area. Laurin and Hoeffner saw Secretariat standing calmly at the gap by the training track, as if he were waiting for a taxi.

Dave Hoeffner climbed out from the car, walking with stealth toward Secretariat, who stood looking at him curiously. He reached out and grabbed the reins. Laurin immediately took off back to the barn, leaving Dave to walk Secretariat home alone. The colt walked like a prince for a quarter mile.

Paul Feliciano unscrewed his face from the mud at the seven-eighths pole and started walking around the oval toward the stable area.

He did not want to return to Barn 5, where Lucien Laurin was waiting for him. Paul Feliciano, twenty, born and raised on Union Street in the Park Slope section of Brooklyn, feared Laurin. Earlier, the headstrong Gold Bag had run off with him, as he had done with other riders, and Laurin had ranted at him. Paul had not forgotten the incident, so he had no illusions about what Lucien would say to him.

It was a ten-minute walk to the stable. By then Secretariat was standing in his stall, with blankets stacked up on his back. His back muscles were tied up so badly he couldn't move. Secretariat wouldn't leave the barn for almost two weeks.

Sometime in late June and July of 1972, Secretariat woke up as a racehorse, ceased being the overgrown pumpkin of a colt, and began to like the business of racing: to get with it when the gates opened, pumping the legs and the neck and tracking the leaders for a while and then—once the legs began to mesh and the rhythm took over—picking up speed, grabbing the bit, and racing hell-bent past them for the wire. Some horses loaf; others refuse to run at all; others spit out the bit and back off when they are in a fight. Others fear close contact, shying away when bumped, hemmed in, or impeded. Not Secretariat.

He began to come alive, and after his first win he started training faster, running faster and harder against the bit. Then he was off to Saratoga, traveling north by van up along the Hudson River to the historic old spa, the mile-and-an-eighth sandbox where the rich play in August, where the beams are still made of wood and the awnings at the racetrack are peppermint striped and the people eat corn on the cob and chicken in the basket.

On July 29, two days before his third start, Lucien sent Secretariat three-eighths in 0:35 under hand-urging, a sharp move at Saratoga, whose surface is not as fast as Belmont Park's. It primed the pump for Monday. Lucien had the red horse entered in the fourth race, a six-furlong sprint for two-year-olds who had never won two races. The purse was $9000, with $5400 to the winner, and he was in with six others. The feature that day was the Test Stakes, the prestigious filly race that Imperatrice and Miss Disco had won in the 1940s. About the time Penny Tweedy and Lucien Laurin headed toward the paddock and Turcotte donned the Meadow silks, one elderly turf-writer who had seen the grandmothers but never the grandson was awaiting quietly the colt's arrival for the fourth.

The cognoscenti give Mrs. Helen Tweedy's Secretariat the nod for potentiality. He has electrifying acceleration, duende, charisma, and star-fire raised to the steenth power. He also is pretty good.

Charles Hatton in the July 19 *Daily Racing Form*.

Wearing tinted glasses and a summer suit, smoking mentholated cigarettes in a holder, his gray hair drawn back, his voice carried along on the soft southerlies of an old Louisville accent, Charles Hatton sat on a bench near the paddock and watched for Secretariat.

Hatton had been coming to the races for more than fifty years, working around them almost as long. His tutor was the former black slave and the rider of Ten Broeck, Billy Walker. Walker had retired as a jockey and was timing horses in Kentucky when Hatton came under his tutorial care. Billy Walker taught him the intricacies of a horse's conformation—the proper angulation of the skeletal parts, the muscular investiture, the set of the eyes and the jowls and the length of the cannon bone relative to the length of the forearm. Horses were anatomical puzzles, all of a piece but in pieces.

Hatton had no way of knowing it then as he sat on the bench, but there was a young racehorse turning the corner of the racetrack—perhaps 150 yards away—who would fulfill some ideal that he had been turning over in his head since Billy Walker put it there more than fifty years ago.

Secretariat walked down the pathway toward

the paddock, toward the towering canopy of trees above the saddling area, toward Harron, who saw the colt and came to his feet. The red horse filled Hatton's eyes of an instant, not striding into his field of vision but swimming into it, pulling Hatton from the bench to a standstill before him.

Hatton had seen thousands of horses in his life, thousands of two-year-olds, and suddenly on this July afternoon of 1972 he found the 106-carat diamond: "It was like seeing a bunch of gravel and there was the Kohinoor lying in there. It was so unexpected. I thought, 'Jesus Christ, I never saw a horse that looked like that before.' "

Hatton followed the youngster to the saddling area. "First thing I know, I look around and there was a circle of people standing there like Man o' War was being saddled," Hatton recalled.

Hatton was in momentary awe. "You carry an ideal around in your head, and boy, I thought, 'This is it.' I never saw perfection before. I absolutely could not fault him in any way. And neither could the rest of them and that was the amazing thing about it. The body and the head and the eye and the general attitude. It was just incredible. I couldn't believe my eyes, frankly. I just couldn't because I've made a kind of thing of looking at horses since before the First World War, when I was a kid, but I never saw a horse like that."

All was of a piece, in proportion, Hatton thought. Secretariat had depth of barrel, with well-sprung ribs for heart and lung room, and he was not too wide in the front fork, nor too close together, and he came packaged with tremendous hindquarters. Hatton noted the underpinnings, stunned at the straightness of the hindleg, an unusual and valuable trait—straightness, not as seen from the front or back, but rather straightness when viewed from the side, from the gaskin through the hock to the cannon bone behind. It was as straight a hindleg as Hatton had ever seen and would serve as a source of great propulsive power as it reached far under the body and propelled it forward.

The value of a straight hindleg in a thoroughbred is roughly analogous to the value of the left arm held straight in a golf swing. A straight left arm gives maximum arc to the backswing and downswing and more propulsion to the clubface, greater sweep and power with minimum effort. "This construction comes to a sort of scooting action behind," Hatton later wrote. "He gets his hind parts far under himself in action, and the drive of the hindlegs is tremendous, as he follows through like a golfer."

His eyes moving up, Hatton looked at the head. The nostrils were large, with great flaring room for breathing large quantities of air rapidly—Man o' War had enormous nostrils, too—and the wide spread between the jowls suggested that it housed an ample windpipe. The cannon bone was not too long—the longer it is, the more susceptible it is to stress and injury, as is the tendon—and the forearm above it was of good length. Hatton noticed the sloping rump, the Nearco mark, but rejected it as unimportant. That sloping rump used to be the emblem of sprinters, but the staying Nearcos had remodeled that conception. Secretariat's shoulders were powerful, and he stood slightly over at the knees—that is, seen from the side, his knees were neither concave, an anatomical disaster in a horse, nor perfectly straight, but rather slightly convex. In this particular he was fine to Hatton, slightly over to reduce the concussion of the hooves on the racetrack.

"It was the thrill of a lifetime."

Hatton and the circle of onlookers parted, stepping back as groom Mordecai Williams led Secretariat to the paddock. Turcotte joined them there, conferring briefly with Lucien on the race and the way to ride the colt. This was not a herd of nonwinners of the type he spread-eagled at Aqueduct two weeks earlier. Two of the colts, Russ Miron and Joe Iz, had shown speed, and Turcotte knew he'd have to catch them if the red horse fell back and ran as he had under Feliciano.

"Don't rush this colt," Lucien reminded him. "Let him feel his way and just come on with him. He has a particular way of running. You can't rush him"

The crowd had made Secretariat the odds-on favorite at $0.40 to $1.00, and Turcotte sat ready on him in the starting gate, clutching a handful of his coppery mane for balance when George Cassidy sprang the latch and sent them on.

Secretariat brushed the side of the gate when

361

the doors sprang open, drifting left and brushing Fat Frank as they left the slip, and Turcotte could feel him trying to get with it. He could feel him chopping and struggling to put his mass in motion. So Turcotte sat chilly on him. Secretariat had broken alertly, but was dropping back as the field made off for the turn. Russ Miron rushed to the lead and through as opening quarter in 0:23 1/5, with Joe Iz a head behind and on the outside of him. Turcotte eased Secretariat to the outside, giving him time to find his stride and room to move when he found it. As Russ Miron raced past the half-mile pole, Secretariat was last, trailing him by four with his own quarter in 0:24. The horses made the bend, and Turcotte had Secretariat five horses wide, giving him the worst of it but no traffic to deal with. The colt started rolling around the turn, picking up speed past the three-eighths pole and moving past Fat Frank, Court Ruling, Blackthorn, and Tropic Action in a matter of jumps, zipping along that second quarter mile in 0:22 3/5, and moving up on Russ Miron and Joe Iz to the head of the lane. By then he was just a half a length from the lead and on the outside.

With Secretariat moving to them, Joe Iz caved in first, dropping back, and passing the three-sixteenths pole Ron reached back and hit the red colt once, right-handed. Secretariat drifted left. Turcotte switched his stick and straightened him out by rapping him once left-handed. Secretariat had Russ Miron in trouble at the eighth pole. Carlos Marquez worked on him vigorously, but

Turcotte eased away from him in the final 220 yards, hand-riding to a length-and-a-half victory in 1:10 4/5 for the six furlongs, his final quarter in 0:24 1/5.

Now the colt began to exact more than just casual interest from horsemen. "Mrs. Tweedy," said Virginia breeder Taylor Hardin, turning to her after the race. "I'd like to apply for breeding rights to that horse. I was the first person to ask for breeding rights to Native Dancer and I was right."

Turcotte liked his race that day, too, though he would not do handsprings back to the jockeys' quarters over it. He had given the youngster the worst of the running, taking him to the high ground at the turn and giving away lengths to two fast colts. And the red horse caught them with a rush when his rider chirped to him. Secretariat ran willingly, responded to the whip, and didn't loaf when he made the lead. The early signs were good. Turcotte also recalled his heavy-headed way of running—stylistically, he was the opposite of the airy-going Riva Ridge—the way he pounded the ground as he reached out for more of it. He had beaten maidens, he had beaten nonwinners of two races, and now he would have to run against the best—the best stakes horses on the grounds, and that meant running against the undefeated Linda's Chief. Secretariat and Linda's Chief were both being aimed for the $25,000-Added Sanford Stakes August 16, another six-furlong sprint.

# A. J. LIEBLING.

# One Jump to Four Miles

*With humor and affection A. J. Liebling wrote about the texture of life in his hometown, New York City. In this piece about jockey Eddie Arcaro, who as a young man rode six days a week at Belmont, Liebling's ear for the richness of everyday, unpretentious language yields an inside view of a jockey's day through the "pungent phrases" and unique jargon of the race track. Not one to romanticize the life of a jockey, Liebling focuses on the mundane— the daily schedule beginning at five-thirty in the morning, the strain of maintaining an ideal riding weight, the details of Arcaro's commitments to various stables and how he earns each dollar at the track, or the technical discussions and arguments in the jockey room between races. Here also is a short history of Arcaro's apprenticeship and an explanation of a few of the skills a jockey must learn, such as gauging a horse's rate of speed, how to "shower down," and the technique of riding "ace-deuce."*

We have better riders in New York than any place else in the United States. The best riders cannot afford to live in the country; there are no horse races there.

Although Eddie Arcaro, the jockey, is only twenty-two, he has a mature, Metropolitan understanding of his public, which is largely made up of investors. When he canters back to the winner's circle at Belmont or Saratoga or wherever he is riding, he peers sadly down his long, pointed nose and touches the peak of his cap with his whip in perfunctory acknowledgment of the applause. He knows that the hatless man in the polo shirt who hangs over the rail screaming "Attaboy Eddie!" has had two dollars on his mount to win; he knows that if he loses the next race, the same fellow may be yelling, "Yah, Arcaro —you bum!" Neither the handclap nor the hiss moves him very much.

What really interests Eddie is his income. As the leading rider on New York tracks last year, he collected about forty thousand dollars. With a win in the Kentucky Derby to start him off and good prospective mounts in the fall two-year-old classics, he ought to do even better this year. Since a jockey's career is usually short, Eddie works hard at his trade, knowing he'll get heavy eventually. He puts his money in annuities.

"You know how old jockeys wind up—with eppes," he once said. "You know, they got nothing." *Eppes* is a Yiddish word, meaning something of indefinite value, which Eddie learned from Jockey Sammy Renick. His talk, like that of all jockeys, is a strange mixture of New Yorkese,

Westernisms (about half the riders hail from the horse-range country), Southern idioms picked up from Negro swipes, and trade terms pertaining to race riding. All these elements are fused into one standard jargon in the jockey rooms, where the boys spend the greater part of their afternoons.

Eddie is five feet three inches tall and can ride at a hundred and twelve pounds. This means he is able to strip to a hundred and seven, for riding weight includes a racing saddle, pad, the jockey's garments and boots, and any extra equipment, like a martingale or blinkers, worn by the horse. Bridle and whip are not counted in the weight. Eddie got his first stable job when he was fourteen, and his view of the world, although sharp, is limited. He has never assumed a knowledge of champagne vintages or a hunt-club accent. Mrs. Payne Whitney is his contract employer, but he has never met her. He thinks well of Mrs. Charles Shipman Payson, Mrs. Whitney's daughter, whom he sees occasionally around stables. "She's a high-class woman," Eddie says. "She never has nothing to say."

During the season he receives scores of letters from people who want inside tips on the races. They generally say that they need the money for an operation, or to lift a mortgage, or to buy themselves a pardon from a penitentiary. Eddie never answers them. He is not a successful bettor himself. When occasionally he backs one of his own mounts, he says it "just seems to jinx everything."

"Anybody is a sucker to bet their own money," he says. Usually, if the horse he is riding looks like a fairly sure thing, the trainer or owner will put a bet on it for Eddie, which costs Eddie nothing. He likes that kind of bet all right.

Arcaro is a sociable sort, but he has little time for pleasure. With the increase in the importance of winter racing, there is a strong inducement for him to work all year round. Arcaro usually knocks off in November every year to mitigate the strain of continual weight-making. In a few luxurious weeks his weight goes up thirteen pounds, which he works off gradually during December and January. In winter he rides in Florida and California, and in spring in Maryland and Kentucky.

Six mornings a week, during the Belmont season, Arcaro rises at five-thirty in his apartment at Jamaica, gets into riding togs, has a cup of coffee, and then drives a long maroon automobile out to the barn of the Greentree Stable, at the end of a hedge-lined, studiously English lane in the stable colony at Belmont Park. The Greentree Stable is Mrs. Whitney's *nom de course*. The stable pays him a retainer of a thousand dollars a month for first call on his services. When Greentree has no horse in a race, he is free to ride for other owners.

At the barn, Arcaro joins the exercise boys and rides one of the Greentree horses out to the track for its morning gallop. He gallops three horses around the mile-and-a-half oval every morning. Sometimes he shakes one out for a time trial. He performs this morning chore in order to hold his riding form. After the gallops he may chat a while with Bill Brennan, the Greentree trainer, or Nick Huff, who is at the same time the stable agent and Argaro's jockey agent. As stable agent, Huff acts as a combined purchasing officer, paymaster, and auditor. As Arcaro's agent, he arranges for the jockey's outside mounts. Eddie starts for home at about eight-thirty and has breakfast there with Mrs. Arcaro. He has been married a year. At breakfast he follows no special diet, but is careful not to eat as much as he wants of anything. Then he takes a nap until noon. He must report at the jockey room at the track at one o'clock, even when his first engagement comes late in the afternoon. After he has ridden his last race for the day, he is free to go.

At the track Arcaro changes from street clothes into the colors of the first owner he is to represent, then sits around or plays catch with other boys in back of the jockey house until it is time to go out to the saddling shed. A valet in a khaki uniform helps Eddie dress. For this service the valet receives two dollars from Eddie each time Eddie rides. If Eddie wins, he must pay the valet three dollars instead of two. On a typical program, Arcaro may ride six races.

A certain Wednesday early this summer was a fair sample of his day. Arriving at the Belmont jockey room, in a white one-story building next to the saddling shed, he changed into the "salmon pink jacket, emerald green hoops, salmon pink sleeves and cap" of Mrs. Ethel Jacobs, owner of the two-year-old General Howes, which he was to ride in the first race. Hirsch Jacobs, Mrs. Jacobs' husband, saddles more winners than any other trainer on the American turf. Jockeys like to ride his horses because, Eddie says, "they always have a chance." A jockey receives only ten dollars for a ride unless the animal wins. If it wins, he gets twenty-five dollars plus ten per cent of the purse. The millionaire establishments like Greentree, Foxcatcher Farms, and the Wheatley Stable retain contract riders in view of the great stake races toward which they aim their seasons. Jacobs has no contract rider, but few of his horses run in the big stake races, and he usually has his pick of the high-salaried riders in the cheap races.

General Howes was wild and hard to ride going to the starting gate for a straightaway dash of five-eights of a mile. But he got off well, led all the way, and won by half a length, making a profit of ninety-five dollars fee and ten per cent of the seven hundred dollars first money. Eddie said, "I bounced the sucker out in front when the man throwed it, and then at the eighth pole I showered down." Jockeys call the starter "the Man." When he pressed the buzzer to signal the start, they say he "throws the gate," or, more colloquially, "throws it." "When he throwed it, I had it," a boy will say to express satisfaction with a start. To "shower down" means to whip.

Eddie had a breathing spell during the steeplechase which followed the opening dash, meanwhile changing into the "pink jacket, black and white striped sleeves, white cap" of John Hay Whitney, the son of Eddie's contract employer. He rode a Whitney two-year-old in the third race and finished next to last. The horses in this race were of a distinctly higher grade than those he had beaten in the first. He then prepared for the feature of the day, the Hollis Selling Stakes, in which he was scheduled to ride the four-year-old chestnut filly North Riding for the Howe Stable. The race was worth $2,750 to the first horse, which would mean a round three hundred dollars for the winning jockey. The Howe Stable has second call on Arcaro's services, for which it pays him three hundred dollars a month. If there is a Howe entry in a race and no Greentree starter, Arcaro must ride the Howe horse. The stable is not large. Most of its horses are a little better than platers but not quite of stake calibre. North Riding is a heartbreaking mare for a jockey. She is very fast but what Eddie calls "a rank, rapid horse that you can't reserve." This means that she goes out to run her head off at the start and that if the jockey tries to conserve her speed for the finish, she stops altogether. There is a horseman's adage, which Eddie accepts, that no horse can run more than three-eighths of a mile at top speed. A horse that insists on running this magic three-eights at the beginning tires and must be coaxed into finishing on its nerve. "When this mare stops, she sticks her feet in the ground," Arcaro says. "If you whip her she sulks. All you can do is hand-ride her and pray." On this day his prayer was answered. North Riding started fast, as usual, but didn't stop. The race was over before the other horses could catch her.

Eddie then went on to ride another horse of John Hay Whitney's, finishing last this time, and two more Jacobs platers, finishing second on one called Celestino and third on another named Mama's Choice. This brought his gross income for the day to four hundred and thirty-five dollars; three hundred for his win on North Riding, ninety-five for General Howes, and ten dollars for each of the four losing mounts. For a week-day, this had been an excellent program for Eddie. Out of his earnings he had to pay fourteen dollars to his valet and fifty-seven fifty to Huff, the agent. A jockey agent, like a valet gets two dollars for losing and three dollars for winning mounts, but he also gets ten per cent of the jockey's ten per cent of the purse. When Eddie won the Kentucky Derby on Lawrin this spring, he received five thousand dollars as his share of the purse and paid Huff five hundred.

After his ride on Mama's Choice in the last race, Eddie had his shower, got into street clothes, and drove his car into New York to meet Mrs. Arcaro for dinner at a place called Leone's. She seldom goes to the track when there is not an important race. The Arcaros like to eat at Leone's, the Hickory House, or Gallagher's—all Broadway places where the food is good and fairly expensive and the patrons include a sprinkling of sporting peo-

371

ple. After dinner they usually go to a "show." Eddie always calls moving pictures shows. He gets to bed by eleven o'clock except on Saturday nights, when, with Mrs. Arcaro, he invariably goes to a night club. His wife, who used to be a photographer's model, is blonde, pretty, and five inches taller than her husband. They met while Eddie was riding at Hialeah a few winters back. "I guess I'm pretty miserable to get along with during the hot weather when I dassn't drink much water on account of my weight," Eddie says. Being thirsty irritates him, but his wife makes allowances.

Since horses generally carry between a hundred and a hundred and twenty-six pounds in races, it might seem to the layman that very small men, weighing around ninety pounds, would make the best jockeys. They would not have to weaken themselves by sweating or dieting. But, as trainers will point out, ten pounds of dead-weight shows a horse more than fifteen pounds of live weight. The difference between the weight of the jockey with his tack and total weight assigned by the handicapper is made up by loading the saddle pad with thin sheets of lead. The trainer's ideal is a jockey who, with saddle and tack, weighs exactly the figure allotted to his horse. A jockey can vary his weight for races on the same day by using different saddles. Eddie has three, of which the lightest weighs twenty-four ounces and the heaviest five pounds. A heavier saddle is considered preferable to lead. Eddie is close to the trainer's ideal and doesn't have to use lead as often as some other jockeys. But an extra three pounds on Eddie's frame would decrease his chances of employment by about twenty per cent. A gain of five or six pounds would be a vigorous push toward retirement. A "heavy" jockey—118 to 125 pounds—gets engagements so infrequently that he is apt to lose his form, after which he gets no engagements at all. Raymond ("Sonny") Workman, considered by most of his jockey-room colleagues to be Arcaro's only peer, is a deep-chested, bull-necked little man of twenty-nine with a roast-beef complexion, who is afraid of getting heavy. He goes on the road like a prize-fighter every morning, wearing rubber garments under his sweater and trousers. When the weather becomes really hot, he often plays eighteen holes of golf in the late morning, wearing the same rubber clothes. He can count calories like a movie actress.

Boys in the jockey room carry on interminable technical discussions during the waits between races, and there is an argument after each race. "If there is fifteen in a race," Eddie says, "you would think to hear them holler that fifteen should of win it. And when you do win, some other kid will come up and say, 'Gee, you was lucky. I should of galloped.' " Angry little men shout they were bumped or shut off by other jockeys, but a boy who hits another in the jockey room is liable to a hundred-dollar fine, so blows are seldom struck.

Eddie rides "ace-deuce," with the left stirrup a

good three inches longer than the right. Most American jockeys ride ace-deuce, the theory being that since they ride with the rail to their left they throw more weight in that direction to keep the horse from running out. They learn the style on the half-mile tracks, where a jockey feels that he is on a continual turn from start to finish. Arcaro rides ace-deuce even in straightaway dashes. He says he is so used to it that if he evened up he would get seasick. He rides with his knees high and gets his grip on a horse with his lower calves. Workman, whose legs are shorter than Eddie's, grips the horse's withers with his knees. He rides ace-deuce, but less ace-deuce, than Eddie, he says.

Arcaro was born and brought up in Newport, Kentucky, a little town across the Ohio River from Cincinnati and only a few miles from the Latonia race track. Like many Italian-Americans reared where they have few compatriots, he talks with the inflections of a local product. His name and his mobile Latin features, with deep brown eyes and large white teeth, hardly seem to fit the Ohio River twang in his voice. His father, who runs a small crockery and restaurant-supply store in New-port, was born in Texas. Eddie started out to be a jockey after one year in Newport High School, when he decided he never would be big enough to make the football team. A Latonia horseman named McCaffrey offered him a job as stableboy. Eddie agreed to work for him for a year in return for food and clothes and a chance to ride.

The boy was with the McCaffrey stable for several months before he got on a horse. He carried water, polished tack, and amused himself in his spare time by twirling a stick and riding exciting whip finishes on bales of hay. This is the traditional stableboy method of learning to handle a whip. He is an ambidextrous whipper now, and can change the whip from the right to the left hand in two strides of his mount. After a while, McCaffrey allowed Eddie to ride the lead pony, the stolid, cold-blooded brute that is used to lead a string of thoroughbreds to and from the race track. A boy riding a lead pony begins with his stirrups long, like a novice in a riding academy. As he gains confidence he shortens his leathers in imitation of the jockeys he sees about him, until finally he is balanced high on the horse's withers like a real race rider. Eddie has never read the elaborate arguments in favor of the forward seat which are written by cavalry officers and published in limited editions. American jockeys have used it for forty years. A new boy around a stable usually is promoted from the lead pony to the back of a quiet old thoroughbred for his first morning gallops. That was about as far as Eddie got with McCaffrey. At the end of the year the boy's employer advised him to go back to school. McCaffrey told Eddie he would never make a jockey.

Instead of taking his advice, Eddie signed a three-year contract with a gyp horseman named Booker, who was taking a small string to the Pacific Coast for the winter racing. "Gyp," as applied to horseman, is a term without opprobrium. Gyp stables try to make a profit, contrasted with the de-luxe establishments that operate at a deficit. With Booker, Eddie landed out in Agua Caliente in the fall of 1931. His contract bound him to serve his employer faithfully in return for twenty dollars a month and found for the first six months, with a ten-dollar raise every six months thereafter. The contract was signed by Booker, Eddie's parents, and Eddie. An apprentice who breaks such a contract may not be employed by another horseman even as a stableboy.

It is the gyp horsemen, for the most part, who "make" riders. They run their horses often and they cannot afford to pay the regular fees for outside jockeys. If they can develop a good apprentice, they get their riding done for nothing. If he continues to improve, they turn a profit by selling his contract to a major stable, just as a minor-league baseball club sells a player to a big-league team. Booker had too few horses to give Eddie a complete education. The curriculum was limited. But Eddie won his first race in Booker's colors, on a four-year-old named Eagle Bird that had never won before. Horses begin racing at two, and a four-year-old maiden is usually phenomenally bad. Eddie says, in the pungent race-track phrase, "Him and me lost our maidens in the same race." Eddie won a few more races during that meeting, but Booker kept selling horses or losing them in claiming races until finally he had no need of a jockey. He transferred Eddie's contract to a kindly man named Clarence E. Davison, who still runs a highly successful gyp stable in the Middle West. Davison paid nothing for the contract. "It was give to him," the jockey modestly states. "I wasn't doing no good."

Davison is a former Missouri farmer who races his horses methodically. "Everybody in the stable had to earn his keep," Arcaro says. "Even the lead pony could run like hell. The feed was counted right down to the ounce and every horse had to be rode out in every race, because even fourth money meant twenty-five dollars on the feed bill." The Davison horses provided a fine range of experience.

In the morning Davison taught Eddie pace. A jockey unable to gauge his mount's rate of speed may run his horse into the ground early in a race. Or else, fooled by a slow pace, he may dawdle along and be beaten by an inferior horse. Davison would tell Eddie to work a horse a mile in 1:46 or six furlongs in 1:16. He would wave to the boy to slow down when he was riding too fast or to come on when the pace was too slow. In the end Eddie caught onto it. When the boy made mistakes in races, like getting pocketed behind other horses on the rail or running a mount into heavy footing to save a couple of lengths and thereby sacrificing in speed more than he gained in distance, Davison never was angry. He took Eddie home with him after the races and drew diagrams of the jockey's mistakes.

At every track where these horses ran, Mr. and

Mrs. Davison would engage a cottage. They made Eddie live with them. Davison never let the boy associate with hustlers or scufflers, the race-track small fry who ingratiate themselves with young jockeys and try to fix races. He never let Eddie shoot pool or smoke cigarettes. "S'all he ever did to me was preach to me," Eddie says now, his tone a mixture of gratitude and relief at his escape. Under the intensive tutelage the young rider improved, and at Sportsman's Park, near Chicago, he won fourteen races in one week in the fall of 1932. That set him up in his own estimation. Before losing his "bug," he rode seventy winners. A rider's "bug," is the asterisk at the left of a horse's handicap on a race program. It indicates that the rider won his first race within a year, or that the rider has not attained his fortieth win and that the horse therefore is allowed a deduction of five pounds from the weight assigned. The bug always remains with a rider until he has won forty races, and it is a bitter jockey-room reproach to say "You had your bug for five years."

In midsummer of 1934, Davison sold Arcaro's contract for $5,000 to Warren Wright, the Chicago baking-powder millionaire who owns the Calumet Stock Farm. The contract had five months to run. Davison had been paying Eddie his contract salary of sixty dollars a month; the Calumet owner started him at three hundred, plus mount money and a percentage of stakes. The Calumet horses moved East to Narragansett Park near Providence, and Eddie engaged a suite at the

Biltmore, the city's leading hotel. Mr. Wright presented him with a Chevrolet because he didn't like to see his contract rider waiting for buses. Later, in one of his first races at Belmont, Eddie won the Matron Stakes on a Calumet filly named Nellie Flag. His ten per cent of the purse was two thousand dollars, more than he had earned in his entire previous career. He was the contract rider for Calumet through 1935 and 1936, then switched to Greentree at a higher retainer.

While Calumet and Greentree are both millionaire stables, neither has had a real champion in recent years. Some horsemen, indeed, unkindly compare Greentree with the White Knight, who kept a mouse-trap on his saddle in case a mouse ever got up there. The stable, they say, has the jockey in case it gets a horse. Arcaro's reputation has been gained chiefly on outside mounts. He is not sure that he has ever ridden a first-class horse. His greatest triumph was this year's Kentucky Derby, but he is not certain that his Derby mount, Lawrin, who is now out of training because of an injury, is a champion. "Maybe the other three-year-olds just ain't so good," he says.

It is the skill with which Arcaro handles all sorts of mounts that makes him a favorite of the ordinary racegoer. Last year he won 96 races on New York tracks, finishing first with about twenty per cent of his mounts. Including his races in other parts of the country, he had 153 winners. Nine other jockeys led him in number of victories, but they were riders on the minor circuits. His 717 mounts won $205,874 in purses.

The most important figure in Eddie's business life, he thinks, is Nick Huff, who tries to get him on horses that can win. "You very seldom hear of a jockey getting in a slump riding good horses," Arcaro says sincerely.

Huff used to be a jockey himself, although not one of the top rank. He is a small-boned, keen-featured little man who wears snappy suits. He always speaks of Eddie in the first person plural, a custom jockey agents share with fight managers. "We won on Lawrin when nobody gave us a chance, didn't we?" he asks pugnaciously. "We could have won The Withers on Menow—Headley wanted us to ride—but on account of our contract we had to ride Redbreast. We are par excellence the best rider in the country, from one jump to four miles."

Eddie knows from his own experience, or has learned in talks with a trainer before a race, just how to handle whatever horse he is riding. One difficulty of race riding is that some horses are opinionated and stubborn. There are the rapid, rank horses that will run only when they're out front, and there are hardened devils that refuse to run until they reach the stretch. Either type will quit if forced out of its natural way of going. There are old horses that have been knocked about on the rail in their youth and won't go near it, and there are rapid luggers that will make for the rail no matter what the jockey does, and often disqualify themselves because they block other horses. Eddie remembers a rapid lugger named Hot Shot; he drew six ten-day suspensions in one year riding that horse. Then there are horses that will run up on the other horses' heels. Such a one was Gunfire, which stepped on the horse in front of it at Washington Park in 1933 and went down. Eddie, who was on Gunfire, came out of the jam with two fractured ribs, one of which punctured his lung. That is the only serious spill he's ever had.

When Eddie has a mount amenable to reason, he likes to break fast from the gate, then take back to third or fourth position, and come through when the leaders tire. You get two horses out there fighting for the lead for a quarter of a mile, you see, and they will kill theirself off every time. Then you can come on and win. But sometimes when you are set for the rush, the horse isn't. You shower down and he sulks. He loses his action and goes limber on you like, and you know he's stuck his feet in the ground.

# THE OLYMPICS AND OTHER SPECIAL EVENTS

# ALEXANDER M. WYAND

# A Frenchman Has an Idea

*The scale of today's Olympic games has become so immense that it may be surprising to learn that the vision and tenacity of one individual—the Frenchman Baron Peirre de Coubertin—were responsible for their revival. When the thirty-year-old De Coubertin proposed his idea in 1892, his goals were familiar ones: the improvement of youth and the furthering of international good will through the gathering together of the athletes and spectators of diverse nations. Although international sports competition was on the rise during the last half of the nineteenth century, it took De Coubertin and other committed Olympians four years of organizing in Europe and the United States before the first games were finally held in Athens in 1896. Ironically, American athletes at first evinced little interest in the games.*

"The important thing in the Olympic Games is not winning, but taking part; the essential thing in life is not conquering, but fighting well."

These words expressed the creed of that remarkable little Frenchman, Baron Pierre de Coubertin, who, some six decades ago, had an inspiration. As a result of that inspiration, we of today have the ancient Olympic Games revived in modern setting.

Baron de Coubertin was educated at a Jesuit school in Paris and at the famous military academy at Saint-Cyr. Apparently Army life did not appeal to him, for he resigned from the academy to prepare himself for a political career. He dropped that, too, and decided to devote his life and modest fortune to the task of improving the youth of France. Memories of the War of 1870 were still fresh—and painful. The youth of France had not distinguished itself in that war. It showed the need of improvement.

In order to prepare himself for his self-imposed mission, the baron traveled extensively and studied the educational systems in the countries that he visited. He made two trips to the United States. Although he, like most young Frenchmen of the time, was not athletically inclined, he came to the conclusion that competitive athletics provided youth with certain elements of basic training that could not be obtained in any other way. He saw in such competitions an incentive to clean living, courageous action, physical proficiency, mental agility, and good sportsmanship.

A few years before (1875 to 1881), excavations by German archaeologists at Olympia had aroused considerable interest in the games of antiquity. De Coubertin's imagination was fired by the thought of those magnificent cultural, religious, and athletic festivals held in the far-off days when Ancient Greece was in her glory—games that were now dead, or had been sleeping, for fifteen centuries. He visualized a revival of the Olympic Games. He felt that the desire to engage in international contests of such magnitude and historic significance would serve as a stimulus to the youth, not only of his beloved France, but of the world. They would adopt the Olympic ideal. All mankind would thus be benefited.

The improvement of youth was De Coubertin's first and foremost concern, but he also had a secondary objective in mind. He saw not merely a reproduction of the historic character of the Grecian games, but also huge gatherings of the peoples of all climes and nations. The mingling of the competitors and spectators and the opportunity to visit and partake of the hospitality of the various large cities in which the games would ultimately be held would exert a tremendous influence in furthering the cause of international understanding and good will.

In November, 1892, when De Coubertin was thirty years of age, he proposed his Olympic idea at a meeting of French sportsmen. The cold response convinced him that he would have to seek support abroad. He commenced the publication of a monthly magazine on sports, and he spent the next year doing spadework among his athletically inclined friends in foreign countries. At the end of this period he asked some of them to join with him in a discussion of the project. He called upon such gentlemen as Professor William M. Sloane of the United States, Mr. Charles Herbert of England,

General de Bontowski of Russia, Colonel Viktor Balck of Sweden, and Franz R. Kemeny of Hungary.

Professor Sloane, a member of the Princeton University faculty, was, like De Coubertin, a firm believer in competitive sports, and he strongly supported the baron's entire program. Mr. Herbert, secretary of the British Athletic Association, was a practical sportsman, and helpful in technical matters, but not too enthusiatic over the Olympic revival. Of De Coubertin's friends these two, in particular, gave valuable advice, assistance, and encouragement. It was decided to invite the various amateur sporting societies of the world to send delegates to an Olympic Congress to be held in Paris in 1894.

Professor Sloane endeavored to arouse interest in the Olympic plan in America. The proposal was given some publicity at a meeting held at the University Club in New York City, in November, 1893. But neither Professor Sloane nor Mr. Herbert in England met with any pronounced success. The idea was too much in advance of the time.

The Olympic Congress was opened in the Grand Hall of the Sorbonne on June 16, 1894. Baron de Courcel, member of the French Senate, and former ambassador to Berlin, presided. In all, seventy- nine deligates assembled before an audience of some two thousand. Belgium, France, Great Britain, Greece, Italy, Russia, Spain, Sweden, and the United States were represented. The hostile feeling between Germany and France as the result of the War of 1870 was still too strong for Germany to send a delegate. Baron von Reiffenstein attended the meeting in an unofficial capacity. Messages of support were received from Australia, Austria, Bohemia, Holland, and Hungary.

After listening to the singing of the "Hymn of Apollo," the words and music of which had recently been discovered at Delphi, the delegates settled down to business. They were in full agreement that the baron's idea merited a thorough trial. It was decided to constitute an International Olympic Committee of fifteen members to handle the matter.

De Coubertin wished to hold the first set of games in 1900 in connection with the International Exposition scheduled for Paris that year. Thus ample time would be available for missionary work throughout the interested countries. The delegates felt that it would be better not to delay the movement but to make a start in 1896, even though that allowed but two years for preparation. De Coubertin recognized the wisdom of the suggestion. His next proposal—to inaugurate the revival in Greece, the home of the classic games—was enthusiastically received. The delegates would have liked to have held the games at Olympia itself, but flood waters had long since claimed the site of the ancient stadium, so they voted unanimously to award the games to Athens, the capital of Greece.

The proposed Olympic Games aroused only mild interest in the United States, although the time was ripe for international athletic competition. There had already been considerable effort at such competition, particularly with England, Ireland, and Canada. The yacht races for the America's Cup, between England and the United States, had a history that extended back to 1851. International rowing, lacrosse, polo and rifle matches had ceased to be unusual.

As long ago as 1844, George Seward of New Haven toured England, racing all comers at distances up to a quarter of a mile. In 1863 Louis Bennett (the famous Deerfoot), a Seneca Indian, created quite a furor in England by outrunning all challengers at distances of approximately ten miles. To add to the novelty, he wore moccasins.

The British national track-and-field championships were inaugurated in 1866, and the American, ten years later. Individual athletes visited back and forth. Lon E. Myers, an American, won the British quarter-mile championship in 1881 and 1885, and also the half-mile in 1885. T. Ray of England won the American pole-vaulting title in 1887 with a near world-record leap of 11 feet ¾ inch.

The tempo was increased considerably in 1888, when no fewer than eleven Americans competed in the English games. They bagged four titles. In the same year an Irish team took part in the American games and duplicated the feat, winning four championships; and in the same year Canada took two.

Eventually, France organized national championship games. In 1891 the Manhattan Athletic Club sent a team abroad to compete both in the British and in the French games. In England three events were won, and a Manhattan man tied for first place in another. At Paris the Americans won everything. In 1894 Oxford defeated Yale, 5½ to 3½, in the first international intercollegiate games. The games were held on the grounds of the Queen's Club in London.

International sport went into high gear in 1895, the year before the scheduled revival of the Olympic Games. Cornell's crew rowed in the British Henley, the cricket team of the University of Pennsylvania played both Oxford and Cambridge, and arrangements were made of two track-and-field meets in the United States. The first meet brought together the intercollegiate champion teams of England and America, Cambridge and Yale, respectively. Yale won, 8 to 5. The second meet was between the London Athletic Club and the New York Athletic Club.

The meeting between the two famous clubs proved a worthy fore-runner of the Olympic Games. It took place on Manhattan Field in New York City on September 21, 1895. Spectators to the number of 8,592 paid from $1 to $3 apiece for the privilege of seeing the contests. The referee was William B. Curtis of New York, affectionately known as "Father Bill," who was one of the pioneers in putting track-and-field sports on a firm basis in the United States. The judges were Baron de Coubertin's friend, Charles Herbert, and Sir Montague Shearman of the London Athletic Club, and Bartow S. Weeks and Wendell Baker of the New York Athletic Club.

Caspar Whitney, the foremost sports writer of the period, predicted that the English would win three, possibly five, of the eleven events on the program. He was pessimistic. The Americans, trained by the celebrated Mike Murphy, swept the boards. They won every event. They took five second places and tied for another. The performances were startling; four world records were smashed, another equaled, and others closely approached.

American sportsmen were elated by the overwhelming victory over England's best athletes. They were justly proud of their heroes, but it seems peculiar that they evinced such little interest in the Olympic Games. Possibly Athens was a little too far from Broadway!

# ARTHUR R. ASHE, JR.

## Jesse Owens

*Jesse Owens holds a special place in the history of African American athletes. His stunning performance at the Berlin Games of 1936—where he won four gold medals—made his name a household word and inspired a new generation of track-and-field stars. As former tennis star Arthur R. Ashe, Jr.—who brought down a long-standing racial barrier in his own sport —recounts, Owens's story highlights the obstacles African American athletes had to transcend in the first half of this century—overt racial prejudice, segregated recreational facilities, banning from participation in major sports, such as the major baseball leagues and the National Football League, and discriminatory policies in housing and employment at universities.*

Jesse Owens was named James Cleveland Owens after his birth on September 12, 1913, in Oakville, Alabama. One of twelve children of Henry and Emma Owens, Jesse was one of nine that survived. He did not grow up in good health, having suffered from bronchitis brought on from drafty winter winds and growths on his legs and chest that doctors could not decipher. Owens was not an especially good student, but he later acquired an ability to express himself quite well.

His family members were very religious, which may have helped him withstand the racial discrimination meted out to blacks in Alabama. Though Owens never had many unkind words to say about his early life there, another black Alabama sprinter contemporary, Eulace Peacock, lamented that "When I look back over my lifetime I can get so bitter about things that happened to me. And actually I should hate white people, but fortunately my family didn't bring me up that way." Young Jesse must have had similar sentiments.

Owens' family moved to Cleveland, Ohio, in the early 1920s, and he again faced a new set of segregated movies and other recreational amenities. At the Bolton Elementary School, his teacher misunderstood Owens to say "Jesse" when asked his name rather than "J.C." in his slow, southern drawl. "Jesse" stuck. At Fairmont Junior High School, he met his future wife, Minnie Ruth Solomon, and discovered the joys of organized sports, mainly basketball and track. He also met his primary mentor and friend, Charles Riley, the school's coach and physical education teacher.

Riley, who was white and of average build—five feet eight inches—may have seen something of William DeHart Hubbard in Owens' speed, because he literally made his young protege his life's work. Owens even lunched at Riley's home, where Riley spared no efforts in making him faster. Within a year, Owens had clocked 11 seconds in the 100-yard dash and at age fifteen he set world marks for a junior high school student of 6′ in the high jump and 22′ 11½″ in the long jump. Riley even arranged for Owens to meet Hubbard, who had set the world record in the long jump in 1925.

In 1930 Owens was in East Technical High School, in a group of blacks that made up less than 5 percent of the students. In two years, he was the hottest track property in the country, bar none. He competed in the 1932 Midwest Olympic Preliminaries but lost in the long jump, the 100 meters, and the 200 meters. He became a father on August 8 when his daughter, Gloria, was born to Minnie Ruth. He then finished high school after setting a schoolboy record in the long jump of 24′ 3¾″. Later, at the National Interscholastic meet at Stagg Field in Chicago, Owens soared 24′ 9⅝″ in the long jump, tied the world mark in the 100-yard dash in 9.4 seconds, and set a new world record in the 220-yard dash in 20.7 seconds. Of East Tech's fifty-four total points, Owens accounted for thirty of them. He was even feted with a parade back in Cleveland. Strangely, not a single black college made an attempt to recruit him, so he wound up at Ohio State after seriously considering a few others.

But Ohio State had a sordid reputation among black Ohioans in the early 1930s. In 1931, William Bell, a black Ohio State football player, was benched in a game against Vanderbilt (Tennessee) that was played at *home*. In 1933, the Ohio State

Supreme Court upheld the university's right to deny housing to a black co-ed, Doris Weaver, because, as school president Dr. George Rightmire said, "Knowing the feelings in Ohio, can the administration take the burden of establishing this relationship—colored and white girls living in this more or less family way?" Rightmire must have been talking about the feelings of white Ohioans.

The black press urged Owens to think twice before entering his choice of schools. "Why help advertise an institution that majors in prejudice?" cried the *Chicago Defender.* Nevertheless, with his 73.5 high school grade-point-average, Owens enrolled in Ohio State in the fall of 1933. He had to share a boarding house apartment with some other black friends, only one movie theater was accessible—upstairs, no university restaurants would admit them, and Owens himself was given the least visible job as a freight elevator operator in the State Office Building. The passenger elevator job was reserved for white athletes. Owens did not complain for he was paying his own way through college; he did not have a free ride as is the possibility today. (In those days, a scholarship was in fact a ready-made job for a student.) But 1933 was not all bad. John Brooks was Big Ten long jump champion at the University of Chicago; James Luvalle was ICAAAA winner in the 440-yard dash; and Eulace Peacock was the national pentathlon victor.

Problems aside, Owens' track potential seemed harnessed until the end of his sophomore season when he exploded with stellar performances on one Saturday afternoon. At the National Intercollegiates in Ann Arbor, Michigan, on May 25, 1935, Owens put on a mind-boggling display that resulted in three world records and a tie in another. The new marks were a 20.3-second clocking in the 220-yard dash, a 22.6-second time in the 220-yard low hurdles, a leap of 26′ 8¼″ in the long jump, and a tied world mark in the 100-yard dash in 9.4 seconds. It was simply the most superlative feat ever accomplished in the history of the sport.

The black press was understandably effusive in praise. Said the June 8, 1935, *Norfolk* (Virginia) *Journal and Guide.* "Owens . . . is without doubt the greatest individual performer the world has ever known." It also noted that coverage in the white daily papers in Birmingham and Atlanta was relegated to page three. Up North, the June 2, 1935, *New York Times* carried a banner headline, "Owens' Record-Breaking Feats Presage Brilliant Olympic Mark" and then reopened a discussion of why blacks make better runners. The *Times* added that " A theory has been advanced that through some physical characteristic of the race involving the bone and muscle construction of the foot and leg the Negro is ideally adapted to the sprints and jumping events." Need more be said about this ridiculous notion that was thought to be just the reverse before Eddie Tolan and Ralph Metcalfe won the sprints at the 1932 Olympics? No matter what blacks did, white experts had to concoct a "theory" to explain it.

Owens' accomplishments overshadowed other outstanding performances by black stars. Willis Ward had defeated Owens in a 60-yard Indoor event on March 2 of that year, and again in the hurdles. In July, at the AAU Championships, Eulace Peacock also beat Owens twice—in the 100-meter dash in 10.2 seconds and in the long jump at 26′ 3″. Owens and Peacock were envisioned as another one-two sprint punch for the upcoming Olympics like Tolan-Metcalfe in 1932. With this kind of talent, it is not surprising that Adolf Hitler was worried about America's "Black Auxiliaries," as he called our black runners.

As controversial as the 1936 Olympics themselves were, problems started for the American team and for Owens even before they left for Berlin. Owens suffered a few personal problems in July 1935 in California, and performed poorly at the AAU Championships in Lincoln, Nebraska. Then he got married and was later told that he may have endangered his amateur standing by accepting a job as a "page" in the Ohio House of Representatives. That taken care of, he fared badly in his studies and found himself academically ineligible for the 1935-36 indoor track season.

Compounding all these problems was a mounting campaign to boycott the 1936 Olympics. On September 15, 1935, Adolf Hitler issued the Nuremberg Laws which stripped German Jews of their citizenship rights and equal treatment under

German Law. The AAU then voted in the fall of 1935 to boycott unless Germany changed its treatment of their Jewish athletes. The American Olympic Committee sent several leaders—including Avery Brundage, its president—to Germany to see for themselves. They came back with high marks for the Germans. What, pray tell, raged the black press, did Brundage and his cohorts see? Brundage remained a despised figure to the majority of black athletes the rest of his days.

Black stars like Owens were also reminded by the black press that, here at home, neither the major leagues nor the National Football League admitted blacks. The New York *Amsterdam News* urged our black athletes to stay put, as did Owens' two hometown black papers, the *Cleveland Call and Post* and the *Cleveland Gazette*. To make matters worse for him, because of his troubles as a "page," the ASU ordered Owens' name removed from consideration for the Sullivan Award, given annually to the nation's most outstanding amateur athlete. Thus Owens' May 25 performance—the most acclaimed athletic feat of the century—went unrewarded by the sport's highest authorities.

Owens had to be slightly unsure since Peacock had beaten him five straight times since July 1935. But then Peacock tore a hamstring muscle at the Penn Relays on April 24, 1936, while Owens regained his form. Owens, by now at five feet ten inches and 165 pounds, broke the world mark in the 100-yard dash in 9.3 seconds on May 16, won all of his events at the Big Ten Championships, and easily qualified for the American Olympic squad at New York City's Randall's Island. His other black teammates were Ralph Metcalfe and Mack Robinson (Jackie Robinson's brother) in the sprints, David Albritton and Cornelius Johnson in the high jump, Archie Williams and James Luvalle in the 400 meters, "Long" John Woodruff in the 800 meters, Fritz Pollard, Jr. in the 110-meter hurdles, and John Brooks in the long jump. The sprinter Louise Stokes and hurdler Tydie Pickett made the women's team. Willis Ward of Michigan, Mel Walker (Owens' Ohio State teammate), and Peacock missed their berths. One favorable note was the designation of Tuskegee as the site for semi-final trials for women—a first for a black school.

The team sailed on the *S.S. Manhattan* on July 15, and arrived in Bremerhaven, Germany, nine days later. Owens was mobbed by German autograph seekers as he and his teammates tried to adjust to the time change. When the Games began a week later, everything seemed in order except for the banning of Howell King, a black boxer, for supposedly pilfering a camera from a store. Then on the very first day, what began as a perceived slight in time mushroomed into legend.

After Hitler watched two German athletes win gold medals, he ordered them to his box for personal congratulations. He did the same for a Finish athlete. Then Cornelius Johnson won the high

jump over David Albritton but Hitler left just before the playing of the American national anthem.
No one will ever know for sure if Hitler was pur-
posely avoiding a face-to-face confrontation in full
public view with a black athlete, but the American
press played the "snub" for all it was worth. According to William J. Baker, "Not until the next
day did Owens win his first gold medal. By then
the president of the International Olympic Committee, Henri de Baillet-Latour of Belgium, had
gotten word to Hitler that as the head of the host
government he must be impartial in his accolades.
. . . Hitler stopped inviting winners to his stadium
box."

The snub to Johnson was eventually transposed
to a snub to Owens that Owens himself initially
denied but later erroneously admitted was true.
Owens won his first gold medal on the second day,
August 3. In the semi-final heats on the first day,
he broke the world record in the 100 meters at
10.2 seconds, but it was wind-aided. In the final
on that Monday, he lined up against Metcalfe and
Frank Wykoff of the United States, and the runners from Germany, Sweden, and the Nether-
lands. He drew the inside lane but officials had
moved everyone one lane out because the distance
runners had chewed up the lane nearest the curb.
But it did not matter as Owens won by three yards
in 10.3 seconds with Metcalfe second. One down,
three to go.

On Tuesday morning, August 4, Owens qualified for the 200-meter finals with Mack Robin-

son. In both of his heats he clocked 21.1 seconds for new world marks around a turn, but trouble loomed in the afternoon long jump trials. American jumpers had won every long jump event since 1896. After Ownes took a practice run through the long jump pit, an official raised his red flag to signify an attempt. Practice runs were not allowed in Germany. On his second try, his take-off foot stepped over the front edge of the board and he fouled again. He had one last try to qualify and here more legend surfaced.

Many accounts had Owens' chief rival, the German Lutz Long, as coming over to him to offer words of encouragement. In the book, *Jesse: The Man Who Outran Hitler,* Long supposedly said, "I Luz Long. I think I know what is wrong with you." In actuality, Long did no such thing and Owens later admitted as much to close friends. But the first version was more dramatic and many sportswriters let him get away with this little slip. In any event, Owens qualified and set up a real confrontation with Long. Owens held a small lead at 25′ 9¾″ after the first round of jumps but Long matched it. Then Owens sailed beyond 26′ and Long failed to keep up. But Owens still had more in reserve though his second gold medal was already in his pocket. On his last solo try, he sprung himself out to a new Olympic record of 26′ 5¼″. Two down, two to go.

Both Owens and Mack Robinson qualified in the morning rain on August 5 for the 200-meter finals. In the finals in the afternoon, Owens and

Robinson crouched next to two Dutchmen, a Swede, and a Canadian. With the starter's pistol Owens catpulted his lithe figure to victory in an Olympic record time of 20.7 seconds. Robinson was second in a borrowed pair of shoes in 21.1 seconds. But the attention once again centered on Owens who had just won his third gold medal, the first since 1900. Three down, one to go. He rested and watched Fritz Pollard, Jr. win a bronze medal in the 110-meter hurdles on August 6.

Ordinarily, Owens would have been finished competing, but he surprisingly found himself having to lead off the 400-meter relay team. The team was told at the Randall's Island trials that the fourth, fifth, sixth, and seventh finishers in the 100-meter trials would make up the 400-meter relay squad. That was Foy Draper, Marty Glickman, Sam Stoller, and Mack Robinson. But at the last minute the coaches changed their minds in a ploy that looked as though the two Jewish runners, Glickman and Stoller, were intentionally overlooked and that favoritism for the University of Southern California (USC) was involved.

Though Robinson had qualified for the 200 meters, he was replaced by Frank Wykoff who was a USC student. The coach of the relay squad was Dean Cromwell, also of USC. Glickman and Stoller had resisted protests back home for going to Nazi Germany in the first place and this was another blow. In addition, Cromwell had Glickman, Stoller, and Draper run in a special 100-meter race next to the Olympic Village to see who would run in what order in the relay. Both Glickman and Stoller finished ahead of Draper in this dry run. But Lawson Robertson, the head coach, decided to drop both Glickman and Stoller in favor of Draper and Wykoff.

According to William J. Baker, Metcalfe and Wykoff thought Owens had selfishly wanted to win a fourth gold medal and had not protested the exclusion of the Jewish runners. Glickman said he vividly remembers Owens saying in a meeting: "Coach, let Marty and Sam run. I've had enough. I've won three gold medals. Let them run, they deserve it. They ought to run." To which one of the coaches snidely replied, "You'll do as you're told." Back home the press concerning the benching of Glickman and Stoller was lost in the euphoria of the team's victories.

Metcalfe, who lost twice to Eddie Tolan at Los Angeles in 1932, finally got his gold medal in the relay; Archie Williams won the 400-meter dash in 46.5 seconds; John Woodruff captured the 800-meter run in 1:52.9 minutes; and James Luvalle, the only Phi Beta Kappa in the field, won a bronze medal in the 400-meters. John Brooks placed sixth in the long jump. All returned home as conquering heroes in an election year that saw black Americans courted as never before.

After a series of economic and occupational mishaps, Owens finally settled down as a representative for the Atlantic Richfield Company, while Woodruff, Pollard, Williams, Albritton, and Metcalfe finished college and went on to respectable lives. Luvalle earned his doctorate in chemistry and became a college professor at Stanford University. Neither Stokes not Pickett won medals at Berlin in the women's events.

In 1950, the Associated Press named Owens as the "Athlete of the Half-Century," an especially welcomed honor since he failed to win the Sullivan Award in 1936, given to the nation's most outstanding amateur athlete. In late 1936, Owens publicly backed the losing presidential candidate, Alf Landon. He also lost his amateur standing because of oral agreements made to cash in on his Olympic fame. Not only did these offers fail to materialize, but he became involved in a series of business disasters that sullied his name for a time. His stature was resurrected by presidential appointments for world tours to promote sports and international understanding. Through it all, his wife Ruth stood by his side.

In 1972 his alma mater awarded Owens an honorary doctorate, and in 1974 the NCAA presented the Theodore Roosevelt Award to him in honor of his college contributions. He was made a charter member of the Track and Field Hall of Fame. In 1976, President Gerald Ford awarded him the highest accolade a civilian could receive—the Presidential Medal of Freedom.

The victories of black Americans at Berlin served as a beacon for all Americans of African descent. The Depression was beginning to ebb and another migration from South to North had started. More runners were competing in more events as the Second World War decimated the college campuses. But the black dominance in sprinting and jumping had begun in earnest despite the plaudits of Woodruff and Williams at Berlin. The increasingly learned coaches of young black speedsters funneled them into the shorter races so they could perform like Jesse Owens. They found inspiration in his exploits.

# ADRIENNE BLUE

## Killer Gymnastics

*Olympic gymnastics was transformed in 1972 in Munich when Soviet gymnast Olga Korbut and her coach, Renald Knysh, introduced two new and dangerous somersaults on the uneven bars and the beam. From that year on, women's gymnastics would be dominated by young girls who possessed the flexible bodies needed to execute daring routines. For those athletes bound for the Olympics, courage became an all-important factor. Rumanian Nadia Comaneci and American Mary Lou Retton followed in Korbut's footsteps by introducing their own innovations. But behind the scenes of the crowd-pleasing routines and the triumphs of the Olympics are troubling statistics of anorexia and other eating disorders among female gymnasts desperate to retain their prepubescent bodies. Adrienne Blue reminds us that there is also a personal cost to consider when viewing the dazzling accomplishments of the Olympic stars.*

Munich, 1972. The smallest gymnast on the team, carrying the huge team bag on her shoulder, is the last one in the line when the Soviet team walks in graceful procession into the Olympic

Sporthalle. This is the team which has won the Olympic title five times in a row. They are all fine gymnasts. But the little one, whom that enormous bag is almost obscuring from view, the little one who only just made the team as a reserve, is about to create a sensation.

The newcomer, Olga Korbut, looks about eleven or twelve. She is virtually straight up and down, a pretty child. On her delicately-boned, four-foot eleven-inch, 84-pound body there is little fat and no sign of puberty. The first surprise of her Olympic gymnastics debut was that Olga Korbut was fully seventeen.

The Soviet team was known for its aloof perfection. This Olga Korbut was an able gymnast too, but she was differnt. She flirted with the audience, winked, tossed that blonde head, strutted. She looked like an innocent child. She behaved like Lolita. Standing in for a member of the team who was ill, Korbut performed in the team competition. She charmed the audience with her gymnastics as well as with her coquettish ways, earning high scores—the lowest a more-than-respectable 9.4 out of 10.0—and qualifying for the second stage of the competition, which featured the thirty-six gymnasts who had performed best in the team competition.

Only two other gymnasts had more points to carry over to the next stage than Olga Korgut with 38.350. She now had a good chance of winning the most sought-after of all gymnastics titles: the all-round, or overall, championship. Her strength was in the optional routines. Hers were imaginative and daring, even dangerous. The reason Olga Korbut was on the team only as a reserve was that despite her ability to do some marvellous, complicated routines, sometimes she muffed the simple compulsory exercises. But things this first day were going well.

Then, suddenly, she made two mistakes during her thirty seconds on the uneven parallel bars. Her feet touched the floor. They weren't supposed to. Her hand momentarily slipped off the bar. Practically beginner's errors. She continued her performance anyway, as gymnasts are taught to do, to the end, but scored only 7.5. Those mundane errors had lost her the chance of an overall medal.

Unable to hide her disappointment, at the end of her performance Olga Korbut wept. Satellite television was watching. An audience of four hundred million saw her cover her face with her hands and cry. It was a touching sight. Hers would become the most famous tears in sport.

The timing was right. A girl who could be graceful and cry, who was a champion without visible muscles, was to many people a welcome sight. It came at a time when in Western countries, many parents had begun to worry that their daughters might want to play football or run the marathon. The idea of women's liberation was taking hold, and even spreading to sport. Billie Jean King was in the news. She and some of the other tennis players had become fed up with the raw deal they were getting compared to male players, and had started their own women's professional circuit, which was thriving. Girls were asking why they couldn't join teams in what had always been boys' sports. The women who competed at the Olympics had attained so high a standard in so many sports that sex tests had been instituted at the previous Games to make sure they were not men in disguise.

A revolution was bubbling up in women's sport. But when Olga Korbut went all girlie on the television screen, there were plenty of people out there not only eager to comfort her, but willing to embrace her as a way of holding back the tide of change—if only she could be a winner.

The next day was like a Hollywood movie. With the audience rooting for her, everything began to go right. She did a half back somersault on the uneven bars which no one else had ever done. The crowd and the judges gasped. It was a difficult, dangerous, innovative manoeuvre. It had taken Olga Korbut, whose short body it was designed specially for, fully two years to learn to do it. She must have practised it twenty thousand times.

The backward somersault she did on the long, four-inch-wide plank called the beam had never been done before either. The judges were anxious: should such perilous innovations be rewarded or banned?

The crowd was exhilarated. They cheered her every move, and Korbut held on to her concentration. Early on, when the judges' marks were low, the crowd in the Sporthalle booed and stomped. At one point, the jeering went on for five tense minutes. In the next event, there were signs that the judges had been affected.

On the balance beam, Korbut was awarded a generous 9.90. Purists said the judges were over-marking her, pandering to the partisan crowd. There were accusations that they overmarked in the floor exercise too.

With those two golds and her share of the Soviet team gold medal, plus one silver medal on the uneven bars, Olga Korbut came fifth overall. The most coveted Olympic title in the sport, the individual overall championship, went to another, more flawless Soviet gymnast, Ludmila Tourischeva, but it was Korbut who had become a star.

Girls by the millions took up gymnastics after Olga Korbut's Olympic debut. They and their parents did not realize that Korbut had made her sport dangerous. They only knew she had excelled at a sport where girls could be girls. No muscles needed—or so it appeared—just grace.

In fact, that was a lie. Strength is as important a factor as skill. Korbut had trained rigorously in a special gymnastics school since the age of ten to build the required muscle.

At her school near Minsk in Grodno, Russia, there were five hundred girls, but only she had learned to do those special somersaults. Her coach Renald Knysh had designed both of Olga Korbut's difficult new moves specifically to suit her body. He had designed them to be dangerous and difficult and to look it—to impress the judges.

Not everyone liked Renald Knysh, a dark-haired man who didn't talk much, and who disliked noise, even applause. But few doubted his devotion to his profession. He kept a cardfile of young married couples in the town who might bear children whom he might train in gymnastics. He worked his gymnasts hard. There were people who said he would stop at nothing to produce champions.

There were rumours that he had staved off Olga Korbut's puberty with drugs. Only a short-waisted, childlike body was flexible enough to do some of the routines Korbut was introducing into the sport. Only that sort of body, unburdened by fatty tissue like breasts, had the right strength-to-weight ratio. The womanly classical gymnasts of old would never have been able to do what Korbut did.

Not only the judges were impressed with what Olga Korbut could do. So were young gymnasts. Korbut and Knysh's new Killer Gymnastics changed the face of the sport. The Korbut somersault and the Korbut loop, once considered daring, still considered dangerous, have virtually became necessary for anyone who wants to win. Ever after, 'girlish' gymnastics would require enormous courage.

Montreal, 1976. Olga Korbut had invented Killer Gymnastics. Now Nadia Comaneci perfected it. With exquisite technique, she won three gold medals and a bronze. She was only fourteen at the time, stood Korbut's height—four foot eleven—but weighed 86 pounds, two pounds more. She was the first gymnast to score a perfect score of 10.0 at the Olympics. They called her Little Miss Perfect.

The distinguished Romanian coach Bela Karolyi had discovered her when she was only six. He was scouting for talent and saw her, in Onesti, Romania, in the schoolyard during recess. He liked the way she moved. As he was going over to talk to her, the schoolbell rang and the children ran into their classrooms.

Karolyi went into every classroom to find her. But how could he tell, the children were sitting down? Finally, he asked each class if they like gymnastics. Nadia Comaneci was one of the ones who shouted, 'I do.' Until then she was an ordinary dark-haired child. Her father was a car mechanic; her mother an office worker. She had a younger brother called Adrian.

Now Karolyi saw to it she had fine training, and took the sport seriously. At the early age of seven Comaneci was entered in the Romanian junior championships; she finished thirteenth. At eight, she won. She was a student at the special gymnastics high school in Gheorgehiu Dej. At just thirteen, she won the women's European championship, one of the hardest of all competitions because the Eastern European nations, who for years have dominated the sport, compete there. In 1976, with two coaches, a choreographer, a physician, an assistant music master, and a masseur to assist her, Nadia Comaneci became, at fourteen years 313 days old, the youngest ever Olympic gold medallist in the sport.

Comaneci made the sport riskier by adding a full turn to her dismount routine. 'The world has me to thank or blame for the Comaneci Somersault and the Comaneci Dismount,' she says. On the blind forward somersault done on the high bar, 'the gymnast doesn't get to see the bar while trying to catch it until the last possible moment.'

In this new Killer Gymnastics, grace was not as necessary as courage. To win, you had to pick up 'bonus points' for risk. The injury level began to go up in the sport. Bones and joints were subjected to impact and squashed and stretched—they were stressed—over and over and over, thousands of times. This was damaging growing bones and joints, possibly stunting growth.

But Nadia Comaneci also had another problem. She began to grow up. To save her career, when at sixteen her breasts budded and she grew taller, Comaneci instinctively stopped eating. She became the first famous anorexic gymnast. The need to stay skinny and childlike—pre-pubescent—has resulted in gymnastics having the highest percentage of anorexia of any sport. Coaches call it the Nadia Syndrome.

Anorexia is not, literally, contagious. But many young gymnasts modelled their behaviour on Comaneci. Two top British champions came down with anorexia. Nearly half of the gymnasts in a key California study were eating less than two-thirds of the recommended daily allowances of vitamin B6, iron, calcium and zinc, all essential for normal growth. More than three-quarters of the college-age gymnasts studied in Michigan in 1986 had some sort of eating disorder associated with trying to stay thin.

In Texas, at the 1979 world championships, Nadia Comaneci showed all the signs of anorexia —among them weakness, pallor, low resistance to infection and injury, wounds that would not heal. Although she was really too ill to perform, Comaneci was told to make an appearance to save the team's chances. She went on, but she made a mistake on a simple move.

Then she was taken to a nearby hospital with an inflamed wound on her wrist which had not healed. The greatest danger to a gymnast of being anorexic is that it makes her weak, prone to injury.

Moscow, 1980. Gymnastics practice, three days before the Olympic Games. Elena Mukhina, aged twenty, the daring world overall champion is practising for the Games. Elena Mukhina has already contributed something new to her sport: she has added a full twist to Korbut's high bar loop, catching the high bar once again and continuing with her routine. This new move, which took two years to learn, has increased the risk of the sport, but it is enthralling to watch. Mukhina must practise every aspect of her performance.

Now, as she practises the floor exercise, probably the least dangerous part of a gymnast's performance, she makes a mistake. In the final somersault of her tumbling sequence there is a standard gymnastics movement called a one and a half or one and three-quarter Arabian front somersault. She has to land on her neck and shoulders and then roll to a standing position. Mukhina has practised the Arabian over and over, probably well over 10,000 times. This time, she lands on her neck too heavily. It breaks.

She is hurried to a well-equipped hospital, she undergoes surgery, her life is saved. But Elena Mukhina is now paralysed from the neck down. For six months she cannot even talk. How could this happen to a world champion?

In her tribute to Mukhina, Nadia Comaneci said, 'As one of the world's top gymnasts, she could be expected to include many elements of high risk, in order to give her a chance of acquiring the necessary bonus points.' In other words, the higher in the scale you got, the more perilous the sport was. Elena Mukhina, who had enthralled world audiences, was, Comaneci said in conclusion and intending no bitter irony, 'a fine exponent of our sport'.

After the accident, she never walked again. After arduous physiotherapy, much of it painful, which she undertakes with the same intensity as she did her championship moves, Mukhina can now sit up in a special chair. She believes that one day she will be able to walk.

In 1986 Olga Korbut, long retired, proposed an

alternative to Killer Gymnastics. Why not, she said, have age categories at Olympic level? Then, girls who had become women could stay in competition. Physically, anorexia would no longer be such an occupational hazard.

We might even see a return of the grace of the classical gymnasts, the grown-ups like the great Czech Olympic champion Vera Caslavska. The pre-pubescent grouping, with its elastic contortions would have its audience; the ballerinas would have theirs. Korbut's ideas are theoretically viable. Unfortunately, it isn't likely anyone will up and change the sport soon, if ever.

No one knows how much of the postponement of puberty is done individually by gymnasts who become anorexic, and how much is inflicted by coaches and sports doctors. In fact, you might say it is all inflicted because what the anorexic is responding to is her coach's message, the audience's message, to stay a child so she can do those Killer Gymanastics contortions.

The Soviets seem to be the first to have discovered that it may be possible to hold off puberty without drugs. Usually, just making sure a young gymnast's body fat is below seven per cent of body weight is enough. Some estimates say it can even be a bit higher. Most competitive gymnasts fall in the eight to nine per cent range. The body weight of most teenaged girls is about twenty per cent fat. Like marathoners, champion gymnasts are particularly thin. Even Lisa Elliott, the British national gymnastics champion, who is nowhere near the top of the world, has only 5.3 per cent body fat. This is close to the level of the Soviet stars.

It is possible that some gymnasts worldwide now use drugs, to delay puberty, or to stunt growth, and to build muscle power. There is no proof, though, and everyone denies it. It may just be that short girls in the West are attracted to the sport, and are sought out in the Eastern bloc.

The 1984 overall Olympic champion Mary Lou Retton, a four-foot nine-inches tall American from the hills of West Virginia, is the first American ever to win an Olympic gymnastics title. She is the first to credit her coach, Bela Karolyi, the Romanian who discovered Nadia Comaneci, but now lives in the United States. Retton tells fond tales of his slave-driving. But so eager was she to train, that she didn't have to be prodded to remove the cast on her fractured wrist early and against doctor's orders. Retton won the Olympic title at the age of sixteen but has the aches and pains of a sixty-year-old. 'When it's cold and damp outside', she says, 'I just ache all over.'

The 1987 world champion, Aurelia Dobre, who won the title at the age of fifteen, is a superb technician, in the Romanian tradition of gymnastics perfection. She looks pert and small, childlike, a typical Killer Gymnast.

Her predecessor as world champion, Oksana Omelianchik, tiny and two years older, has made innovations in the floor exercise that are breathtaking and a little scary. Her immediate change of direction after her first tumbling pass steps up the pace of floor exercise. Omelianchik, who trains in Kiev, brushes aside talk of anorexia or special diets or drugs. So does her coach and the head of the Soviet team. Long hours of training, they say, are the only secret of gymnastics.

# RICHARD HARTEIS

## November 1—New York City Marathon Day

*The New York City Marathon is not only one of the most grueling tests a runner can face but also a vehicle for hopes, fears, and personal reflections. In this piece Richard Harteis invites the reader to experience first-hand the emotional exhilaration and physical pain of running the race. Here are recounted in detail the sometimes madcap festivities, the poignant moments of extreme effort, the fleeting encounters between the spectators and the runners—such as the Hasidic children in Williamsburg with faces that were "bowls of cream set with cherry cheeks and coal-black eyes" or the ten-year-old girl who passes a cherished stuffed koala bear to an exhausted Harteis as he runs through Harlem—and the writer's inward reflections as he struggled to complete the twenty-six-mile run.*

Fort Wadsworth Park was a mob scene, as though a Super Bowl football stadium had emptied out onto its staging fields. Runners were converging from all parts of the world and from all points of the compass. The morning chill was already beginning to burn off, and runners were stripping themselves of plastic bags and old sweats. A number of runners sported less-than-traditional outfits. Two were dressed head to foot in Arab robes and veils and paraded around like Saudi royalty. One black boy was dressed like a French chef with a cream puff hat, apron, and white uniform. He even carried a three-layered wedding cake, which I hoped for his sake was made of cardboard. Six guys formed the twelve legs of a fairly realistic centipede snaking around a flatbed trailer on which drill sergeants directed warm-up exercises. It was hard to tell if the more exotic running outfits were a result of the Halloween holiday, or if some esoteric statement was being made. Carnival.

The prerace material had announced, "There will be more than three hundred portable toilets and the world's longest urinal at the start. Please don't use the bushes!" There were such long lines, however, that every tree larger than a fire hydrant was occupied. Grace kept marching from one john to another, sure we would find one that had shorter lines. But when we came to the main tent she decided we should check in first and tap a kidney later. We fed ourselves into roped-off funnels leading into the tent. At the end of each line a volunteer stood with an electronic wand that she ran over the code strip at the bottom of our bib number. The wand made a little beep when it got the number, like a fancy checkout register at the grocery store that "reads" your purchases and gives you a computer printout of the price of peas.

As we rang through the line the volunteer bean

counters wished us good luck, then Grace and I queued up for the johns beyond the tent. The doors on the little houses were marked "Men" or "Women," but the distinction had long since become academic as both sexes shifted from one leg to another in anticipation. No sooner did a runner come out, bursting into breath like a whale surfacing from the ocean depths, than another runner hustled into the foul box, regardless of the designated gender on the door. This was not a polite line of beauties clutching their evening bags during intermission at *Aida*. It was like elbowing your way through a shopping center the day after Christmas as groups funneled their way into single file. Runners just coming on the line were nervous. You could feel the latecomers willing the lucky occupant to get on with it. As they got closer to their goal, however, runners in the front of the line became sweetness and light, since now it was clear they'd make it before the call to the start. Occasionally, a round of applause sounded for some sluggard whose olfactory nerve was apparently shot but who finally released his booth for someone else.

"How's your ankle feeling today?" Grace asked from the line she was standing in.

"It's a little less stiff, but it still hurts. There's no way I'll do this nonstop, I guess."

"I pulled my knee last week," the girl in front of me began.

"Your ankle will warm up," Grace said. "Just keep moving, Richard, no matter what. Don't let your body go into a walk, keep jogging even if you're going slow as a snail. Once you stop running it's hard to get started up again."

"Twenty-six miles is a long way, Grace."

"Forget twenty-six miles," she said. "Just think of one mile at a time until you float across the finish line. Peachy." She gave me a little punch in the stomach.

From time to time a pleasant young guy came on the PA system to tell us how much time we had left, making announcements about the day. "Here comes the Goodyear blimp, ladies and gentlemen, that cigar-shaped cloud just coming over the Verrazano Bridge. What a view they must have up there."

People spread over the fields of Fort Wadsworth like a Hollywood movie set of Moses leading his people out of Egypt. I'd never seen such a crowd before, a World Series sell-out where everyone in the stadium is a player. The expectation in the runners was almost visible.

"Ladies and gentlemen, please don't forget to keep drinking lots of water. It's going to be plenty warm today, so you've got to keep replacing those fluids."

Tables were set up everywhere, honeycombed with paper cups that water boys and girls replenished from thirty-gallon cans.

"Now, ladies and gentlemen, we're going to get going here in just a few minutes. We want all the men with runner numbers under 15,999 to begin at the blue start. All other runners will begin at the red start. Please don't go onto the bridge plaza until your start color has been called. We're going to give you plenty of time to get to the starting line, so when we call you please move gently. When you are called, line up near the pace sign that indicates your predicted finish time for the marathon."

If I could average 10 minutes for each mile, I figured I could finish in 260 minutes—60 into 260, 6 into 26—let's see, my estimated time would be 4 hours and 20 minutes. With an extra 10 minutes for the 0.2 miles added by the queen cheering from her balcony, and it looked as though I might run the marathon in 4½ hours, just what I had signed up for. Clever, the way they print out your schedule for you upside down at the bottom of your bib number so you can read it as you run: 5 miles at 51 minutes; 10 miles at 1 hour and 43 minutes; half marathon at 2 hours 15 minutes; 20 miles at 3 hours 26 minutes; 25 miles at 4 hours 17 minutes; and finish in 4 hours and 30 minutes. I wouldn't be burning up the track at that pace, but it was as fast as I'd gone on my longest run. I wondered if 10-minute miles would be realistic for 26 miles.

"Okay, folks," the announcer called out. "This is what we've all been waiting for. Would the red starters please begin to move onto the toll plaza. And slowly, please. We won't be going anywhere until everyone is in place."

A tidal wave of 4,489 women and several thousand men swelled over the little knoll to the toll plaza and lined up behind the pace signs strung on poles high over the crowd. I looked for the sign that indicated ten-minute miles. Happily, there were men and women, young and old, who also planned on a four-and-a-half-hour marathon. There were plenty of runners with such modest expectations among the blue starters as well, but as this was my first marathon I was placed with the women. For the first eight miles the red and blue runners would run a parallel but separate course. At Lafayette Avenue, however, red and blue starters would join up together for the rest of the marathon.

When the blue runners were called to the start with the red, it was like standing in the middle of a beehive, a general buzz of nervous chatter and good wishes almost overwhelming the PA system. At the instructions of the announcer, runners began passing clothes they wished to discard to the sidelines. Old sweats went hand over hand like beers at a ball game. Twins from Arizona decided their long-sleeved tops would be too hot, and we all joined around to rip their arms off. Very little sweat-shirt was left to cover the leopard brassieres they wore underneath.

Helicopters were hovering in place over the Verrazano Bridge, and several blimps floated up a little higher. Sailboats glided up and down the river, tugs passed under the bridge spraying jets of water hundreds of feet into the air. At the very top of the bridge perhaps fifty lilliputian-sized cameramen were filming the human ribbon that lay at their feet waiting to unwind. A string of sailors holding hands stretched across the starting line like a paper cutout. As the good mayor fired up his hyperbole my nerves got the better of me. I stopped listening and felt my eyes start to sting. The whole scene was as overwhelming as they promised. I had lost my personality, felt small and inconsequential, but in a mystical way somehow I was powerful—powerful as the whole of the human mass that had come together for this event, like the core of a nuclear reactor going critical. One body, one voice. A lot of people around me felt the same way. It wouldn't have mattered, but I didn't want the beauty of what I was feeling to start me crying. It was like trying to stop the hiccups by an act of will until a good scare does the trick.

Boom. The cannon scared me shitless, as they say, and I no longer had to worry about my dignity.

For five minutes we ran in place like a hoard of Chinese foot soldiers until the thousands ahead of us began to move across the bridge. Finally the wind whispered to us, the dragon's tail came alive, and we were off.

"Have a good journey," Grace said to me, careful of the word "journey" as though she had been waiting to give me a secret piece of advice. "Been nice knowing you," we used to say in the old days as we lifted a glass of bourbon. There wouldn't be anything artificial about our recreation today, though—this was to be the ultimately natural, maybe once-in-a-lifetime high. She gave me the sly big Bancroft smile, and I pulled her up for a kiss. I also made the sign of the cross the way we used to do before leaving the locker room at half-time, the way I still do when I'm sure the plane is going to crash. My heart was speeding at a rate that had nothing to do with running. The sun was bright, the air sharp, and the water all diamonds below us. We couldn't ask for a better day.

"*Look* at those guys," Grace said in feigned disgust at the two hundred men who had stopped along the railing and turned their backs to the runners going by. "You know they just saved it up so they could say they had a pee off the Verrazano Bridge."

"Penis envy, Grace," I said.

"Ha. I've seen women stop too."

Occasionally, someone would accidentally tramp on the person in front of him or bump into a runner trying to get by. It was a little disconcerting to be in such a crowd of people having to depend on the common sense and good will of the pack to move things along safely. The queasiness of driving on an L.A. freeway. This crowd was a sample of humanity like any other, though, and sometimes the accident was no accident at all. Some creep would push by, passing on the right, say, as he bumped his way ahead: "Excuse me, I believe this is *my* stag ahead there. Or would you prefer that I rip your ear off?"

Today of all days, of course, the plastic stays in my ankle braces began to slide up and threaten to pop out as I ran. I bounced on one leg for a minute every now and then to push them back down, risking a ten-car pileup every time I did. It was impossible to move off to the side the way you were supposed to do. My ankles, especially the left, and the connective tissue to the heels were still burning like crazy, hadn't warmed up yet. It was like taking a paring knife up the side of a papaya and scraping the hard seed just under the soft flesh. The braces had pulled me through all summer, and I felt like a child whose favorite blanket had just been snatched away for the cleaners.

"These braces are giving me fits, Grace," I said, hopping on my right leg to adjust the left brace. "Listen, if I have to stop don't let me hold you back. If you want to pull out, just go ahead, okay?"

"Maybe after the bridge I'll pick up my pace," she said. Beads of sweat had formed on her upper lip.

As we came to the end of the bridge I heard a little click-click-click, and when I turned around one of the plastic struts lay on the road getting trampled by runners twenty feet behind me. Pain in the ass. But they had cost forty dollars and had saved my career as a runner this summer. I wanted to keep them.

I made my way back as though I were swimming up Niagara, a few curses hurled at me along the way. When I picked up the struts I decided to leave the damn things out, at least until I got over the bridge. I tucked the supports into the waistband at my hip. My feet felt naked, but at least I was no longer worried about being run over by ten thousand marathoners. When I looked ahead sweet Grace was just moving down the curve off the bridge. She waved and gave me the last big smile I would see till the race was over. I was on my own.

Some purists consider running with radio earphones to be antisocial, like going to a town meeting and reading a newpaper. All summer long, though, good rock and roll had helped me stave off pain and boredom as I ran the deserted country roads in Connecticut. Sometimes a particularly pounding Rolling Stones song carried me into another lap just as I was about to give it up for the day. Music had become as indispensable as my ankle braces. When Grace disappeared down the exit ramp onto 92nd Street I tuned in my headset as though I were lighting up a good Cuban cigar after a pound and a half of rare prime rib.

Ah, those were the days, weren't they? We never thought of cholesterol, or lung cancer, or angioplasty. It never crossed our minds that vegetarians were less likely to suffer from gallstones, that calorie needs decreased with age, that before you added salt to your meal at the table you should probably at least *taste* your food to see if it was needed. The worst that could happen from a night of debauchery in the Big Apple could be cured with a shot or two of penicillin. It never occurred to us that Mick Jagger would turn forty, that

Diana Ross might look old one day, that John Lennon would ever die.

But find the right song, turn it up loud enough, there you are again cruising down a country road to a polo game in autumn, top down of your mom's '65 Mustang, full bottle of Jack Daniels at your side. Or you're blasting through the suburbs of Paris on the back of a friend's motorcycle headed for the Cannes Film Festival. He's teaching you how to ride, your arms surround his black leather jacket at the waist. Better-looking than a young Brando, and he has invited *you* for a weekend in Cannes. How will you hide the crush that is growing as you fly into the wind down to the Côte d'Azur holding on tight to your friend? Strawberry fields forever.

Running with a radio didn't take you out of the race, it just added to the joy of the ride. It was like a good movie score that helped your heart follow the action. Aretha Franklin was demanding a little R-E-S-P-E-C-T when I danced off the bridge and landed in Bay Ridge. By then I had become mesmerized by a girl dressed in metallic green running shorts. On each cheek of her well-endowed derriere she had printed the word "go" in large gold letters, and watching her run was like having a private cheering section: go go, go go, go go.

I wasn't ready for the throng that greeted us when we came off the bridge—a rambunctious crowd lining the sidewalks. This is a working neighborhood of Irish and Italian and mostly Norwegians, who first came here in 1636 fleeing religious persecution. "Ten thousand Swedes lay in the weeds all chased by one Norwegian" is a rhyme you might hear as children jumped rope. Each May 17 the neighborhood still celebrates Norwegian Independence Day. Anything for a party.

Half the guys in the crowd pulled on a can of beer, women too. Little old ladies sat waving from cheap folding chairs in front of their row houses. The local fire station apparently had one of their own in the race. A sentry was stationed in the bin of a cherry picker, which telescoped from the back of a fire truck. When he picked out their boy in the crowd sirens went off, lights flashed, and the whole company went into an uproar. Mongrels of every possible genetic combination sported red and blue kerchiefs about their necks like cowboys. Some had balloons tied to their collars. Church was over, the day was sunny, and this was the best show in town.

All along 4th Street groups of children like flocks of chicks huddled together and stuck their tiny arms into the flow of runners. Their mothers stood behind watching over what had become a ritual, like organizing a line of seven-year-olds for their first communion. This was more than just "getting five." The runners were heroes for these kids, and they wanted to touch us, simply to touch us, as though we might bring good luck or some of our strength might flow into them. I thought of that cereal advertisement that portrays gorgeous athletes working out before their morning Wheaties until the jazzy lady comes on and sings, "Go tell your mama what the *big* boys eat."

It might sound a little wacky or sentimental, but this energy surge seemed to flow both ways. We felt that we were in touch with some sort of grace or power too as we touched the children. A jogger would pull over to the side and put out his hand as he ran by, pat, pat, pat, pat, pat, pat, pat, pat, slapping all their little mitts and taking in the bright smiles, the astonishment, and sometimes the fear on the faces. He found it hard not to straighten up a little and tighten his form as he ran through this mill of glad hands.

Ahead, an army of volunteers in yellow slickers manned the first station holding water out to runners. Sweepers couldn't keep up with their numbers, and the street was paved with crushed dixie cups, making it somewhat hazardous to swing in for refreshment. We'd been encouraged to drink at every station and throw water on ourselves as well to stay cool, but I had hardly worked up a sweat four miles into the race. The volunteers seemed to be competing for customers, and no sooner did they give up their cups than they came back with others, faces full of expectation.

"Thanks," I said to the small black girl from whom I took my first drink, running in place as I downed the water. "I needed that." Her eyes widened and she looked down at her feet. You'd have thought I'd said she was more beautiful than Whitney Houston.

I was having a great time watching the spectators watch us. Certain runners were an obvious hit: a midget running on bandy legs, three little steps for each one of mine, a guy with his hair dyed green, a well-toned sixty-year-old with canvas, brush, and an ammo belt filled with oils, painting a fairly respectable portrait of New York as he ran along. Five miles into the race, and none of the runners was in any particular distress. The burning in my ankle had subsided. Everyone was chugging along well, and the crowd sensed our ease and high hopes. No particular drama evident. But when the Jolly Green Giant, or Michelangelo, or a runner in a tuxedo and top hat came by, the crowd pointed and laughed, sending a ripple of applause up the line, as if a pack of circus dogs in clown outfits had entered the center ring.

My radio headset produced a psychological distance between me and the crowd, something like wearing dark glasses. It didn't matter, since most of the crowd's attention went to a little old lady running the race or some guy with mountainous shoulders pushing himself along in a wheelchair. There were thousands of regular, middle-aged runners like me, and I was a little shy, just as glad to be lost in the crowd. If I needed a lift, however, all I had to do was to look someone directly in the eyes, and immediately that person began to whistle, or clap, or call out to me, just me.

It was one-sided in an odd, silent way. None of us seemed to talk to the crowd, an unwritten convention whereby we must pretend to concentrate on the effort of running. But if we looked at a pretty girl or some black dude or a grandma from San Juan, somehow our eyes let them know we were proud, that we wouldn't mind hearing what they thought. The black dude would give the thumbs up, or maybe the pretty girl would still be clapping if we turned around to catch her eye again. Even at great distances, I've read, the eyes are the most distinguishing feature about a person, even more recognizable than body shape or posture. Windows of the soul indeed.

A lot of runners had their names on their shirts, and this got a rise from the audience. "All right, Mike" or "Go, Karen, looking good" would follow you along the course if you happened to be running beside Mike or Karen. And, of course, many couldn't resist making a statement on their T-shirt, from the blatantly commercial "Don White's Ford, Why Pay More?" to the blatantly personal phone number listed under "Single, great in bed." There were team shirts, his and her shirts, and shirts that portrayed the front of a penguin, the Union Jack, or Martin Luther King, Jr., standing on a mountain. A hundred or more devotees of a fashionable guru were running with the yogi's words stenciled on plain white T-shirts. The runners didn't seem overly eager to proselytize, relying on the billboards they were wearing to spread his message. These were not your standard Moonie or Hare Krishna disciples pressuring you to come feast at the temple. But I had to admit I liked the shape of the guru's mind spelled out on their T-shirts and gave him a silent blessing back.

"Om." The sound reverberates through the universe, they say, triggers an independent harmony to help check chaos, rippling through the world like circles on a pond when a stone is dropped in the center. The harmony was resonating in my soul, all right, as I ran through the crowd lined up in Walt Whitman's old neighborhood. I knew that it would be touch and go later on. But for the moment a feeling of great well-being and peace had come over me, and I was singing the body electric.

The endorphin high people talk about has never been my experience. For me, the pleasure I feel when I'm warmed up and alert and running painlessly on a bright day is more like the animal joy I see in Mikey when he's chasing sticks in the river. He would swim out into the current and paddle logs back to the shore until he drowned if we weren't careful. Whatever is going through my mind as I run may be intense, but the very weird thing is that for hours on end I am not aware that *I* am thinking it, have pretty much lost conscious personality as though thought had a life of its own or was being spun out in the mind of God. It's the reverse of astroprojection. Thought has become organic, like blood perfusing my muscles as I run. I become so much a part of the world the loneliness of being locked inside the body never occurs to me. It's easy to become a little anthropomorphic at such times. It isn't just the crowd urging me on, nature itself is conspiring in my happiness. The breeze turns cool and friendly, the day embraces me, and the maples in Sunset Park send up banners of color, wave over the heads of the runners.

The crowd senses something of this too, I think. The festival is contagious. One is likely to have a good time on such a day, maybe meet someone, get lucky. A day to follow one's instincts.

One of the nice diversions for me as I slipped into cruise control and made my way down Fourth Avenue was picking and choosing from the people in the crowd who had brought gifts for the runners. Water was offered at the aid stations, but every so often a spectator stood a little into the street proffering a basket of Hershey Kisses, orange or apple slices, hard candies, grapes, chewing gum, or sour balls. I passed up a well-heeled couple handing out cups of fruit compote in front of their brownstone for a couple of Red-Hot-Dollars a little kid slipped me. Some spectators tempted us with huge jars of Vaseline, which runners dipped into and spread erotically on their crotch or nipples or wherever they had begun to chafe.

A lot of people in the crowd had set up suitcase-sized ghetto blasters to keep the runners jumping to the Pointer Sisters or Prince. Every so often, though, a full-fledged street party was under way with a live reggae band or cottage-industry rock group. The neat demarcation between spectators and runners collapsed, and you might find yourself dancing with folks who had spilled into the street. Mardi Gras in Rio. Pushcart vendors sold hamburgers, gyros, Italian sausages, shish kebabs, and any kind of beer you wanted. The smells drove me crazy. It was about lunchtime, and I could barely resist pulling out my taxi money and stopping for a quick dog and sauerkraut. But I had a more important stop to make.

In the past half hour as I ran, the nagging small sensation that announces a full bladder had become a rather big nagging sensation. I tried to remember how often they said portable johns would be set up. Sometimes an astute spectator carried a sign reading, "Pit stop, one mile" or "Johns just ahead," but I hadn't seen such a sign for some time. I could have held on a little longer, but a walled-in parking area in front of a school came along fortuitously, and I ducked behind the wall.

It's pretty hard to pee while jogging in place, so I decided to put aside my purist notions and stood fast there behind the wall in blessed relief. It felt odd to stop the rhythm of running. It was also a little disconcerting that my urine had turned pink. A year ago when I first found out I had cancer of the bladder, that had been the first symptom. The urologist discounted the symptom as overly athletic sexual activity: "Happens all the time in young men, nothing to worry about." But when the urine turned the color of Gallo Hearty Burgundy another urologist decided to investigate the question a little more carefully.

The doctor was very happy to inform me that

mine was one of the least malevolent forms of cancer, but I found that little consolation. True, I wasn't dying of AIDS, but the nasty tumor in the bladder often returned. I might lose a kidney someday, or have to be refitted with plastic plumbing. It might even be the thing that ultimately does me in. On the other hand, it might never return at all.

Our old friend Jules Hallum has written poems about the act of dying in World War as good as anythng I've read. "We all get our turn," he's fond of saying about the inevitable meeting with the Grim Reaper. But you age a little when you know you're closer in line to your appointment. You begin to take stock and plan a little more carefully for the future. It scared and saddened me when my own dear parents insisted on being there for my operation. It seemed wrong that they should feel responsibility for me even into their own old age. But they said they were coming whether I liked it or not. I guess you never stop being a parent no matter how old you become.

My friend May was promised by a poet friend that she would be young forever—not biologically or chronologically but the way it really matters, he said, spiritually. She gets furious when death comes sniffing around in her life and threatens to turn her into an old woman. She won't give an inch. I tell her she'll always be beautiful, wrinkles or no, that I'd rather have dinner with Melina Mercouri than Madonna any day of the week, and that I bet if the truth were known, Ms. Mercouri would prove to be the better woman in other social encounters as well, despite Madonna's lace jumpsuits and tassled brassieres.

Dueling scars are no longer fashionable, but it doesn't make us less attractive, I think, to admit that life has touched us. Often the contrary is true. You have to be able to sense when something really has you at risk. You have to try to be a little balanced and keep things in perspective. Auden told the story of Bert Savoy, the famous female impersonator, who was watching a thunderstorm with some friends. " 'There's Miss God at it again,' Bert exclaimed and was instantly struck dead by lightning."

This time around, as I inspected the Gallo Rosé splashing against the wall, I felt pretty certain I had just traumatized myself a little by running with a full bladder and made a mental note to stop more often. Go to the back of the line, your turn hasn't come up yet. But the pit stop made it clear why I'd been warned to keep moving, no matter what. In the two minutes I stood ruminating on meeting my maker all my muscles decided to freeze up as though they'd suddenly become aware of what I was putting them through. I longed to sit down for a minute. Auden's words came to me again, a late poem in which the flesh is "praying for Him to die,/so setting Her free to become/irresponsible Matter."

It isn't too hard to talk yourself into keeping at it when fatigue and pain tempt you to stop. It's very tough, however, to get back in gear once you've stopped running and the oxygen-starved muscles finally get a breather. It's like being frozen in a block of ice and having to break out by an act of will. Mind over matter, one of those times that prove the marathon is more a spiritual than physical challenge. The tendons in your groin, hip joints, and calves catch fire like silk rent by flame. Experience tells you the agony will eventually pass, but first you must walk through the fire and immolate your pain.

Offer it up, take a cold shower, try to think of something else, the nuns would counsel when the temptation of sins of the flesh came up on the agenda during my boyhood. As I ran I tried to forget my aches and pains by using the same distraction technique. I concentrated on remembering what part of the course I'd come to as I turned down Bedford Avenue. The Marathon Guide said I'd be "following the footsteps of history," that this was to be a first-class history course as well as a premier race course, so I had to pay attention and enjoy the lesson.

If I remembered rightly, I had already passed the Fort Greene monument for the Prison Ship Martyrs. Eleven thousand colonists had died on British ships docked in Wallabout Bay during the Revolutionary War, about half as many as were running in the race today, a toll hard to imagine from the faraway, romantic war. How many of these poor ghosts trailed the runners like unseen coaches in the core of their fatigue?

If the guide was right, I ought to be coming into

Williamsburg, where "Brooklyn's booming in-
dustrial section got its start." When they opened
the bridge in 1903, however, the diaspora made
it perhaps the largest settlement of Hasidic Jews
in the world, and sure enough little family
groups of Hasidim stood like flocks of starlings
along the sidelines viewing the race in silence.
The men wore black fedoras to cover their yar-
mulkes, black coats and trousers with white
shirts buttoned to the neck. Many wore beards,
and single foot-long locks of hair fell in front of
their ears like ropes to pull them to Abraham's
bosom. The women were dressed in equally drab
attire. Dark stockings, skirts, and sweaters covered every bit of skin save the face, which was
naked of makeup or even natural expression. Only
the children revealed their parents' love of life,
pride in family. The exquisite creatures were
dressed in crushed velvet, subtle navy-blue or for-
est-green capes trimmed in black with fine stockings and shoes. The curl locks on the men looked
goofy, but on the boys were quite precious. Their
faces were bowls of cream set with cherry cheeks
and coal-black eyes. They were the most beautiful
children I had ever seen, with an unworldly aura
of privacy about them. You could almost feel the
effort it took to overcome shyness and offer a runner a piece of orange or a candy. Their parents
would coax them into the street for the exceptional encounter, their black eyes luminous with
excitement under thick lashes. When a runner accepted their gift they jumped back to their moth-

441

ers like little crickets, filled with surprise and pleasure.

Williamsburg was certainly the quietest stretch of spectators so far, but the silent intensity as they stared at us or offered dignified applause made me feel as though we'd done something important. Serious work, liebling. Congratulations.

Polish and Russian immigrants had set up shop in the community of Greenpoint next door to the Jews of Williamsburg, and it was a far livelier crowd that greeted us as we ran down McGuinness Avenue. Gold onion domes competed with Gothic steeples on the skyline. Lampposts were decorated with red, white, and blue balloons. The residents were very good at parades, had a highly developed "sense of occasion," as Chester Kallman used to say. In 1969 a little-known Polish archbishop made a triumphant visit to this community. Some years later a local street was rechristened John Paul II Square when he became pope. Just ahead the Pulaski Bridge, named for the Polish hero of the American Revolutionary War, marked the halfway point of the marathon —13.1 miles and feeling good again after my pit stop. The body was running smoothly, with the normal level of pain in the left ankle.

My right hip had developed a burning ache to compensate, I suppose, for my favoring the weak ankle. A hernialike pain began to flare up in the appendix area when I thought about it, but my form hadn't gone out of whack in any serious way. There was no discounting the fatigue, though.

Mid-marathon, I sure felt I had spent more than half of myself in the race. Today was certainly going to require a marathon effort. *There's* a new adjective for you, Richard, I thought, to qualify the rare, sustained, and extraordinarily difficult. A marathon friendship, or a marathon marriage. "I coundn't bear the party," one might sigh with hyperbolic flare. "It was *marathon* boredom." Or "Have you seen the new tax forms this year? Absolutely marathon."

A middle-aged woman tugged on my shirtsleeve trying to pull me out of my rumination. A group of young blacks on the corner started cheering and throwing fists into the air. "Who's ahead?" she shouted again, when I took off my earphones.

Just a little more than two hours into the race it was incredible to think that someone had just proved victorious when I still had better than half the race to run. I put on my headset again and was able to tune in to the sports announcement.

"Some guy from Ethiopia has already won it. Two hours and eleven minutes. Ibrahim Hussein or something like that."

"Yeah, yeah," she said. "What about the *women?* Who's leading the women?"

"I didn't catch it," I shouted to her. The lady had fifteen years on me easy, but she pulled away like a mildly bored Porsche owner leaving a Pontiac Firebird in the dust.

The dark horse among the women in today's race would later be described by *Running News* this way: "Priscilla Welch's strategy, to go out fast and literally get lost among the men, worked to perfection. She was invisible for most of the race, constantly obscured by an ever-shifting phalanx of half-a-dozen men. . . . But receive a trophy she did, arriving at the finish in 2:30:17, a long shot away from the other women." At forty-two, Priscilla Welch is one year my senior. Gulp.

I wondered if the crowds would begin to drift away now that the race had been won, but there didn't seem to be any rush to empty the streets. There were still thousands to watch us stomp over the metal grating of the Pulaski Bridge. I liked watching the runners myself. Once again I was savoring the attraction of bodies in running gear, the silky shorts cut high above a runner's thighs, the simple T-shirt or tank top, the goofy shoes that flatten out like duck feet. I passed one guy in bright green tights, red sneaks, and a white tank top, part of the Italian contingent. In a way he was more naked than if he hadn't been wearing anything.

In spite of all the good will from the fans lining the streets of Brooklyn and Queens, I was beginning to wonder if Manhattan was ever going to appear at the end of the rainbow. I'd been at it for two and a half hours now, about as long as I'd ever run before, and I was beginning to feel as though I were in one of those dreams where you fall and fall and fall and never have the satisfaction of hitting earth.

A lot of runners were beginning to show some wear and tear now, and the encouragement from the spectators was genuine, not the bright congratulation thrown out earlier in the race when we were still fresh and optimistic. Pain and sweat streaked the runners' faces. Some panted or made little cries as they favored an injury or simply pushed against gravity. The fans got a little louder, a little more insistent when some poor soul came struggling by doing his or her best not to let the pain win. The blind guy who was chatting up a storm with his running partner just a few miles back tagged along in silence and only reached out occasionally to touch his partner for bearings.

It was something like having the flu. You feel just awful. How does the old chestnut go? "First I was afraid I was going to die, then I was afraid I wasn't." But unlike children who have no sense of history and cry all night with an earache because they can't imagine a world without earache, adults are able to endure pain because they have experienced earaches before, can extrapolate their personal history. All they have to do is forget the exploding eardrum for twelve or fifteen hours, and by sunrise it will all be over.

Very simple.

Perhaps the weirdest sensation was to have an exquisite pain whose source I couldn't identify. More than the awful heaviness, it felt as though some window decorator had skewered my thighs with metal ramrods to support some particularly lurid pose. I couldn't exactly visualize where the trouble was coming from, and was like a paraplegic who has to reach down to feel if the accident

445

has left him with any legs. Pain is a very difficult serpent to trace as it slithers through the body's high grasses. A man with severe prostatitis only knows the agony begins below the belly button, a lady with gallstones may feel certain she is dying of uterine cancer. How little we know of what goes on between our neck and our knees. The pain we suffer is like orgasm, each time unique, mysterious, without replication. Describing it is like explaining sight to a blind person. Even the skilled anotomist has difficulty connecting the reality of what the body is feeling inside with the color maps he is able to devise for the body's geography.

As I meditated on the curious state of my upper thighs, a part of me sat down in an easy chair and pulled out the old notes from my first surgical rotation. In my mind I flipped through the various diagrams I'd drawn to see if they offered any clues. Fractures, vein stripping, different sorts of tumors and the various procedures to accommodate their individual growth patterns. And then, ah-ha, I was finally able to put a picture with the pain I felt.

A "hip replacement" is only a funny term for gluing a peg with a silver ball into the upper femur and slipping the restored piece back into the hip socket—it's like carpentry, simple as plugging a new caster into a rickety office chair. It sounded a little medieval when you explained it to patients, but the operation had those octogenarians walking around good as new time after time. When they first came in they always described the same type of amorphous pain that was warming my own hips and legs as I ran on the streets of Queens. It looked as though the extra pounds I'd been carrying around these past few years were finally beginning to warp my body's architecture, and the girders were sagging a little.

I thought of my favorite deejay in D.C., an old black dude named Jerry Washington who spins the blues on Saturday mornings. Nothing better to start off your day on a weekend. I put on my headphones and Mikey and I start up the neighborhood hills, running with the Howlin' Wolf, Otis Redding, Sam Cooke, or maybe Lightning Hopkins, and the music warms my soul like a bush burning for Moses. The blues pour through me and I want to cry, "Oh, my prophetic soul."

For the millionth time I asked myself why I had gotten into this mess. I wondered if some degree of masochism was a prerequisite for trying to run a marathon, the way, at a very deep subliminal level, a thin thread of sadism must run through the psyche of the surgeon.

Fifteen miles into the race, however, if there was some unconscious, more esoteric reason why I was putting myself through all this, I'd have given anything for a clever psychologist to pop out from the sidelines and tell me what it was.

An English pundit writing about the London Marathon recently describes it as mass idiocy, the looniness of the long-distance runner. "We are not talking here about a few blisters, a stitch, and a temporary urge to expectorate heart, lungs and stomach. We are talking of hypothermia and hyperthermia; of tissue exhaustion and debilitating dehydration; of torn muscles, snapped tendons, fractured bones; of long-term damage to joints, bringing the risk of arthritis, of blood blisters requiring toenails to be punctured with red-hot needles; in general, of a self-inflicted beating to the body from which it takes, at best, weeks to recover." He concludes his analysis by dragging Jim Fixx through the mud again, as well as the "Unknown Soldier" of jogging who first pulled into Athens and promptly dropped dead after announcing the defeat of the Persians at Marathon.

Normally, this kind of snotty commentary would prompt a hot letter to the editor extolling the race as a challenge to the human spirit, but as the Queensboro Bridge finally opened into the last miles of the marathon, the cynical journalist sounded like Joshua to me. This was perhaps the first time I said to myself, "Maybe you should just stop. Maybe it would be okay to just stop." And again fate dropped a rose before me making that impossible.

As we started up the red carpeting that covered the grating on the bridge, a severly handicapped girl sat on a homemade wagon inching her way backward against gravity. She couldn't control her legs or arms very well but was able to push ahead with her feet. One of the Italians who had come over on the plane in a group stood jogging in place, watching her slow progress. His dark hair was slicked back like a swimmer's, his skin-tight leotards proclaimed bold calves, thighs, and buttocks in red, white, and green, like some Sicilian version of Superman. When it was clear the girl wasn't going to let him push her up the bridge, he bent over a face become monstrous with her effort, kissed her full on the mouth, and went on his way.

"Now that's Italian!"

Spectators were not allowed on the bridge, and for the first time in the race all the noise and hoopla from the crowds fell away. The silence was eerie as we ran high into the air approaching Manhattan. No automobiles, no foul exhaust fumes, as though war or some civic disaster had forced the population to desert the city. Giant girders pushed into the blue sky, iron struts twisted into a mammoth black honeycomb arching over distant waters. It was hard to believe the bridge was a manmade thing. In that deep silence my thoughts became almost physical objects. I was a slow-gliding hawk, my shadow playing over the World Trade Center, the Chrysler Building, the Empire State, high city of shiny metal beyond filth or poverty or fear.

Not long ago, at another race, mysteriously, a young athlete ran off the course and leaped over the handrail on such a bridge. The papers described it as one more tragic death brought on by the stress of competitive sports. But as I ran across the bridge I could almost imagine trying the thin air, like Icarus, climbing higher and higher in his ecstasy toward the brilliant sun.

The mind shuts down at such dangerous moments, a kind of psychological self-preservation. When there are no neurons left to translate the pain, a torture victim will mercifully pass out, and I suspect there must be some similar overload mechanism to handle mania. I was winging around in such euphoria that I grew faint. As we came off the bridge onto First Avenue thousands of New Yorkers smashed through the silence in greeting, like the blast of hot air an express train makes when it roars through the subway.

Marathon guides describe a sense of self you sometimes achieve in the race that is "elemental, childlike, and somehow connected to the essence of who you are." This stripped-down self made its way down from the blue heights and back into the exhausted runner on the bridge. The runner was a little stunned, unable to take it all in for the moment, and began to cry.

I realized I had better be a little careful or some well-meaning health-care worker might tackle me and force me onto a first aid cot. Coma and hyperthermia weren't the only symptoms of dehydration. I was a little terrified suddenly with the thought that maybe my emotional volatility was the result of some metabolic crisis I was going through. Like a melancholy Irishman lost in his "vin triste" who finally pulls himself together and closes up the bar, I ran to the next water station, drank a cup, and threw several more over my head and shoulders. My shirt and shorts were completely soaked and clung to me like cellophane.

The sun was still bright, but a breeze had come up making the water uncomfortably cold. I looked like a shipwreck survivor as I fished out a couple of hard candies that had worked their way into my crotch and turned into sticky orange paste; or more, I thought, like an orangutan hanging around in his own muck on display for all the chic New Yorkers who dallied over brunch along First Avenue.

It was a straight shot up to Harlem now, four miles to the Willis Avenue Bridge for a token jog through the Bronx, then back through Harlem for the home stretch down Fifth Avenue and through Central Park. Looking uptown from the foot of First Avenue was as bleak an experience as looking into space on a night without moon or stars. I became conscious of my hip pain again and decided another Advil would be permissible. It was hours since the last dose when I started the race, well within the guidelines printed on the bottle. I also pulled into one of the portable johns that had appeared along the course. My urine didn't seem to be bloodstained anymore, so I was doubly relieved as I let the door bang behind me and started back into the race.

At the seventeen-mile marker I was able to put the hip pain in the background again and enjoy the "easy listening" station I had found on the radio.

There were far fewer people lining the streets now as we left the restaurant district in the 70's and 80's. This far north along First Avenue the

451

excitement seemed to peter out, and people drifted into other Sunday amusements, doing the New York Times crossward puzzle, maybe taking a nap, or catching up on their laundry. Occasionally, a policeman standing alone beside a sawhorse barrier made a valiant effort to cheer on the runners, but with most of the crowd gone it sounded a little silly. Paper cups and trash filled the street. The wind was growing colder.

At nineteen miles my muscle tissues cried out for oxygen the way children at play refuse to give up the thin last light of days that have already become diminished by the earth's sad distance from the sun. My tired bones seemed to translate the wilted city, the planet tilting and growing cold. I was coming to the legendary twenty-mile point in the marathon, in just one mile would confront the fabled Wall. This was what I had really trained for, preparing to face the unknown of my personal limits. The final miles of the race lay waiting for me like summer storm clouds building to a black head over the long heat of day.

I was amazed that runners of every age and both sexes still remained in the race, that it wasn't all just forty-year-old amateurs. We were a sickly lot by now, like refugees staggering across the border before the military junta sealed it forever. The field still remained a fair cross section of the runners that had started off together four hours ago on the Verrazano Bridge.

The little strip of Alexander Avenue that carried up into the Bronx was littered with broken glass, garbage, and other ghetto debris. The buildings were worn down with years of filth and disrepair. As I came over the Madison Avenue Bridge into Harlem, the northernmost point in the marathon course, someone had posted a hand-painted sign that read simply, "Say no to death." It didn't say otherwise the devil will get you, or advertise any particular Christian sect. A ghetto philosopher was simply painting the big picture as we came running into his slum pushing ourselves to the max. I thought of the old guy in a wheelchair at the outset of the race who had had only enough energy to wave his hand a little at the wrist like the pendulum of a clock as the runners passed him by. He wasn't strong enough to clap his hands, but there he was just the same, sitting in the sunshine, part of it all, cheering the runners on to the finish line. Say no to death. It was more moving than I could have believed. And harder to subscribe to than I would have believed, as well.

It seemed like hours since I had seen the last marker announcing nineteen miles and the prospect of meeting the Wall. Could I be banging my head against the Wall even now? Time and space had become hallucinatory, a kind of Einsteinian melt-down. The coordinates fixing reality were subsumed into an overriding fifth dimension of nightmare.

Spectators filled the streets again as we ran deeper into Harlem, lots of people carrying on as if it were Carnival. Groups of women stood outside the storefront churches in feathered hats and purple sequins, clapping in unison under a sign that proclaimed in neon lights that "God is Love." Other ladies took it all in with greater aplomb, watching from within a cloud of marijuana that wafted over to us like incense as we ran by. Ahead of me I noticed a little black girl about ten years old hiding something in her hand, sizing up each runner that came by with great white eyes. She was shy as a squirrel and wasn't going to have any luck giving away the piece of candy or orange or whatever she was offering by hanging back so carefully. As I came up to her I slowed down to see what secret she was hiding. A tiny toy koala bear, brown and furry, peeked up over her small fist. She didn't say a word, but it was clear I was being introduced.

"Pretty late in the day to still be running a marathon, wouldn't you agree, Mr. Bear?" I thought. "Would you like to wrap your huggie arms around my little finger and help me finish this goddamn race?"

In an instant I had taken the koala from her hand and was running ahead again. Suddenly I had the awful feeling that maybe she wasn't bestowing this toy on some special runner she was waiting to find, that maybe I had just mugged a schoolgirl for her little mascot. But when I turned back to find her in the crowd she gave me a shy smile and waved to me as though I were her secret lover. I clipped Mr. Bear to my shirt and blew her a big kiss that lit up her face.

I wouldn't have parted with that toy bear for

anything in the world, but that kiss almost did me in. For almost five hours I had been pushing straight ahead, stop after stop, in single-minded forward motion toward the finish line. Twisting my body at the waist to look back at her sent a wrenching pain through my groin muscles that was like being processed in a meat grinder. I swallowed the last Advil I had rationed for the race and rumbled on a hundred yards or so like a car that has suddenly blown a tire and is struggling to keep from running off the road. It was difficult to get back into the rhythm that had become as mindless as breathing. After a while the pain was beginning to wear off a little, the way the sting eventually fades out of a burn, when a second miracle nearly undid me. My heart started flopping around like a seabird in an oil slick when I looked up to see the twenty-one-mile marker just ahead.

Oh Jesus, oh Jesus. Some sweet genius had simply deleted the infamous twenty-mile marker from the course to help us over the psychological hurdle of the Wall—out of sight, out of mind. I had already broken through, it seemed, was already beginning mile twenty-two of the race.

My spirit began to ricochet off the walls and leap up into the trees, but all I could bring myself to do physically by way of celebration was give a single high-pitched burst of a laugh. The guy in front of me winced like a monk startled in the midst of prayer. At this point in the race runners were saving their energy, and you rarely heard a peep from anyone. Last year two hundred people were treated at the twenty-mile medical tent in spite of all the balloons and hundreds of green megaphones given out to boisterous children. The cots were filled with runners with a range of ailments from muscle spasm to collapse. Beyond mile twenty the body had spent its reserves and was running on something other than blood and oxygen. All the guidebooks will tell you that the body has nothing left to give now, and the only thing that enables you to keep it from falling into a heap is will power. Physical stamina has nothing to do with the race at this point. And this is precisely the challenge that veterans of the marathon have entered the race again for, to see what their bodies and souls will make of it all this year, to see if they can't reverse time by doing even better than they did last year.

For me, no particularly gargantuan act of will was fueling my body's effort. I didn't need to consciously prod myself along. The little engine driving my soul kicked into overdrive and produced something like dream power. It simply happened while I looked on, like levitation. You try for hours, work yourself into a splitting headache, and when you finally give up, sure enough the knife slowly rises from the table, or you notice that your feet are floating six inches off the floor.

At one level, of course, every yard was very real agony and hard won. Pain emanated from any number of sources, and my exhausted body was begging me to pull off the road and sit under a tree for a while.

I was certainly in my body, but not necessarily *of* it, I guess, like that contemporary cartoon of a movie that illustrates so nicely the Cartesian dualism of mind over matter. In the postnuclear world of *Beyond Thunderdome* society is run by a nasty little midget named Masterblaster who rides around on the shoulders of an idiot giant and makes him do his bidding. This rather successful partnership has kept the world in slavery, producing energy out of pig manure, until it meets up with Mel Gibson and Tina Turner, queen of the Thunderdome gladiators—can any tyrant, regardless of IQ, really have all his marbles if he messes with Tina Turner? The body's travails are interesting. There may be a certain curiosity about how precisely we fall apart trying to run 26.2 miles. But in the end who wants to hear the gory details down to the last blister?

The doctor puts on his concerned face with his white jacket to listen to the tired aches and pains of humanity once again. Who *isn't* arthritic, or nursing an ulcer, or having a tough time taking care of an invalid at home? Everybody has something. It's why we all understand the blues. Don't we have a moral obligation to tell an off-color joke every now and then? Why belabor the "affliction, the fear"? Why would I want to hear the trouble you went through having your baby, for example, when I've got the sweet little rug rat in my arms?

The next four miles would be as tough as anything I would ever do in my life, but I decided to keep myself tuned in to that part of me sitting

457

on my shoulder, like Masterblaster overseeing the production of methane in the bowels of the city. I tried to take in the scenery, the way I did those Sundays Dad would pile us all into the car and we'd drive into the country to visit our favorite dairy for ice cream. Just out for the ride.

One of the sweet things I noticed was the sympathetic look in the eyes of spectators who chose to stand along the final few miles of our trial. The compassion in those eyes was mysterious, beautiful. God's own sweet grace seemed to play across their faces like light dappling a forest.

Another puzzle preoccupied me as we left Fifth Avenue and entered Central Park. Twenty youngsters sat deserted in their wheelchairs like cabbages that someone had forgotten to protect against an unexpected frost. These "floppy" babies had grown into "floppy" children. Their heads undulated on little stems, their limbs waved slowly like seaweed on the ocean floor. Nurses had parked them along the curb several hours ago, perhaps, and they could only wait in the cold until someone decided to wipe their noses or take them back in again. One little boy with thick black eyebrows and lashes looked at me as he pushed himself up in his chair. His skin was unblemished ivory, as though he hadn't grown past his smooth baby skin. By working hard and turning his arms like a windmill he was finally able to right himself. He gave me a big drooly smile, as though he had just won the New York middleweight wrestling championship.

"All right," I shouted to him. "Way to go."

I pretended to miss a step and fall into a stumble. I screwed up my face and began flapping my arms around, mirroring *his* effort as though I had cerebral palsy too, or was a fledgling that had fallen out of the nest. I was mocking him, all right. Goofing around, yes, but I was teasing him in a way I wouldn't have tried unless I happened to be his older brother or unless a marathon had worn down my self-conciousness. But he was a big boy, didn't take it amiss. He started to laugh and laugh, and so did the girl sitting beside him, like two sweet little geese honking at the moon.

Now as I came deeper into the heart of Central Park there were exhausted runners lining the road who had already finished the race. They limped along slowly clutching the silver thermal capes about them and eating a Milky Way or an apple or a bagel. Garbage containers were filled with green Perrier bottles that had been shoved into their hands at the finish line, enough rosebud vases to supply every café table in Manhattan.

"Hang in there," the newly triumphant called out to those of us still marking time in limbo. "It's not far now." Runners gave exhausted grunts that seemed to respond, "Easy for you to say." There were plenty of fans in the crowd who realized that, if anything, the latecomers needed a cheering section more than those who had finished the race hours ago. Even though the stadium seemed to be emptying, the fans were going to stay until the last batter was retired, the last inning played out.

"Just a mile and a half," some guy shouted to each runner who traipsed by him. He waved them on like a frantic traffic cop in rush hour. "Move it, lady. Move it. Move it. Move it." I forced a smile just like everyone else that came poking by. Except for pit stops, I had been running nonstop for exactly five hours.

As we turned the corner onto Central Park South the guy running beside me looked over and smiled. Number 13287. A nice smile and bright eyes. He wore a singlet, shorts, and headband all stamped with the New York Marathon logo: a stick man running on a big red apple. His mustache and goatee were flecked salt and pepper, and his glasses were the wire-rimmed FDR type. But I could tell he was about my own age.

I could tell my sidekick wanted to talk to me, wanted to share a sense of pride and relief and valediction. Maybe he was running alone like me, maybe he didn't have anyone waiting for him at the finish line either. William would be waiting for me at Paul's apartment instead, since there was no telling how long it would take me to finish, or *if* I would finish.

Even when I get off an airplane and no one is scheduled to meet me, I still find myself looking around expectantly. Everyone else is hugging his wife while the kids cluster about yapping for a present. Everywhere there are little bursts of reunion, a child running to Grandma, someone shedding tears, while you stand around like the ghost of Christmas past. Having someone meet you almost seems to be part of the landing procedure, and if you pick up your luggage in silence by yourself, somehow you haven't really arrived.

We ran facing straight ahead, oblivious to the spectators cheering us on, hopeful for any sign of a finish line.

"How you doing?" my running mate asked, and gave me the same shy smile.

"Okay," I said. "How about you?"

"I'm doing great," he said. "It's been a beautiful run."

I had let my form slip a little now and bowed my head as I ran. I thought of the past hours, feeling the weight of the day settle on my soul. How many miles had I run to prepare for this moment? How many mornings did I pull myself out of bed and start by lacing up my jogging shoes?

The pace and vigor of my strides had diminished, but I knew I would make it to the finish line in respectable form, all I ever really hoped for during the months of preparation. One of those terribly hot summer days when I was training, a song came on the headset that was a simple idiot refrain set to atomic bomb rock and roll. As I came to Ryan's Hill I set the volume on maximum until my ears nearly bled, making a conscious decision to let the stupid lyrics function as a prayer. For all their banality they suited some personal song of gratitude that was welling up in me. Louder, brighter, stronger, I danced to the very crest.

As I began the final mile of the New York City

Marathon, however, I was not dancing, I was not singing. Now it was a little hard to concentrate on anything other than running, as though I had gone blind. My body seemed to lack the energy required to run and talk and take in the pageant igniting up ahead all at the same time. But I knew in a short while I would be able to feel the joy of it fully and was amazed by the fact.

"You know, I'm dying," I said, "but it really wasn't as bad as I thought. I mean, it could have been a lot worse."

And miraculously enough, an enormous red, white, and blue banner announcing the finish line eventually appeared around a bend. A giant clock floated over the banner like the crown of heaven. I felt as though I were running toward the clock in slow motion—could "feel this channel widen as I swim." I was as confused as any longhorn in a roundup trying to figure out which running chute to feed myself into without getting trampled. There was such a great crush of runners and timekeepers and volunteers and onlookers I didn't quite understand what was happening.

In what must surely be the most exquisite anticlimax of my life, I somehow managed to pass under the banner in the middle of my partner's farewell. "Been nice running with you." He smiled and waved goodbye. Only when a pretty girl placed a silver medal with a blue and white ribbon around my neck did I realize that I had actually run the New York City Marathon.

Tomorrow's *New York Post* would rank my new

friend just ahead of me even though we both passed through the chutes at exactly five hours fifteen minutes and five seconds. They could have ranked me last for all I cared. I had run the entire New York City Marathon and crossed the finish line standing up. I couldn't get over what a wonderful thing had just happened.

The dust of the long day's run washed from my eyes. I was able to focus on things, "to see the extraordinary data" once again as the crowd thinned out and I slowed down to a limp.

People began to look after us now, and no one raised any objection to the care they offered. The simple act of walking again was a shock. Every abused muscle and ligament took its little revenge for the nasty trip it had been forced to endure. A television commercial for Anacin would have a million scarlet arrows pointing to every joint and bone in my body.

One volunteer fastened a silver cape around my neck, and another smacked a big red apple into the palm of my hand. Congratulations from the City of New York. I bit in with a chomp, and it was just as sweet as having dessert with Eve in the Garden of Paradise. The taste was almost visible.

# Sonny Kleinfield

# A Month at the Brickyard: The Incredible Indy 500

*Automobile racing is the most dangerous sport of all, and the Indy 500—revered as "racing's mother church" and feared for its tight curves that allow little room to regain control of a car after a spin—has claimed the lives of thirty-five drivers. In this piece writer Sonny Kleinfield takes the reader behind the wheel of a racer with Johnny Parsons, a qualifying driver, and reveals some of the secrets of winning—and sometimes just surviving—the race. As Parsons observes, "driving the track is like playing music. You have to find a rhythm." What makes a great driver like Parsons? Superb eye-hand control, excellent vision and depth perception, good musculature in the wrists and neck for absorbing the vibrations of speeds that can reach nearly two hundred miles per hour, intense concentration, cool judgment and resignation when an accident is inevitable, and an extra dose of courage.*

On the third day of practice, fourteen men are running their winged things around the tight ribbon of bricks and asphalt, seeking speed cautiously on the nasty, low-banked corners and long

464

straightaways. Drivers and mechanics use the practice period to iron out problems with the car and to build confidence in their abilities. There is a ceaseless bellowing of snarling exhausts; the air is sharp with the peculiar acrid smell of heavy-duty racing oil.

The racers screaming past all bear commercial names. Alex Foods Special. Sugaripe Prune Special. Spirit of Indiana Special. Leader Card Racer. Scio Cabinet Special. Schlitz Special. Indianapolis is the meat market of professional auto racing, where expensive cars are the equal of moving billboards. Their flanks are covered by the decals of every company involved in their creation.

The big track is one of the hardest these drivers run on. Built for much slower-moving cars, it is narrow, just fifty feet wide in the straightaways and sixty feet wide in the turns. The bends are sloped at only nine degrees, twelve minutes. There's little room to regain control of a car after a spin. Some drivers hate the track and dread driving on it. Auto racing is the most dangerous sport in the world, and Indy cars are possibly the most frightening machines around. Every driver knows that unexpectedly, in a matter of minutes, he could be turned into a vegetable or snuffed out. The track has put fear in many drivers, and it has taken the lives of thirty-five. Driving the track is like playing music. You have to find a rhythm.

Fingering matter from his eyes, Bill Finley mutters, "Today maybe we'll find out if this son of a bitch'll run. Every new car is sick. That is my

465

premise. We must take the car and find out what it needs to make it well and healthy. Some cars need more medicine than others."

Johnny Parsons booms out of the fourth turn and scrambles down the main straightaway, the car about three feet below the outside crash wall, the best position from which to approach the first corner. The car has four forward speeds that can get it up to top speed ("full bore") of around 205 miles per hour. In ten seconds. The cockpit is more cramped than a coffin. The seat is custom-molded to reduce fatigue. Five dials fill the panel facing Parsons, indicating lubricating-oil pressure, engine-waste temperature, engine revolutions per minute, lubricating-oil temperature, and turbocharger pressure. There's no speedometer; the closest thing to it is the dial for engine revolutions. Some teams stick a two-way radio in the driver's helmet to let the driver pass information to the crew while he's on the track, but it's hard to hear with the snorting of the cars. Parsons doesn't use one. Down the main straightaway, with the huge grandstands climbing over the course—inside and out—and flipping shadows over the pavement, Parsons feels as if he is "driving down a narrow hallway in a house and getting ready to make a sharp left turn into the bedroom."

A gate is ten feet from the first turn. Just before Parsons reaches it he steers the car to within six inches of the outside wall; then he twists the wheel less than an inch in the other direction, enough to bring the car gently downward. The throttle is about four inches deep, deeper than on most cars. "This is my security blanket. I like to know I have a lot of control over the car's speed." A quarter of the way into the turn, Parsons lifts up on the throttle around an inch for a fraction of a second. He lightly brushes the brakes. "Mainly to know they're there." There's no shifting of gears. He brings the car down till the inside tires creep about an inch onto the wide white stripe that runs around the inside of the track. Called the "line" or "groove," it is the quickest way around the Indianapolis Motor Speedway and following it involves entering and exiting the turns in as near a straight line as possible. This cuts the friction between tires and asphalt and doesn't require as much reduction in speed. You stay outside on the straightaways, inside on the turns, follow a straight line.

Top cornering speed is about 180. Parsons keeps his head back and looks halfway, four hundred feet, into the curve, so he gets a good feel for his trajectory. All the turns have the same radius and banking, but every one is different. Turn one feels narrow. By the time Parsons is halfway into the corner, he is back at full speed. Since the next straightaway is short, Parsons stays close to the wall—within a foot of it—throughout its length. Inside the cockpit, Parsons is constantly talking to himself, criticizing his performance. Too low in that corner. A bit close to the wall there. Keep it steady. Don't touch the brakes too much. That's a little low. Keep it high. He peppers himself with questions. Can I take that corner just a shade faster? How are the tires? Are they a little soft? Is the steering weak or strong? How's the oil pressure? Brakes? Is the car smooth? What's the engine temperature? Can't I get around any faster?

Parsons comes into turn two lower than he did the first turn, about two feet from the wall, because there's a slight hump (from the tunnel that burrows under the corner to allow traffic to enter the infield of the track). The hump is so slight that it's invisible to the naked eye, and you could crawl out on your hands and knees and not be able to find it. But to a racing driver blasting along, the hump feels like he's just run over a clock-radio. So acute is Parsons' sensitivity that he can feel if anything is loose on the car. He can tell if one of the tires is low on air, even a couple of pounds. "Tires are like the nerves on your fingers." He also has quite a nose. He can sniff if a bearing is about to burn out before it registers on the oil gauge.

No brakes before entering turns two and four, because the car's speed doesn't build up as much down the short straightaways. Parsons now ducks to the bottom of the second turn, letting up slightly on the throttle, and then drifts out near the wall. He relaxes his grip for the trip down the backstretch, the best place to check the gauges and look in the rearview mirrors to see if someone is overtaking you. Without any outer grandstands, the back straightaway seems about the width of a living room.

Tooling around the Indianapolis Speedway in a race car is nothing like ordinary motoring on the expressway. The basic idea is to go so wickedly fast that the car barely stays on the road and comes as close as possible to skating off into the wall without actually doing so. The man who gets around the fastest is the man who drives closest to the brink of disaster. You need an uncanny instinct for the exact play of a car at racing speed and in all kinds of racing situations. You have to know tricks like slipstreaming, which is a way to hitch a ride on a faster car. Getting right behind a car and into a low-pressure area creates a vacuum effect. This gives a tow to the trailing car, allowing it to run faster. Only thing is, the freeloader has to be within inches of the other car. All around the track, Parsons is being cooked by heat, dulled by fumes. The wind tears at him. The noise batters at him. He's on the lookout for birds. A bird can knock out a driver.

A superlative blend of eye-hand control is probably the trait that most separates an Indianapolis driver from drivers in lesser levels of the sport. Racers deal in inches and half inches. At 180 miles per hour, the car directly in front of a driver might spin out, and there is only a second perhaps to size up the situation and get out of it. The throttle jams wide open going into a turn. Perhaps a second and a half before the driver is stuffed in the wall. One of the basics of auto racing is to know when you're going to have an accident and accept it. The ordinary motorist, in emergencies, goes into a panic. In a crash that would send the motorist's blood pressure through the ceiling an Indy driver is all calm. Clobbering walls is part of his job.

"When an accident occurs, the first thing is to try to steer your way out of it," Parsons has said. "In a race, you try not to 'lock it up,' slam on the brakes, because this will flatten the tires and force a pit stop to have them changed. Lose you several laps. And once you lock it up, you're out of control. You can only go straight. You can't steer the car. You lock up a car only if there's no other choice. It makes sense to do it if you have to. If you hit another car with the wheels turning, you'll probably sail right over it. With the wheels locked, you're liable to smash into him and bounce off. A car out of control is unpredictable. Usually, when a car spins out in front of you, you aim right for it, because it won't be there by the time you get there."

Parsons is short and well-built, neither heavy nor thin. He has thick wrists and a thick neck. The result of years of exercise, isometrics, lifting weights, a hundred and fifty neck rolls every morning, they have been developed for one purpose—to absorb the stress of a racing car at speed. He has twenty-forty vision, which aviator glasses correct to twenty-twenty. Once he had his eyes tested for how fast they respond to stimuli and the results were unbelievably high. Race drivers have great vision. Have to. Nothing foggier than twenty-twenty corrected vision is allowed on the Speedway. Drivers are run through a tough physical of the sort jet fighter pilots must face. Emphasis is on reflexes and depth perception. There are some drivers who would never pass an army physical who get on the track by learning to adapt to their handicaps. Three one-legged drivers have shown up, one of them managing a sixth place. But one-eyed drivers are out. No depth perception. Yet in the 1920s, when medical exams were more lax, a man named Tommy Milton came to the Speedway, and before he was through, he had two Indianapolis victories to his credit. Milton drove with his head cocked, and though he neither admitted nor denied it, the word was that he had vision in just one eye.

Pounding down the backstretch, Parsons is thinking of nothing but getting the car around as fast as possible. "Concentration is the key," he has said. "Every second that you don't concentrate completely you are losing time. We call concentration lapses 'brain fade.' When I'm out on the track, I forget people are watching me. Race drivers are only thinking of their cars. That has to be hammered into you, and you learn it best by hitting a lot of walls."

Off the racecourse, Parsons bangs around in a scruffy-looking 1970 Ford Econoline. Top speed is 100 miles per hour. Handling isn't so hot in the wind. Parsons hates being a passenger and does everything he can to avoid a trip in which

471

he's not behind the wheel. He drives about ten miles over the speed limit. "You don't know what's going to happen on the highway. On the track, you drive offensively. Everyone's a pro there. On the highways, you drive defensively. You look out for nuts. I never feel scared on the racing track. I've had some real chills run up and down my spine on public roads."

Gripping the wheel harder, Parsons barrels into the third turn, the roughest on the course, where southerly winds can shove a car off the corner. You have to really fight the car in turn three. To cancel the breeze, Parsons works the car down beneath the white line onto the rough inside apron.

Courage plays a part in racing, though drivers differ in their boldness. There are so-called "strokers" or "coast and collectors" who know they have small chance of winning. They plug away, saving their engines, just hoping to finish the race and collect some money. Parsons has said, "I drive cars to the limit. As fast as they'll go. Finishing fourth or third is not worthwhile. I've done that. I want to win." Parsons drives cars into the ground. "Give me a race car that will go 200," he says, "and I'll drive it 200."

Parsons hugs the wall in the short chute between three and four. No brakes, a slight easing on the throttle, and he floats into the fourth corner. The smoothest of the four corners, a beautiful turn. Parsons wishes all the turns were the fourth turn. A lot of grandstands border the turn, making it, like the first corner, seem narrower that it is.

Parsons feels as if he is leaving the bathroom and returning to the long hallway leading to the bedroom.

"Every day I'll try to go a little faster. You sneak up on speed. If you climbed into a car and went 185 without working up to it gradually, you'd probably get sick. You concentrate so hard you tire quickly. There are other races that are more physically draining than Indianapolis, but there are no other races as mentally draining. You're constantly alert for possible changes in the track or in the car. Every year the track is different. The weather alone changes the way it runs. I'm always checking my opposition. I make mental notes on every driver. A driver I trust I'll run within four inches of. If I don't trust someone, I'll stay two feet away. I'll never try to pass him in a corner. I'm always seeing how I can gain a few feet. You don't try ridiculous things, but you must be aggressive. The winner of the race must drive as fast as his car will let him. Not unsafely, but maybe a little past the point of safety."

A car whips by. Another. Another. Parsons growls through the exit of the fourth turn, his foot nailed to the throttle, the engine up to full bore. He comes steaming down the main straightaway and whistles past the starting line. In the pits, a crewman hits a stopwatch with his thumb. It shows 50.9 seconds, a speed of 176.917 miles per hour. "He's got to go faster," the crewman says.

# EPILOGUE

# GRANTLAND RICE

# Through the Mists

*We end this collection of great sportswriting with a piece by the "dean of American sportswriters," Grantland Rice. Writing during what is called the Golden Age of Sports—the twenties (which was, claims author Robert Lipsyte, actually a golden age of sportswriting)—Rice transformed his profession by popularizing embellishment and the use of metaphor in reporting. Glancing back nostalgically over his long years covering sports, Rice sums up his philosophy. With generosity he applauds those who try but don't succeed—those who know "the matchless gift of fortitude." Along the way he aptly demonstrates his signature style of interpolating verse. As he admits, "verse and sport together make up the menu perfectly." Listen to this singular voice of a bygone era.*

### These Are My Dreams

My dreams are not tomorrow—nor
  yesterday.
For yesterday is gone, and on its way.
And by tomorrow it may be much too late
To find my way through darkness and
  through fate.

When you have reached a certain span in life,
Today is all that counts, for fun or strife.
The past is blurred with fogs and mists and
    myth.
The future is too brief to bother with.

I dream today with no vain, vague regrets
For yesterday—and all its unpaid debts,
With no fear of the future's fading sun,
Since it may end before this rhyme is done.

I dream of romance and a song that rings
Above the duller, elemental things,
Not caring what may happen to skies dark
    or blue,
If I can know that just one dream comes true.

Having spent 64 of 74 years in the maelstrom of
sport, I seem to have spent the vital segment of
my life in crowds of 50,000 and 100,000 people.
As I look back, the picture is a vast canvas of tumult and shouting, where, on many occasions, I
was seeking a "solitude I could call peace."

It's been an endless highway of thrills. I look
back on countless examples of gameness, smart-
ness, stamina, uphill struggles—and with them all
the varying tides of luck that test human character.

I see them walk by in a dream—Dempsey and
Cobb and Ruth, Tunney and Sande and Jones—

Johnson and Matty and Young—Alex and Tilden and Thorpe—was there a flash of youth That gave us a list like this, when our first tributes were sung?

Man O'War waits for the break—Shoeless Joe Jackson's at bat. John McGraw barks from the line—Hagen is taking his swing. Gehrig is watching the pitch—Greb is outclawing a cat—Milburn and Hitchcock rise up—taking the ball on the wing.

Where the old dreams move along—shadows that drift to and fro—Moving on back through the years—I've seen a pretty good show.

And what does it all mean? It means that sport —games, hard competition played under the rules, is the greatest thing a country can know. Sport offers the greatest fund of national entertainment. It offers relief from the drabness and dullness of making a living. It is a cure for lonesomeness, the dark spectre so many people face. Because it builds character, sport can also help in curbing the current curse of juvenile delinquency. About adult delinquency, I'm not so sure.

Most of the headliners in sport that I've known have been decent humans. Exceedingly few have been dull or stupid. They have all had the proper rhythm, the right angles. What are the most important qualities that should belong to a champion? In no particular order, I've found them to be:

  Confidence
  Co-ordination
  Concentration
  Condition
  Courage—at impact
  Fortitude—stick-to-it-iveness
  Determination
  Stamina
  Quickness
  Speed

To a degree, these ingredients belong to any topflight business man, doctor or lawyer just as they belonged to a Dempsey, Jones, Cobb or a Ruth. There is also the highly important factor of innate Ability. Yes, and Luck, too, is worth cultivating.

*Dame Fortune is a cockeyed wench, as someone's said before, And yet the old Dame plays her part in any winning score. Take all the credit you deserve, heads-up in winning pride, But don't forget that Lady Luck was riding at your side.*

Two other qualities often identified with a leader—intelligence and education, are missing from this list. Neither, I've found, is necessary for a champion. Intelligence usually denotes imagination which can be a positive deterrent, especially in heavy contact sports . . . or golf. However, awareness, a form of intelligence, is something I've found in most champions. I mention intelligence and education together because the two are often confused. There may be a yawning gap between an intelligent person and one who happens to be educated.

In all these years I have run across only two big scandals in sport—the World Series corruption of 1919 and the far deeper basketball scandal of recent years. There have been minor incidents that were little more than some deflection from the code.

The West Point sacking was not, in my opinion, a matter of cheating in any game and was badly handled at the Point. The scandal was as much with the higher-ups at the Academy as it was with the football squad.

There is little chance for any big scandal, outside of boxing, with the alertness shown by most of those in control plus the public sense of moral indignation that is unusually strong.

Over the same span of years I have seen politics with far more than its share of crookedness including governors and others high in the affairs of state. The statesman is differnt. But there are so few statesmen. Politics, unhappily, is loaded with crooks and cheats a hundred to one over those honest servants of the public's welfare.

Sport today is, however, much more commercial and much more stereotyped than in my heyday. I doubt if we will ever again have the devil-may-care attitude and spirit of the Golden Twenties, a period of boom, screwballs and screwball antics. The almighty dollar, or what's left of it, hangs high. The magnificent screwballs have been crowded to the wall. The fleet Washington outfielder who, when asked to race Mickey Mantle against time before a recent Yankee-Senators night game, replied, "I'll do it . . . for five hundred dollars" is testimony to the times.

While I saluted the golden days of the amateur in sport, I've watched the professional take over almost completely. I have a keen sympathy and understanding for those sportsmen whose game must lay midway between the pro and amateur label. It is the rare bird who can hustle a living in today's going and still find time to excel as an amateur. That's why I thrilled with the rest of America when amateur Billy Joe Patton shot everything from an ace to a 7 in the 1954 Masters golf tourney, and finished just a shot off the collective heels of Ben Hogan and Sam Snead. The fact that Patton played every shot for 72 holes stiff to the pin and let the devil do his worrying was a tonic today's cash register game needs desperately.

While sport has been a big part of my life, I must admit that verse has meant even more. Frank Stanton, in his tribute to poetry, gave the answer:

"Had it not been for thee,
Life had been drear to me

And all its flowered ways untraveled and
  alone—
No song in any stream,
No daisy in a dream,
And all that makes life beautiful, unknown."

Verse and sport together make up the menu perfectly. Nothing else is needed where brain and brawn, heart and ligament are concerned. Rhythm, the main factor in both, is one of the main factors in life itself. For without rhythm, there is a sudden snarl or tangle.

It has long been my belief that each of us needs a certain philosophy of life. As for me, I was around 12 when I first discovered Shakespeare. Two years later I found the brilliantly lighted domains of Keats, Shelley and Carlyle. I was about 20 when I had full contact with Homer and Rudyard Kipling.

While in my 'teens I ran across two proverbs or injunctions which have traveled with me ever since. One is from the Bible: "Judge not, that ye be not judged." The other is from the Koran, "Know thyself." Just why they should have had such an appeal at such an age I'll never know. The first one changed slightly to, "judge not too swiftly that ye be not judged too swiftly in turn." This Biblical injunction has served me often down the years. It was an order not to be in too big a hurry to condemn.

I discovered also that "Know thyself" carried a decisive message. Why spend all your time studying the faults and virtues of others while learning little of what you actually are? "Know thyself," meant the destruction of self-pity, the end of alibis and excuses, the placing of the blame where it belonged. I learned that good rarely comes from kidding yourself.

Another part of my philosophy stems from Ralph Waldo Emerson's "Self-Reliance" and "Compensation." There I learned that often when things are at their worst, brighter days are just beyond. Conversely, when skies are bluest, then is the time to look out for black clouds. It was a check either way—not to become too optimistic when everything looked good—not to get too low and depressed when everything seemed black.

There's an old song entitled, "The Life That Loves the Valleys Is Lonely on the Hills." I would certainly be lonely on the hills. And I would always feel at home in the valleys. I'd rather look up to some peak than to be on some peak looking down on those who need help. Of course, those on the peak sometimes need help too. Often they, in their loneliness, are the more bewildered. They expect a way of life they can't have—or a happiness that an unsound philosophy has made impossible.

I recall so well the time I read Keats' "Endymion" and saw this line: "Time, that ancient nurse, rocked me to patience." I thought then, here is all the philosophy of life.

Because so much of my life has been wrapped up in sports in which victory is the most important thing, I have come to applaud success . . . but without losing regard for the vanquished. Many coaches miss the philosophy of Hughie Keogh who had this to say: "The rules of sport are all founded upon fair play. . . . You can't pay off people in the square set with technicalities." "Square" in Keogh's day meant decent, solid—not today's bebop "square" meaning "not with it."

Human nature is often perverse—which is one reason why it remains so interesting. When arguments develop between square shooters and the chiselers, much of the public drifts to support the chiseler. Winning is important. But to win at any cost, through any form of trickery one can devise, is never worth while.

While watching every type of record smashed, with more to follow in the briefer time left, I've found that all records were made to be broken. Previous marks have fallen with a crash on land, on water, and in the air. Year by year, each record has only been the incentive for another. Today when anyone sets a new mark, he puts up a sign which reads, "There's Your New Target."

If this happens to marks that can be measured or timed, doesn't it apply to the individuals— to ball players, football players, fighters, golfers and tennis stars? It must. The old-timer looks back on the stars of his youth as much faster, stronger and better than those of today. I don't agree.

There have been ball players in recent years to match all but the great exceptions of Ty Cobb,

Babe Ruth and Honus Wagner. The Dodgers and Yankees of 1953 and 1954 were full of players better than most of the names who played for the 1906 Cubs or the 1910 Athletics.

In the New York area alone, the '54 season saw two, perhaps three present day stars who may take their place with the immortals. I mean Duke Snider, Willie Mays and Mickey Mantle. With Brooklyn's Snider climbing the center-field walls to haul in certain home runs . . . and breaking these same fences with his bat; with Mays contributing glittering heroics each day (I write this in late June '54 with the Giants bidding fair to make a shambles of the National League) with his basket catches, his rubber arm, booming bat, and, most important, his contagious, irrepressible zest; with Mantle commencing to play the ball George Weiss and Stengel *hoped* he'd play as DiMaggio's replacement in the Yankee's center field—well, how good can you get? All three boys, incidentally, are the direct results of growing up with a bat, glove and a ball, practically from the cradle. All three stem from fathers who didn't or couldn't make the big step themselves but who saw in their sons the potential realization of their own dreams. I don't know of a country in the world—or another field—where this type of thing could happen, except right here in a democratic, sports loving America.

The best doesn't belong to the past. It is with us now. And even better athletes will be with us on ahead. When we arrive at the top athlete, the

Jim Thorpe of the Year 2,000, we should really
have something. But by that year I will have slight
interest in what the field has to show.

## The Long Road

Here is my traveler's cloak, dusty and torn.
For half a century it has known the road.
Once it was clean and new, now it is frayed
   and worn.
The end is near, beneath a heavy load,
But from the valley to the topmost hill,
The sky is blue, the birds are singing still.

Yes, I have seen my share along the way,
Ruth, Jones, and Tilden, and the mighty
   Cobb,
The fists of Dempsey with their deadly
   sway,
The speed of Owens on the record job,
And coming on still driving like the surf,
Milburn and Hitchcock ripping up the turf.

I've seen my share upon a busy trip,
I've looked at Johnson's fast ball outspeed
   time.
I've seen Pete Alexander's deadly whip,
And I've seen Matty in his golden prime.
And there was Grange, the ghost, of super
   rank
The Four Horsemen—and Nagurski moving
   like a tank.

One by one I watch them march on by,
From vanished years they move across the
  field,
Sarazen, Hagen, Pudge and Thorpe and Cy,
Louis and Paddock decked with sword and
  shield,
The mighty thousands who have done the
  same,
To leave this epitaph—He Played the Game.

The long line forms through life's remem-
  bered years,
The flaming heart—cold brain and firm
  command
Of nerve and sinew, blotting out all fears,
The will to win beyond the final stand,
These are the factors in each hour of need
That mark the pathway of the Winning Breed.

But there is more than winning to this game,
Where I've seen countless thousands give
  their best,
Give all they had to find the road to fame,
And barely fail against the closing test.
Their names are lost now with the swift and
  strong,
Yet in the final rating they belong.

For there are some who never reached the
  top,
Who in my rating hold a higher place

Than many wearing crowns against the
   drop
Of life's last curtain in the bitter race.
Who stand and fight amid a bitter brood,
Knowing the matchless gift of fortitude.

Far off I hear the rolling, roaring cheers.
They come to me from many yesterdays,
From record deeds that cross the fading
   years,
And light the landscape with their brilliant
   plays,
Great stars that knew their days in fame's
   bright sun.
I hear them tramping to oblivion.